NEIGHBORHOOD POLITICS

GARLAND REFERENCE LIBRARY OF SOCIAL SCIENCE
VOLUME 1063

NEIGHBORHOOD POLITICS
CHICAGO AND SHEFFIELD

LARRY BENNETT

GARLAND PUBLISHING, INC.
NEW YORK AND LONDON
1997

BKL 7652- 7/2

Library of Congress Cataloging-in-Publication Data

Bennett, Larry, 1950–
    Neighborhood politics : Chicago and Sheffield / Larry Bennett.
        p.   cm. — (Garland reference library of social science ; v. 1063)
        Includes bibliographical references and index.
        ISBN 0-8153-2112-0 (alk. paper). — ISBN 0-8153-2113-9 (pbk. :
alk. paper)
        1. Neighborhood government—Illinois—Chicago. 2. Neighborhood
government—England—Sheffield.   I. Title. II. Series.
JS713.B45 1997
321.8'3—dc21   97-17787
                                                          CIP

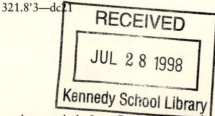

Cover photographs by Larry Bennett depict replacement housing on former council estate in Sharrow, Sheffield, England (top), and non-profit housing in Uptown, Chicago, Illinois (bottom).

Paperback cover design by Robert VanKeirsbilck.

Printed on acid-free, 250-year-life paper
Manufactured in the United States of America

In memory of Edna Bennett, 1914–1995

CONTENTS

List of Illustrations and Maps......................*ix*

Introduction and Acknowledgments ....*xi*

1. Neighborhoods, Community, and Grassroots Action *3*

2. Comet and Hearth Flame, Cauldron and Cup of Tea.......*25*

3. Urban Renewal in Uptown.........................*75*

4. Sheffield Comes to Sharrow........................*97*

5. Sharrow in the 1980s: The Trials of
   Community Development *123*

6. Uptown After Renewal: Contested Territory,
   Hotbed of Movements............................*165*

7. Neighborhood Identity, Neighborhood Change,
   and Grassroots Action *215*

8. Uptown, Sharrow, and Beyond.....................*241*

Appendix..*263*

Index...*267*

ILLUSTRATIONS

Storefront church, new construction, and federally subsidized
apartment building on Winthrop Avenue *38*

Argyle Street *41*

Asian produce garden *41*

For-purchase housing sponsored by an Uptown non-profit
organization, Voice of the People *42*

London Road *56*

Corner shop and terrace houses near the Sheffield United
Football Ground *57*

Lansdowne Estate *60*

Renovated ("enveloped") terrace houses in the Sharrow Street area *61*

Broomhall Flats *132*

New housing on the Broomhall Flats site *142*

The elegant front...
...and fortified rear of a 6-flat condominium renovation in
Heart of Uptown/Sheridan Park *225*

MAPS

2-1: Uptown *36*

2-2: Uptown's Racial & Ethnic Mosaic (1990) *40*

2-3: Sharrow *55*

2-4: Sharrow's Racial & Ethnic Mosaic (1991) *63*

3-1: The Uptown Chicago Commission "Meltzer Plan" (1962) *79*

3-2: Uptown Urban Renewal Project I (April 1968) *81*

4-1: Proposed Sharrow Highway Improvements *100*

4-2: Highway Proposals Through Heeley Bottom *111*

7-1: Heart of Uptown/Sheridan Park *220*

INTRODUCTION
and
ACKNOWLEDGMENTS

This book is the outcome of a small project that grew and grew. In the fall of 1990 the Chicago-based Policy Research Action Group (PRAG) commissioned me to do a study of the Uptown area, to which my wife, Gwyn, and I had moved in 1988. We had become modestly involved in local neighborhood issues, and I was interested in testing my ability to do an in-close investigation of a neighborhood with a reputation for persistent internal political strife. The first fruit of this work was a report for PRAG, "Uptown: Port of Entry, Hotbed of Movements, Contested Territory," which I completed in mid-1991. Meanwhile, in conjunction with my university's Foreign Study Program, I spent the fall of 1991 in Sheffield, England. With the luxuries of uncommitted time and no specified research agenda, I set about familiarizing myself with Sheffield and its neighborhood structure. At the back of my mind was the prospect of identifying a Sheffield neighborhood with sufficient historical and institutional parallels to Uptown to make for a provocative comparative analysis. As I note in Chapter 1, comparative research has emerged as a growth field in urban studies; though at this point, textured neighborhood-level comparison has not been characteristic of this work.

Armed with a general sense of Sharrow's neighborhood history, notes from a few suggestive interviews conducted in the fall of 1991, and a supertanker load of anxiety, I returned to Sheffield in the summer of 1993. The bulk of the Sharrow research was conducted in the summers of 1993 and 1994. Although much of my attention in 1993 and 1994 was devoted to Sharrow, Uptown did not stand still. Consequently, I have pursued a variety of Uptown developments, controversies, and contacts since the main portion of the Uptown interviewing was conducted in 1990-91. In the chapters that follow I have attempted to link a detailed account of these two areas' neighborhood trends and organizational developments to the academic and public affairs literature interpreting the roles of neighborhoods and community organizations in contemporary cities.

Among the daunting aspects of examining Sharrow and Uptown are their ambiguous contextual parallels. Routine municipal services, housing, and environmental issues are matters of great concern in each neighborhood, and often for approximately the same reasons. However, their respective local governmental arrangements—Chicago's mayor-centered city government set amid a complicated structure of independent local jurisdictions, Sheffield's council-centered municipal government set within a broader structure of regional government—operate in distinctive ways. And furthermore, Britain's unitary state insures that municipal governments are more directly subject to shifts in national policy than are their American counterparts. Yet even this point must be made in a guarded fashion: since the early 1980s the national regimes in both Britain and the United States have exhibited analogous ideological movements. As a practical matter, rather than devoting specific sections of this text to discussions of the continuities/discontinuities in governmental arrangements, national urban policies, or even salient terminologies, I have chosen to incorporate reference to these contextual variations directly into the discussions of the two cities and two neighborhoods.

A number of individuals and institutions have made important contributions to this project. In London, Khalid Khan and Susan Monks provided a most amenable staging area for my forays to Sheffield. In Sheffield, Patrick Seyd and Debora Green have been great friends. Among my Sharrow contacts, Margaret Howard, Mick Kerrigan, and Ann Wilson have been wonderful companions as well as informative sources. In particular, Margaret's and Mick's records allowed me to discuss the Broomhall Tenants Association and the Sharrow Street Residents Group in a much more comprehensive way than otherwise would have been the case. In Uptown, Rob Bagstad, Jill Donovan, and Denice Irwin have provided me with far more than local information. Two DePaul undergraduates, Ellen Gorney and Marilee Penn, were very helpful informants—passing on to me their field notes from internships in a pair of social service agencies. DePaul University made much of my research possible, via a College of Liberal Arts and Sciences summer research grant in 1993, as well as University Research Council research expense support in 1994 and a research leave for the fall of 1995. I did a considerable part of my early background research on Uptown in Chicago's Municipal Reference Library (whose collection has been relocated to the Harold Washington Library). At the Municipal Reference Library Tom Callanan was extremely helpful and supportive of my work. I was also the recipient of expert assistance from the staff of Sheffield's Local Studies Library. In preparing this manuscript the team at Jade Publishing has been remarkably adept with map preparation and text formatting. A friend and colleague, Phil Nyden, got me started on this project and over the years has been a provocative co-interpreter of Chicago's far North Side. Janet Abu-Lughod's criticism of the manuscript-in-progress has been pointed and illuminating. As an editor, David Estrin has been masterly: supportive, concise in his opinions, and open minded. Lastly, I wish to thank Gwyn Friend: as strategist, first-draft critic, and simply, as herself.

NEIGHBORHOOD POLITICS

CHAPTER ONE

NEIGHBORHOODS, COMMUNITY, AND GRASSROOTS ACTION

On the evening of July 15, 1968, a public meeting brought together several dozen residents of the Uptown neighborhood on Chicago's North Side. Uptown is familiar to most Chicagoans as the poor relation among the city's otherwise affluent north lakefront neighborhoods. In the late 1960s Uptown was an economically mixed area in which well-to-do residents on the community's east side—that is, along Lincoln Park and just back from Lake Michigan—lived in uncomfortable proximity to a large, low-income population inhabiting blocks of rundown apartment buildings extending about a mile to the west and away from the lakefront. Those attending this particular gathering were sitting in on the deliberations of the Uptown Conservation Community Council (CCC), a board comprised of Uptown residents with the mandate to review the City of Chicago's long-awaited urban renewal plan for the community.

The urban renewal hearing turned out to be a tumultuous affair. Although the eight-member CCC summarily approved the urban renewal proposal, the council took action before a crowd of "restless, placard-bearing residents" whose signs assailed the "phony consensus on urban renewal."[1] Following the CCC's actions, approximately 150 people marched to Castlewood Terrace, a posh street near Lincoln Park where one of the CCC members, Joe Sander, lived. Observing the crowd milling outside his home, Sander—who was known to be sympathetic to the concerns of the urban renewal opponents—ventured out onto his front porch and spoke to the gathered protesters. Sander punctuated his remarks with the promise to meet with Mayor Richard J. Daley and to suggest that the mayor expand the membership of the

CCC to better represent all elements of the Uptown population. Following their confrontation with Sander, the crowd dispersed. A newsletter circulated by local opponents of urban renewal included several accounts of the events of July 15, as well as the following poem:

> *Topple the church, and knock down the steeple,*
> *Bulldozers really don't care about people.*
> *Build some tenements for the poor*
> *Tear down forty houses…and build back four.*
> *Stack all the poor in a big high-rise*
> *Build some slave quarters in disguise.*
> *Where we walk to school each day*
> *The living dead now work and play.*[2]

Several thousand miles to the east and just under three years later a similar public meeting occurred in the working-class neighborhood of Sharrow, within a mile of Sheffield, England's city centre. Sharrow was a tightly packed enclave of brick "terrace" and "back-to-back" houses that had been built at the turn of the century. Since the 1950s Sheffield's municipal administration had been demolishing inner city slums and replacing old two-and three-story terrace blocks with apartment towers neatly spaced amid landscaped garden areas. Sheffield's municipal leadership prided itself in its forward-looking redevelopment efforts, and indeed, until the late 1960s there was little resistance to the municipal authority's program of central-city rebuilding. However, in 1969 opposition to redevelopment emerged in the Walkley area of central Sheffield, and in February 1971 the authority announced a twelve-year clearance schedule that would take an additional 28,000 units of housing.[3] About 4,000 residences would be cleared in the vicinity of Sharrow, a neighborhood including many homeowners, as well as numerous renters of long standing.

On March 18 approximately 200 people attended a meeting convened by the Sharrow and Heeley Neighbourhood Association (SHNA), a community group that had previously sought to foster improved race relations in these adjoining neighborhoods.[4] At this meeting the crowd approved the formation of a steering committee to organize a new community group whose efforts would be directed at determining the precise nature of Sheffield municipal authority plans for the neighborhood, and, if possible, to work with the city government in making local improvements. The steering committee was convened by a local minister, John Peaden, who was active in SHNA. Within weeks the steering committee evolved into the Sharrow Action Committee (SAG), which for the next several years sought to reshape Sheffield authority redevelopment plans for Sharrow.

II

At its core, this book is my effort to unravel the meaning and consequences of these two neighborhood conflicts. I am a resident of Uptown and have taken a professional interest in studying the neighborhood, its organizations, and its conflicts for about five years. In the fall of 1991 I visited Sheffield for three months, beginning at that time to collect information on Sharrow. I have since made two more extended visits to Sheffield to elaborate my examination of Sharrow activists, organizations, and issues. As an urban studies specialist with a particular interest in neighborhood issues and grassroots politics, my starting point in conducting this research was to determine whether or not the seemingly parallel stories of Uptown and Sharrow are, indeed, as analogous as at first glance they appear to be.

There surely are intuitive grounds for supposing that opposition to redevelopment in Uptown and Sharrow sprang from comparable local roots and promoted similar agendas. One of the most commonly circulated pieces of public affairs conventional wisdom, both in North America and Europe, holds that in the years following World War II a kind of municipal hubris infected the leadership of cities on both sides of the Atlantic. Elected officials, planners, and business figures observed cities that, at the least, had suffered from decades of neglect, or in more extreme cases, had been severely damaged in the war years, and these policymaking elites began to hatch plans for urban rejuvenation. The resulting redevelopment schemes are typically characterized as having been overly ambitious in their physical designs and largely insensitive to the needs of their resident populations. In some cities the effort to execute these plans only exacerbated the process of urban decay; in other cities pitched social conflict resulted from the efforts to force redevelopment down the throats of unwilling neighborhood residents.[5]

In more pessimistic renderings of this scenario, emphasis is placed on the folly of the post-war urban rebuilders, who sought to restructure their cities in the absence of a thoroughgoing comprehension of under-lying urban processes, while possessing a full measure of the arrogant will to impose their designs on their fellow citizens.[6] More optimistic interpretations of this story note that neighborhood-centered redevel-opment conflict produced an outpouring of new, locally rooted move-ments, which, in the long run have contributed to the revitalization of many urban areas.[7] Like many such pieces of conventional wisdom, there is an overall complementarity between this scenario's main points and the general outlines of policymaking and political conflict in post-war cities. Yet at the same time, the appealing simplicity of this narra-tive homogenizes striking variations in national urban policies, local government structures, and neighborhood cultures. Might it, in fact, be the case that the intuitive plausibility of this scenario obscures as much as it reveals? By pairing two neighborhoods whose initial responses to urban redevelopment appear so similar, I aim to devote close attention to detailing their experiences in light of the main features of this grand scenario of post-World War II redevelopment conflict. However, before proceeding with further discussion of Uptown and Sharrow, it will reward us to examine the intellectual context that has shaped not just the post-World War II programs of urban redevelopment, but just as surely, the reassessment of post-war rebuilding, contemporary urban conditions, and neighborhood action constituting what I have described as the conventional wisdom of redevelopment policy, con-flict, and rejuvenation.

III

In order to reconstruct the ebbs and flows of intellectuals' analysis of urban neighborhoods, we must return to the late nineteenth century and reimagine the industrial cities of that time. But before reentering those cities, we should devote a moment to clarifying two terms: "neighborhood" and "community."[8] In the first case I refer to a piece of urban territory whose residents and other "users" ascribe to it an identity—typically through naming it—and which may harbor certain distinctive physical features—specific building types or complementary economic uses, possibly well-defined physical boundaries—or distinctive social features—residents of a particular race, ethnicity, occupational grouping, or social class stratum. Community, which in everyday conversation is routinely used as a synonym for neighborhood, may also be given a more abstract and value-laden content: a network of social ties, behavioral norms, and collective practices that defines a cohesive group of people. Some neighborhoods may be places where community, in this latter sense, exists. Many neighborhoods will not be such communities, and it is with this proposition that the story of intellectuals and urban neighborhoods begins.

Between 1800 and 1900 established urban centers such as London, Paris, and New York grew from substantial cities of several hundred thousand residents to metropolises of several million in population. Emerging industrial cities such as Manchester and Chicago grew from villages to great cities. The forces that produced these changes in urban scale—the articulation of increasingly complex and geographically expansive markets, new production techniques, and massive immigration flows—have been the subject of much research and analysis. But at the time, observers were equally impressed by the chaotic physical and social conditions that accompanied the rise of these and other great cities. In an essay devoted to reinterpreting the "social differentiation" perspective of the early urban sociologists, Ira Katznelson recalls a central concern of this era: "What were the new cities of the nineteenth century like? The various portraits...show a city of high indeterminacy and of bewildering alterations to established ways of life and patterns of social relations."[9] In the increasingly differentiated metropolises of the nineteenth century, markets, occupations, and social identities multiplied at an alarming rate, giving rise to the fear that old bases of social solidarity—family, village, trade, and religion—were on the verge of obsolescence. Describing and interpreting this new mass society, whose central features were precisely those characteristic of the exploding city, quite predictably assumed an important place among the main concerns of the new social science discipline of sociology.

In the view of Ernest Burgess, one of the founders of the "Chicago School" of urban sociology, as critical as differentiation to understanding the growth of the industrial city was "disorganization," which he likened to

> ...a tidal wave inundating first the immigrant colonies, the ports of first entry, dislodging thousands of inhabitants who overflow into the next zone, and so on and on until the momentum of the wave has spent its force on the last urban zone. The whole effect is to speed up expansion, to speed up industry, to speed up the "junking" process in the area of deterioration.[10]

Burgess thus specifies that it is the process of growth that disorganizes urban society, which in turn may be apprehended via various indicators of individual breakdown: "disease, crime, disorder, vice, insanity, and suicide."[11] In such a milieu, the retention of community—conceived as that binding network of social ties—was unlikely. Yes, the expanding Londons and New Yorks, Chicagos and Sheffields, were fertile grounds for the formation of neighborhoods, but to the eyes of many early sociologists, social reformers, and social workers, these ethnicity-, occupation-, and class-defined enclaves were not necessarily the sorts of communities that would produce orderly urban citizens. Thus, at the point in time—and in the development of great cities—when intellectuals and professional observers began to investigate urban life, a considerable part of their interest in this subject derived from the conviction that the cities they knew were inimical to the nourishment of community.

Not all observers of the industrial city so evidently disapproved of its indeterminacy. By the mid-nineteenth century Bohemian quarters had become a characteristic locale within the growing metropolises, and through the art of individuals such as Charles Baudelaire a studied appreciation of the city's anonymity, "flow," and unpredictability emerged as a recognizable, if minority taste.[12] At the turn of the century the German sociologist Georg Simmel gave a lecture entitled "The Metropolis and Mental Life" in which he carefully balanced the costs ("nervous stimulation," "indifference," "tendentious peculiarities") and benefits ("independence," "freedom") of life in the great city. Simmel's summing up is absolutely equivocal, his lecture closing with the comment that "it is not our task either to accuse or to pardon, but only to understand."[13]

Notwithstanding the artist's appreciation of urban indeterminacy, or even Simmel's measured response to the various effects of rapid urbanization, most of the intellectual and professional energy devoted to understanding early twentieth-century urban conditions sought to define and implement strategies that would give more structure and predictability to cities. In the United States the founders of the settlement house movement sought, via an array of educational and recreational programs, to give coherence to the lives of urban immigrants. Housing reformers contended that only by insuring sound shelter for the masses of new urban residents could cities count on a healthy, law-abiding workforce.[14] In Britain, as early as the mid-nineteenth century, a series of parliamentary measures sought to enforce systematic improvements in municipal service provision, with special emphasis on sanitary measures.[15] At the end of the century, the visionary Ebenezer Howard proposed an entirely new mode of community, the "Garden City," as a corrective for the ills of the English industrial city.[16] Yet Howard was, himself, but one in a line of British reformers seeking to promote more hospitable physical settings for industry, housing, and recreation. As we shall see in Chapter 2, even before World War I the Sheffield municipal government was sponsoring "council estate" developments intended to provide more commodious physical quarters for the city's working-class population.

In both North America and Europe the early decades of the twentieth century constituted the city planning profession's period of incubation. The previous century's experience of rapid urbanization had delivered urban problems to the forefront of national domestic agendas, and by the inter-war 1920s and 1930s the modernist architectural ethos had begun to coalesce into a widely accepted set of precepts for giving shape to a "city of tomorrow." From a technical standpoint, through the development of concepts such as use zoning and the "neighborhood unit," planners appeared to be on the threshold of imposing a previously unattainable degree of order on the twentieth-century city.[17]

In retrospect—and particularly when one bears in mind the neighborhood/community concerns of the early sociologists—the emerging planning perspective on cities, neighborhoods, and their residents is oddly contradictory. On the one hand, it is perfectly evident that an important element in the motivation of many planners was the sustenance of community, particularly by way of inserting amenable residential neighborhoods within the overall physical structure of the still-expanding metropolis. However, as one reviews the drawings of early twentieth-century visionaries, such as Le Corbusier, or the illustrations accompanying innumerable mid-twentieth-century planning documents, the new neighborhoods imagined by these architects and planners are strange places indeed. When one looks for inhabitants within these magnificent settings—geometrically precise high-rise towers set in lush parkscapes, high-speed roadways linking the metropolitan complex's distant corners—one's eyes settle on outdoor cafes where tuxedoed waiters serve relaxed urbanites tending cappuccino or cocktails. Possibly, the renderers of these opulent urban visions mistook the professional and managerial classes for the entirety of the urban population. Or could it be that the imaginers of these seemingly post-industrial inner city spas assumed that the urban population en masse would adopt the worldly mindset of Charles Baudelaire?[18]

Following World War II, planners were given the opportunity to execute their designs in three dimensions. In the United States, the federal government's urban renewal program provided substantial support for the redevelopment of downtown and adjoining areas. Across Europe, the devastation of the war necessitated ambitious rebuilding schemes. Although the reaction of neighborhood residents to redevelopment was, at first, indifferent, a peculiar outgrowth of redevelopment planning was investigation and, one might say, the rediscovery of community within some of the most benighted urban neighborhoods. To note but two examples of this literature, young sociologist Herbert Gans moved into the West End area of central Boston in the mid-1950s, and several years later (following the clearance of the neighborhood) produced an account of "peer group society" that argued a generally well-functioning and even well-liked neighborhood—an "urban village"—had been demolished in the name of urban renewal.[19] A nearly contemporaneous study by two English sociologists, Michael Young and Peter Willmott, of the Bethnal Green area of East London, produced much the same result. Young and Willmott's interviewees located themselves in a tight set of communal relationships, in considerable measure sustained by the women of the community, that gave vitality and security to an old, economically troubled area. In spite of their strong attachments to Bethnal Green, the bulk of these families were slated for relocation to a new housing estate on the eastern fringe of London.[20]

By the 1960s, as the emergence of organized neighborhood resistance to redevelopment became a familiar feature of urban political conflict, the Gans/Young and Willmott perspective—that functioning communities were indeed possible within great cities, that oftentimes these communities were coincidental with what outsiders and professional experts labeled "slums"—gained wide acceptance. I would argue further that this insight, once it entered the mainstream of professional urban affairs discourse, produced an associated notion, which I term "neighborhood salvationism." At its core, neighborhood salvationism proposes that neighborhood, and if possible, community preservation, is a crucial ingredient in maintaining vital cities. At the same time, neighborhood salvationism has taken a number of forms, and by examining their varying emphases, as well as their points of contradiction, we will have come very close to specifying why the strategies and fortunes of neighborhood organizations have assumed such a large place in contemporary discussions of central cities and their futures.

Undoubtedly the most influential critic of post-World War II city planning has been Jane Jacobs, whose *The Death and Life of Great American Cities* remains the essential text for opponents of large-scale redevelopment plans. Jacobs' critique of orthodox planning derived from a conceptualization of the city that reversed the analytical mode characteristic of planning experts. Rather than imagining a whole and, through careful planning, integrated regional structure, Jacobs constructed the city "outward," using as her fundamental unit the residential block. If, in Jacobs' view, a city's system of residential blocks was characterized by diverse physical uses and human traffic, and if through this diversity there was sustained a threshold of "eyes upon the street," public safety and economic vitality would result.

Jacobs is typically viewed as a precursor of the neighborhood consciousness that emerged in U.S. cities by the end of the 1960s, and in particular, some commentators have described her work as an appreciation of ethnically rooted urban villages.[21] However, if one reviews the arguments of *The Death and Life of Great American Cities* with care, I believe that quite a different interpretation of neighborhood amenity may be discerned. For example, in one of the book's early vignettes, Jacobs reflects on the role of Bernie Jaffe, a neighborhood storekeeper and arbiter of street interactions outside his business.[22] Jacobs does not explain Jaffe's behavior as an outgrowth of his intimate ties with local residents, but rather as the rational behavior of a businessperson aiming to sustain his enterprise. The motivation that precedes seemingly public-spirited action is self-interest rather than magnanimity. Indeed, throughout *The Death and Life of Great American Cities* Jacobs derides the consequences of willfully public-spirited gestures, while consistently noting the benefits of self-interested behavior within a dense network of human contacts. Jacobs' version of neighborhood salvationism is thus more pragmatic and commercially directed than is often understood. Still, it is a form of neighborhood salvationism.

The work of Harry C. Boyte is another matter altogether. Boyte, who with *The Backyard Revolution* initiated a series of books promoting and interpreting grassroots action, endows neighborhood people with wisdom and ambition far beyond anything imagined by Jane Jacobs.[23] In Boyte's conceptualization, ethnic and other intimate neighborhood ties are necessary structurers of public-spirited action:

> The citizen movement largely grows out of those
> places in modern society which have not been

destroyed by the force of contemporary life—families, religious groups, civic traditions, ethnic organizations, neighborhoods, and so forth. And the movement incubates an alternative vision, seeking to preserve people's heritage while it changes society.[24]

As such, there is far-sightedness in the local person's disinclination to ground action in political ideology, great integrity in the unwillingness to accept the dictates of distant politicians, bureaucrats, or policy analysts. Furthermore, through the grounded action of local activists, significant shifts in large-scale public policy may emerge. *The Backyard Revolution,* as well as Boyte's subsequent work, is laced with examples of reproducible local action, running from issues campaigns to community development corporations and credit unions. In this version of neighborhood salvationism, the starting point is the activist's sense of justice and human need, while the end point of locally generated reforms transcends by far the boundaries of particular communities.

A third variant of neighborhood salvationism emerged from the European experience of social unrest in the 1960s. According to sociologist Manuel Castells, local activism carried a potentially transformative weight far in excess of Boyte's estimate. Influenced by the seemingly revolutionary climate of Paris in May 1968, and observing a group of national polities which for generations had included explicitly anti-capitalist political parties, Castells argued that "urban social movements" were an emerging product of government service provision geared to underwriting capitalist production and sustaining a pliant, city-based workforce. Thus, if locally grounded conflicts over redevelopment, government-sponsored housing, or governmentally supplied social services could be linked to the ideological program of leftist political parties, there was the possibility of a "decisive step forward in the constitution of an offensive of the dominated classes."[25]

In a sense, the respective neighborhood salvationisms of Castells and Boyte are inversions of one another—the former viewing neighborhood action as trivial unless linked to revolutionary ideology, the latter distrusting ideology as romantic nonsense and seeking reform via sensible local initiatives. By the 1980s, Castells had reconceived urban social movements by uncoupling them from revolutionary political parties. Nevertheless, even in *The City and the Grassroots*, an encyclopedic discussion of grassroots action across centuries and continents, the proposition remains that local action may hold the kernel of broadly transformed social relations.[26]

In the early 1990s a group of American intellectuals began to formulate a program for social renewal which they have called "Communitarianism." The fundamental proposition of the Communitarians holds that an ethos of individual rights has strained the American social fabric, producing a widespread alienation from government and other legitimate institutions, and engendering in a minority of the population a reflexive, socially subversive lawlessness. The Communitarians' ambitions extend to a far-reaching reinstitution of orderly, social responsible behavior. Nevertheless, much of the groundwork necessary for propagating Communitarian practices, for developing a "responsive community," will derive from local action. For example, leading Communitarian Amitai Etzioni calls "...for individuals who organize social activities in which interpersonal and social bonds can be initiated. These may range from church choirs to weekend outings, from groups that discuss books to groups that organize charity events."[27] Unlike Boyte's "new citizen movement," which links local action to an overarching agenda of economic redistribution and minority political empowerment, or Castells' proto-revolutionary urban social movements, the Communitarians seek social reformation rather than transformation. Their program aims to relegitimize family-, church-, and community-grounded institutions as both means and end. Indeed, a striking feature of Etzioni's otherwise expansive charting of the Communitarian program, *The Spirit of Community*, is his reticence in defining the content of his underlying social principles. Yet, quite like Boyte and Castells, the Communitarians propose to use locally generated groups and movements to achieve broad social gains.

The wish to use and fortify neighborhood institutions is such that, as this survey has demonstrated, a variety of programmatic and ideological positions can be expressed via one or another form of neighborhood salvationism. Indeed, it is not merely glib to observe that writers of nearly every political persuasion are able to discern value in the maintenance of healthy, neighborhood-based institutions. In practice, the experience of building grassroots initiatives in real communities suggests that these implicit ideological disagreements over the uses and consequences of grassroots action are not simply matters of interpretation. What some of the main lines of development in actual organizing suggest is that just as the intellectual interpretations of local action vary, the premises, aims, and consequences of local organizing efforts are also decidedly variable.

In North America, the most influential community-building tradition has been the organizer-centered, confrontational method pioneered by Saul Alinsky. Alinsky's signature organizing efforts, such as the Back of the Yards Neighborhood Council (BYNC) and The Woodlawn Organization (TWO) in Chicago, coalesced around existing local institutions—in particular church congregations—and devoted much of their energy to a sequence of campaigns against neighborhood "oppressors"—in the case of BYNC, local meatpackers and the City of Chicago; in Woodlawn, unresponsive residential landlords, the University of Chicago, and (once again) municipal government.[28] Alinsky, either directly or by reputation, influenced a subsequent generation of organizers, and there are few students of neighborhood activism who do not admire his irascible anti-authoritarianism. However, many observers of neighborhood organizing have been uncomfortable with the long-term records of Alinsky-inspired groups. Harry C. Boyte has criticized Alinsky-inspired organizations for failing to move beyond a localized issue focus and for often falling under the domination of their professional staff.[29] Historian Robert Fisher, having discussed the BYNC's retreat to neighborhood protectionism in the 1950s, concludes his portrait of Alinsky-style organizing in *Let the People Decide* with this comment:

> But as events in the Back of the Yards were to prove, relying on the skills of an organizer and the influence of traditional community leaders was not very democratic, and the programs that nonideological,

populist-style organizations like the Back of the
Yards Neighborhood Council pursued were not only
undemocratic and ineffective in addressing economic problems, they could be racist and reactionary
as well.[30]

Critics of Alinsky-style organizing have tended to attribute its
flaws to Saul Alinsky's tactical precepts: the emphasis on organization
building around matters of people's self-interest, the use of confrontation to generate resources and member loyalty, and the avoidance of
alliances with external movements. Reflecting on a variety of neighborhood movements in the 1960s, Ira Katznelson, in his study of neighborhood conflict in New York City, *City Trenches*, contends that
grassroots action in the United States has been undermined by a more
fundamental problem. In Katznelson's view, Alinsky-style groups along
with virtually every other neighborhood-grounded movement for social
transformation have been cut off from workplace-focused populist
action. This lack of contact, which Katznelson contrasts with the experience of European industrial democracies, has weakened both union
activity and neighborhood action, and even more fundamentally,
removed from the neighborhood agenda social class-derived issues. As
a result, in the United States most neighborhood activism centers on
disputes rooted in ethnic- and race-grounded antagonisms.[31] Relatedly,
the national Democratic Party, which since the 1960s has been torn by
race-derived conflict, has been unable to sustain a program of social
democratic measures.[32] Given these circumstances, it is Katznelson's
view that neighborhood institution building almost invariably works to
sustain rather than challenge existing social conditions.

In the last generation, the emergence of enclave consciousness—or
in popular terminology, NIMBYism (as in "not in my back yard")—has
broadened the scope of neighborhood organizing but also attenuated
the presumed link between grassroots mobilization and community
building. The essence of enclave consciousness is locally based mobilization in opposition to various forms of development, from traffic-
generating commercial projects to low-status uses such as sanitary
facilities, which is content to deflect unwanted land uses onto other

neighborhoods or towns.[33] In a national polity such as the United States with its strong tradition of local government, enclave consciousness builds on a revered history of individual communities exercising self-management. However, given the overlapping character of the United States' status and residential hierarchies, the pervasive exercise of pressure on decisionmakers to avoid unwanted development produces a characteristically unequal distribution of private and public amenities. One observes a disproportion of desirable uses—upscale residential projects; low-density, well-manicured office complexes; arts centers—in more affluent areas, and less desirable uses—social service agencies; transportation terminals; waste facilities—sited in poorer, less politically connected areas. The irony of such a patterning is that the local areas (as a rule, but not exclusively, municipalities) well endowed with desirable land uses are, thereby, also well supplied with fiscal resources. Relative to their neighbors in lower-status areas, affluent citizens of desirable communities may thus shoulder lighter tax burdens while receiving more generous public services. In the words of economist and Clinton administration Department of Labor Secretary Robert Reich:

> If generosity and solidarity end at the border of similarly valued properties, then the most fortunate can be virtuous citizens at little cost. Since most people in one neighborhood or town are equally well off, there is no cause for a guilty conscience. If inhabitants of another area are poorer, let them look to one another. Why should *we* pay for *their* schools?[34]

In short, enclave consciousness expresses a sense of community whose scope is neatly circumscribed by political and economic boundary lines. While enclave consciousness, as a rule, works to benefit economically advantaged neighborhoods and municipalities; as a characteristic mindset, it undermines communal ties in all manner of places.

The contemporary interest in neighborhood-based action is the legacy of a long intellectual history, which has itself been influenced in the past half-century by several different approaches to local organizing.

Observers from a variety of ideological camps appreciate neighborhoods as potential sites for vigorous community life, though it is also evident that these observers draw disparate lessons from the experiences of grassroots movements and, prescriptively, seek to direct neighborhood action in different directions. In so doing, they wish to promote particular varieties of community within urban neighborhoods. These divergent intellectual currents are further complicated by the unpredictability inherent in neighborhood organizing. Not only does the social and physical composition of neighborhoods change over time, which of itself may reshape a specific group's agenda, but organizational leadership and its attitudes toward local improvement also evolve. And of course, these shifts may be in response to broader neighborhood changes. Practically speaking, this means that the observer of the Back of the Yards Neighborhood Council in 1955 might come to quite a different assessment of the group than a predecessor evaluating the same organization a decade earlier.

Modesty and good sense prevent me from claiming too much for a research project examining several community groups in two neighborhoods. In the following chapters of this study I will not be able to disentangle all of the perspectives, disagreements, and variables noted in the last few pages. Nevertheless, it was with this body of issues in mind that my Uptown and Sharrow research was initiated, and, based on several years' work in these two neighborhoods, I am confident that by tracing the evolution of their principal organizations, by examining in depth several of their defining conflicts, and further, by comparing their experiences, some very striking insights on neighborhoods, grassroots organizations, and community building will emerge.

IV

At this point I wish to revisit the agenda of this book and note the particular questions I pose in fashioning the chapters to follow. In the first place—and with particular reference to material presented in Chapters 2 through 4—we will examine the political and economic environments that shaped post-World War II redevelopment policy in Chicago and Sheffield. Chapter 2 surveys the long-term patterns of development in these two cities and, within the context of each city's broader political-economic climate, the histories of our two neighborhoods, Uptown and Sharrow. Chapter 3 details the urban renewal process in Uptown and recounts the grassroots opposition to its methods and to its objectives. In Chapter 4 we make a parallel investigation of Sharrow, noting how redevelopment planning occurred, examining the rise of grassroots action in response to redevelopment proposals, and outlining the impacts of redevelopment. Through these paired narratives I focus on two points: (1) the degree to which we can identify a comparable planning and redevelopment "logic" in the two cases and (2) the degree to which the grassroots reaction to redevelopment plans shared agenda and tactics.

As a shaper of this research's line of inquiry, the pairing of Uptown and Sharrow grew out of their initial responses to redevelopment, their demographic diversity, and their sustaining a high-level grassroots activism over an extended period of time. It is this latter feature that centers the narratives presented in Chapters 5 and 6. In these two discussions I trace the long-term trajectories of grassroots action in the two neighborhoods. This is accomplished by following several of the organizations that emerged during the original redevelopment era and examining the evolution of their agendas and tactical methods, as well as their neighborhood impacts. In essence, the focus of these two chapters is the question of community building: to what extent have the efforts of local organizations resulted in the forging (or reforging) of strong community ties within Uptown and Sharrow?

In Chapters 7 and 8 we withdraw from the focused empirical investigations of the preceding four chapters to consider a series of issues growing out of the neighborhood case studies. In Chapter 7 I look at the relationship between neighborhood identity and change from two vantage points: first, by exploring how the dynamics of real estate speculation produce Uptown's unstable identity—especially when contrasted with Sharrow's more fixed circumstances; second, by examining different approaches to grassroots mobilization and their effects on local residents' sense of community. In Chapter 8 I note a variety of broader political implications growing from the examination of these two neighborhoods: the ambiguous link between day-to-day race relations and organization building, the comparability of women's activation in Uptown and Sharrow, the "ideology of gentrification" observable in Uptown, and finally, the diminished political force of left-wing populism in each of these neighborhoods.

V

In the last decade a multitude of social scientists have begun to investigate urban issues by way of comparative analysis, through comparison of national governmental and public policy arrangements, by examining how groups of cities have responded to shifting economic and public policy environments, and through accounts of local power structures.[35] Beyond the neighborhood and community themes that I have explored in a previous section of this chapter, this book is also written with this emerging comparative urban studies literature in mind. By looking very closely at the neighborhood affairs of Uptown and Sharrow I seek to ascertain some of the critical points of commonality and contrast at the very local level of urban politics. In the past, students of urban social movements such as Manuel Castells have devoted attention to neighborhood-level politics, but in the main, this literature has tended to infer its lessons from larger theoretical constructs rather than allow local areas, organizations, and conflicts to "tell" their own stories. Without conceding the prospect of deriving larger points from the case studies of Uptown and Sharrow, it is my intention, in the first instance, to give voice to the local subjects of this book.

I also wish to make clear that while my pairing of Uptown and Sharrow is based on a considered analysis of several features that these two neighborhoods share, I will not claim that the chapters to follow result from precisely calibrated measurements of neighborhood-level variables. Rather, my method has been to follow parallel lines of public debate, organizational development, and conflict; accumulate detailed information on my array of subjects; and offer cautious generalizations. At the beginning of this decade I had begun an examination of gentrification and organizational development in Uptown; and, given the time to observe Sheffield in some detail, I set out to determine if I might find a roughly comparable neighborhood in the latter city. Given what I knew of Uptown, I fixed on Sharrow due to its roughly contemporaneous redevelopment controversy of the late 1960s and early 1970s, its demographic diversity, its continued grassroots action in the 1980s, and the hints of gentrification on its western and southern fringes. Ultimately, I found that gentrification had not proceeded to any great degree in Sharrow, nor was this the source of significant neighborhood conflict. However, given the other three points of comparison—and my sense that the contrasting experiences of gentrification might in themselves be instructive—I carried through my comparative investigation of the two areas.

I consider this book, for the most part, to be an example of what sociologist John Walton (reflecting the work of Charles Tilly) has called an "individualizing comparison," in which I examine the parallel and divergent experiences of Uptown and Sharrow in order to pinpoint the circumstances that control each case. To put this notion more concretely, each neighborhood's particular course of events is used to inform the other case by underlining its unique or, in some instances, analogous features. In the concluding chapter I move beyond individualizing comparison and identify several local features of one or both neighborhoods that may be linked to larger political trends. To acknowledge, once again, Walton's categorization of comparative analytical strategies, in this instance I am making "encompassing comparisons" that seek to note how local matters in Uptown and Sharrow reflect, share characteristics with, or contribute to broader political trends in the United States, Britain, and elsewhere.[36]

It is my hope that a considerable portion of this book's readers have been mildly bored (though not mystified) by the last three paragraphs and are mainly interested in getting on with the investigation of Uptown and Sharrow. My aim is to write a book that intrigues general readers and activists, as well as social scientists. Having bowed to my fellow academics and outlined the structures that give shape to the account that follows, I too am anxious to revisit Chicago and Sheffield and to introduce Uptown and Sharrow.

NOTES

1. Patrick Butler, "UCCC Okays Project I of Uptown Urban Renewal Plan," *North Town*, July 21, 1968.

2. *What's New? Que Pasa*, July 16, 1968, p. 2, Chicago Historical Society Uptown Files. The poem is attributed to Joan Bailey.

3. Geoffrey Green, "People, Politics and Planning," *Yorkshire Architect*, November-December 1969, pp. 209-211; "24,000 Homes to Go in City 12-year Plan," *The Star*, February 5, 1971.

4. Robert Poulton, "Sharrow Residents to Start Action Group," *The Star*, March 18, 1971.

5. John H. Mollenkopf, "The Postwar Politics of Urban Development," pp. 117-152 in William K. Tabb and Larry Sawers, eds., *Marxism and the Metropolis: New Perspectives in Urban Political Economy* (New York: Oxford University Press, 1978); Mollenkopf, *The Contested City* (Princeton, N.J.: Princeton University Press, 1983); Robert Fishman, *Urban Utopias in the Twentieth Century: Ebenezer Howard, Frank Lloyd Wright, and Le Corbusier* (Cambridge, Mass.: MIT Press, 1982), pp. 265-277; Susan S. Fainstein, Norman I. Fainstein, Richard Child Hill, Dennis R. Judd, and Michael Peter Smith, *Restructuring the City: The Political Economy of Urban Redevelopment* (New York: Longman, 1986); Peter Saunders, *Urban Politics: A Sociological Interpretation* (London: Hutchinson, 1983), pp. 297-324; Dennis Judd and Michael Parkinson, "Urban Leadership and Regeneration," pp. 13-30 in Judd and Parkinson, eds., *Leadership and Urban Regeneration* (Newbury Park, Ca.: Sage Publications, 1990).

6. Robert A. Caro, *The Power Broker* (New York: Vintage, 1975).

7. Roberta Brandes Gratz, *The Living City* (New York: Touchstone, 1989).

8. Suzanne Keller provides a detailed account of the variables influencing people's sense of neighborhood in *The Urban Neighborhood: A Sociological Perspective* (New York: Random House, 1968). The classic interpretation of "community" is found in Ferdinand Tonnies, *Community and Society* (New York: Harper & Row, 1963).

9. Ira Katznelson, "Reflections on Space and the City," in John Hull Mollenkopf, ed., *Power, Culture, and Place: Essays on New York City* (New York: Russell Sage Foundation, 1988), p. 288.

10. Ernest W. Burgess, "The Growth of the City: An Introduction to a Research Project," in Robert E. Park, Ernest W. Burgess, and Roderick D. McKenzie, *The City* (Chicago: University of Chicago Press, 1967), p. 58.

11. Burgess, "The Growth of the City," p. 57.

12. Jerrold Seigel, *Bohemian Paris: Culture, Politics, and the Boundaries of Bourgeois Life, 1830-1930* (New York: Penguin, 1987), pp. 97-124.

13. Georg Simmel, "The Metropolis and Mental Life," in Richard Sennett, ed., *Classic Essays on the Culture of Cities* (New York: Appleton-Century-Crofts, 1969), p. 60.

14. Allen F. Davis, *Spearheads for Reform: The Social Settlements and the Progressive Movement 1890-1914* (New York: Oxford University Press, 1970), pp. 3-83; Richard Plunz, *A History of Housing in New York City: Dwelling Type and Social Change in the American Metropolis* (New York: Columbia University Press, 1990), p. 21-49.

15. Leonardo Benevolo, *The Origins of Modern Town Planning* (Cambridge, Mass.: MIT Press, 1971), pp. 85-104.

16. Stanley Buder, *Visionaries and Planners: The Garden City Movement and the Modern Community* (New York: Oxford University Press, 1989).

17. Mel Scott, *American City Planning Since 1890* (Berkeley: University of California Press, 1971), pp. 110-269; Peter Hall, *Urban and Regional Planning* (Harmondsworth, U.K.: Penguin, 1980), pp. 42-98.

18. Le Corbusier's drawings are the classic expression of this image. See *The City of To-morrow and Its Planning* (New York: Dover Publications, 1987). I also have in mind the following planning report: Department of City Planning, *Development Plan for the Central Area of Chicago*, August 1958.

19. Herbert J. Gans, *The Urban Villagers: Group and Class in the Life of Italian-Americans* (New York: The Free Press, 1965).

20. Michael Young and Peter Willmott, *Family and Kinship in East London* (Baltimore, Md.: Penguin, 1965).

21. This was Herbert Gans' reaction to Jacobs' book. His review of *The Death and Life of Great American Cities* is reprinted in *People and Plans: Essays on Urban Problems and Solutions* (New York: Basic Books, 1968), pp. 25-33.

22. Jane Jacobs, *The Death and Life of Great American Cities* (New York: Vintage, 1961), pp. 60-62.

23. Harry C. Boyte, *Community Is Possible: Repairing America's Roots* (New York: Harper & Row, 1984); Harry C. Boyte and Sara M. Evans, *Free Spaces: The Sources of Democratic Change in America* (New York: Harper & Row, 1986); Harry C. Boyte, Heather Booth, and Steve Max, *Citizen Action and the New American Populism* (Philadelphia: Temple University Press, 1986); Boyte, *CommonWealth: A Return to Citizen Politics* (New York: The Free Press, 1989).

24. Harry C. Boyte, *The Backyard Revolution: Understanding the New Citizen Movement* (Philadelphia: Temple University Press, 1980), p. 36.

25. Manuel Castells, *The Urban Question: A Marxist Approach* (Cambridge, Mass.: MIT Press, 1980), p. 433.

26. Manuel Castells, *The City and the Grassroots* (Berkeley: University of California Press, 1983).

27. Amitai Etzioni, *The Spirit of Community: Rights, Responsibilities, and the Communitarian Agenda* (New York: Crown Publishers, 1993), p. 125.

28. Sanford Horwitt, *Let Them Call Me Rebel: Saul Alinsky—His Life and Legacy* (New York: Vintage, 1992), pp. 56-76, 390-424.

29. Boyte, *The Backyard Revolution*, pp. 191-198.

30. Robert Fisher, *Let the People Decide: Neighborhood Organizing in America* (New York: Twayne Publishers, 1994), p. 65.

31. Ira Katznelson, *City Trenches: Urban Politics and the Patterning of Class in the United States* (New York: Pantheon, 1981).

32. Thomas Byrne Edsall, "Black vs. White in Chicago," *New York Review of Books*, April 13, 1989, pp. 21-23.

33. Sidney Plotkin, "Community and Alienation: Enclave Consciousness and Urban Movements," pp. 5-25 in Michael Peter Smith, ed., *Breaking Chains: Social Movements and Collective Action* (New Brunswick, N.J.: Transaction Publishers, 1991).

34. Robert B. Reich, "Succession of the Successful," *New York Times Magazine*, January 20, 1991, p. 42. (The emphasis is in the original.)

35. Timothy Barnekov, Robin Boyle, and Daniel Rich, *Privatism and Urban Policy in Britain and the United States* (New York: Oxford University Press, 1989); Robin Hambleton, *Urban Government in the 1990s: Lessons from the USA* (University of Bristol School of Advanced Urban Studies, Occasional Paper 35, 1990); Michael Keating, *Comparative Urban Politics* (Aldershot, U.K.: Edward Elgar, 1991); Dennis Judd and Michael Parkinson, eds., *Leadership and Urban Regeneration* (Newbury Park, Ca.: Sage Publications, 1990); H.V. Savitch, *Post-Industrial Cities: Politics and Planning in New York, Paris, and London* (Princeton, N.J.: Princeton University Press, 1988); Susan S. Fainstein, *The City Builders: Property, Politics, and Planning in London and New York* (Cambridge, Mass.: Blackwell Publishers, 1994); Alan DiGaetano and John S. Klemanski, "Urban Regimes in Comparative Perspective: The Politics of Urban Development in Britain," *Urban Affairs Quarterly* 29 (September 1993): 54-83; DiGaetano and Klemanski, "Urban Regime Capacity: A Comparison of Birmingham, England and Detroit, Michigan," *Journal of Urban Affairs* 15 (No. 4, 1993): 367-384.

36. John Walton, "Theoretical Methods in Comparative Urban Politics," in John R. Logan and Todd Swanstrom, eds., *Beyond the City Limits: Urban Policy and Economic Restructuring in Comparative Perspective* (Philadelphia: Temple University Press, 1990), pp. 248-249.

CHAPTER TWO
COMET AND HEARTH FLAME,
CAULDRON AND CUP OF TEA

Chicago and Sheffield are, in different ways, cities of the nineteenth century. At the dawn of the 1800s Chicago was an out-of-the-way meeting ground for Native American, English-, and French-speaking traders. Over the next 100 years Chicago, like a comet, rushed through a sequence of developmental stages: from trading village to commercial center, and from commercial center to the industrial capital of the central United States. Sheffield's trajectory of growth was less dazzling, more like a slowly building hearth flame, as a group of adjoining villages coalesced, and after mid-century the region's traditional "light trades" of cutlery and metalworking were joined by a new "heavy industry," steelmaking. Through the second decade of the twentieth century and World War I, steelmaking insured Sheffield's steady population growth and general economic well-being.

Both cities have experienced more ambiguous fortunes over the course of the twentieth century. Like Sheffield, Chicago's population continued to grow in the early decades of the century, with the initial break in the city's arc of expansion coinciding with the Great Depression. Following World War II, Chicago experienced the depredations that have befallen most of the great cities of the U.S. Northeast and Midwest: loss of business and middle-class residents to adjoining suburbs, the regional relocation of major industries, and a substantial decline in the quality of central city life due to residents' falling incomes and deteriorating municipal services. Sheffield's twentieth century has had more of a staccato quality, wartime periods of economic health punctuated by stretches of hard times. However, contemporary Sheffield's situation of massive deindustrialization has stamped the future with a particularly forbidding aspect.

Uptown and Sharrow may be thought of, respectively, as cauldron and cup of tea. Each neighborhood is a product of the last decades of the nineteenth and the first decades of the twentieth century. From its origins, Uptown has been a colorfully heterogeneous neighborhood, mixing a dash of quite prominent Chicagoans with a larger, often transient population, its residents occupying a remarkably diverse physical environment of mansions, rooming houses, nightspots, and more recently, looming high-rise residential complexes. Sharrow, reflecting the character of greater Sheffield, is a dowdier place. Though its physical character matches Uptown's in variety—small manufacturers, rows of early twentieth-century "terrace" houses, and again, stands of 1960s-era high-rise blocks, for most of its history Sharrow has been the quieter and more homogeneous of the two neighborhoods. It has been since the mid-1950s that a series of immigrant streams has made Sharrow one of Sheffield's most ethnically diverse areas.

Comet and hearth flame, cauldron and cup of tea, these pairs of cities and neighborhoods obviously bear the mark of histories shaped by the same broad-scale factors: the arrival of industrial capitalism in the mid-nineteenth century, ensuing population expansion and rapid physical development, more recent economic stagnation and physical decline. Yet coinciding with these common shapers of local development are an array of distinctive features: the divergent public policy environments represented by the United States and Britain, contrasting local government structures, and possibly of particular salience, very different local political traditions. And as this introduction has noted, the specific histories of Uptown and Sharrow—though each is a neighborhood set within a large industrial metropolis—have been quite distinctive. Nonetheless, in the aftermath of World War II, each of these cities turned its attention to inner-city reconstruction, and by the late 1960s both Uptown and Sharrow were slated for major redevelopment projects. In this chapter we examine the contexts that gave rise to these neighborhood-focused redevelopment initiatives.

II

One of Chicago's characteristic civic homilies identifies the city's rise to greatness with its advantaged geographic features: set on the shore of Lake Michigan, provided with a seemingly endless prairie ripe for development, blessed with outstanding transportation connections. However, as historian William Cronon's vivid account of Chicago's early growth, *Nature's Metropolis,* demonstrates, this common interpretation of Chicago's development is thoroughly misleading.[1] In the early nineteenth century, the shore of Lake Michigan was a water-logged desert of inhospitable sand dunes. Due to the Midwest's brutal climatic fluctuations, for months of each year the adjoining prairie became an impassable muck. As for Chicago's transportation advantages, these were largely man-made and accomplished via the promotional efforts of pioneer-entrepreneur-politicians such as the city's first mayor, William B. Ogden.[2] In the city's early days, had it not been for the local infusion of New York City capital (which was invested due to Chicago's status as western terminus of the Great Lakes-Erie Canal trading corridor), the city's rise to prominence might not have occurred. In short, Chicago's comet-like growth had much more to do with access to capital, local boosterism, and the explosive development of its surrounding region than to Nature's beneficent design.

TABLE 2-1
CHICAGO POPULATION

1840	4,470	1920	2,701,705
1850	29,963	1930	3,376,438
1860	112,172	1940	3,396,808
1870	298,977	1950	3,620,962
1880	503,185	1960	3,550,404
1890	1,099,850	1970	3,366,957
1900	1,698,575	1980	3,005,072
1910	2,185,283	1990	2,783,726

Sources: Chicago Fact Book Consortium, eds., *Local Community Fact Book Chicago Metropolitan Area* (Chicago: Chicago Review Press, 1984); 1990 U.S. Census.

Nonetheless, as Table 2-1 demonstrates, Chicago's nineteenth-century trajectory of development was impressive indeed. By mid-century the network of rail lines that linked Chicago with the urbanized East Coast and the regions to its west was in the making. During the 1860s, Chicago became an important supplier of the Union armies occupying the border states and the Deep South. Building on the impetus provided by the Civil War, the city's post-war assemblage of commercial and industrial enterprises produced even more impressive growth. Directly following the Civil War, the city's various meatpackers organized the Union Stockyards; and with the subsequent development of railroad refrigeration cars, the city's packers forged a continent-embracing empire that reached far to the west and southwest in collecting cattle, and sped a huge volume of dressed meat to the urban centers of the Atlantic seaboard.[3] Not only was Chicago the hub of a continent-spanning rail network; local firms such as the Pullman Palace Car Company produced the rolling stock that rode this first national transportation network. And by the end of the century, with the development of the complex of steel mills on the city's far South Side, Chicago—like Sheffield—became a significant steel producer.[4]

Unlike Sheffield, Chicago's multitude of heavy industries occupied significant niches within the city's economy; they did not define its economic base. Chicago's rail connections made it the ideal site for mail-order retailers such as Sears & Roebuck and Montgomery Ward. Out of the city's early grain exchanges emerged a significant, locally based financial sector.[5] And again, through a confluence of natural and man-made advantages, Chicago became an important center for conventions and trade shows. Contributing to its prominence as a place to visit were its renowned "fairs" of 1893, the World's Columbian Exposition, and 1933-34, The Century of Progress Exposition.[6]

As one might anticipate, the rapidity of Chicago's expansion produced a variety of local stresses. In the latter decades of the nineteenth century Chicago was site to any number of radical labor movements, with the unrest surrounding the Haymarket Massacre of spring 1886 giving rise to the international commemoration of May Day.[7] However, the Haymarket incident was neither the first nor last point of focused labor agitation in Chicago. Just a few years later, and providing a sober counterpoint to the city's self-approving Columbian Exposition celebration, Pullman Palace Car Company employees set in motion a rail workers action that spread across the country.[8] After the turn of the century, the relations between meat-packers and their employees were extremely volatile, with bitter strikes in 1904 and the winter of 1921-1922, the latter marked by days of violent confrontation outside the Union Stockyards. By the 1920s, labor-owner relations in the stockyards were complicated by an additional factor, the significant recruitment of African American workers in the preceding decade, who—for the most part—were nei-ther welcomed by nor inclined to join the unions representing white stockyards workers.[9] Racial uneasiness on the city's near South and Southwest Sides had already produced a week's rioting in mid-sum-mer 1919, during which 38 people (including 23 African Americans) were killed.[10] Finally, it is a commonplace among neighborhood rem-iniscences of this era that only the fool wandered too far afield from one's particular residential enclave.[11] Given such worker-owner, racial, and ethnic cleavages, it is not surprising to encounter com-ments such as Rudyard Kipling's, who asserted that having visited Chicago, he "urgently desired never to see it again."[12]

In the final two decades of the nineteenth century, such com-mentary contributed to the rise of a powerful reformist impulse among Chicago's business, professional, and civic notables. Chicago was a leader among American cities in the formation of settlement houses, with Jane Addams' Hull House representing just one of sev-eral neighborhood centers aiming to bring stability and, to some degree, Americanization, to the city's huge immigrant population.[13] This was, indeed, a mighty task, because as early 1870 more than 80 percent of the city's residents were foreign born or the children of at least one foreign-born parent.[14] As late as 1930, the U.S. Census reported that two of three Chicago residents were immigrants or their direct descendants.

The settlement house advocates' social ministrations to the poor and newly arrived were neither the only nor possibly even the most influential strain of Chicago reformism. As the 1880s gave way to the new decade, the city's business leaders looked from their mansions along Prairie Avenue to observe a city of great paradox. On the one hand,

Chicago had recovered from its devastating fire of 1871 and achieved an economic prosperity that was quite astounding. On the other hand, this pulsing, ever-expanding city was a physical mess: its lakefront increasingly the domain of rail lines and other noxious industrial uses, broad stretches of the West and South Sides given over to monotonous, jerry-built residential areas. Indeed, possibly more than in any other American city, the residential enclaves of Chicago's business elite were threatened by the very factories, terminals, and waste sites that fed their wallets and defined their social eminence.

To celebrate both Columbus' "discovery" of America and Chicago's rise from the ashes of October 1871, the city's leadership sponsored the storied Columbian Exposition of 1893. The centerpiece of this world's fair, the White City of neoclassical pavilions, grand statuary, expansive plazas, and evocative canals provided the prototype for the "City Beautiful" movement in American city planning.[15] As to Chicago's future, the Columbian Exposition also inspired the group of rising civic leaders and reformers that would underwrite Daniel Burnham's preparation of the Plan of Chicago, which was completed a decade and a half later in 1909. This latter document, which, like the Columbian Exposition, was of tremendous significance in shaping the early development of city planning in the United States, wed a City Beautiful vision of urban elegance to more pragmatic considerations such as transportation planning and the structuring of the urban region. Yet again, in explaining his intentions in defining a new, prosperous, and more orderly Chicago, Burnham returned to the city's sprawling diversity, contending that effective planning would carry the city "a long step toward cementing together the heterogeneous elements of our population, and towards assimilating the million and a half people who are here now but who were not here some fifteen years ago."[16]

Although Burnham's Plan of Chicago ultimately won the endorsement of Chicago's municipal government, it—like the World's Columbian Exposition—was privately sponsored. In the early decades of the twentieth century, Chicago's initial forays into the development of habitable residential accommodations for its working population, likewise, represented expressions of civic commitment by the city's leading business figures. For example, in the late 1920s Julius Rosenwald, president of Sears & Roebuck, financed the development of the Michigan Boulevard Garden Apartments on the edge of the city's South Side "Black Belt." The contemporaneous Marshall Field Garden Apartments, located in the "Little Hell" Italian district on Chicago's near North Side, as their designation attests, were the godchild of the city's leading retailing family.[17] Only after World War II did a public agency, the Chicago Housing Authority, take on the task of building decent-quality, low-cost rental housing.

This pattern of public planning via the medium of private initiative persisted in post-World War II Chicago. The city's initial redevelopment program, which concentrated on the near-downtown portions of the South Side Black Belt, was promoted by a private civic group, the Metropolitan Housing and Planning Council, and executed by a consortium of private investors and local institutions, including Michael Reese Hospital and the Illinois Institute of Technology.[18] Later "neighborhood" urban renewal projects including Hyde Park on the South Side, and on the North Side, Lincoln Park and "Sandburg Village," were similarly driven by major private sector interests.[19] Chicago's privatistic approach to post-World War II urban renewal contrasts with the experiences of cities such as Boston, New Haven, New York, and San Francisco, where a more formidable public planning/redevelopment agency directed rebuilding efforts. In part, this contrast is attributable to Chicago's never having bred a powerful planning chief such as Edward Logue, Robert Moses, or Justin Herman.[20] In the 1950s and 1960s, Chicago's Mayor Richard J. Daley simply would not have countenanced such a situation, but beyond Daley's power and personal inclinations, the city's longstanding political culture is another source of its particular approach to public planning.

Although political scientist James McGregor Burns has offered the fanciful nomination of the Albany, New York, Democratic Party organization for inclusion in the Smithsonian Institution as that distinguished collection's representative specimen of the political party machine, many aficionados might lean to Chicago's Cook County Democratic Party.[21] What most casual followers of Chicago politics do not realize is that before the Great Depression, Chicago's political system contained competing political machines. Over the half century spanning 1880 to 1930, the city's volatile population mix had produced vying political parties whose constituencies could be roughly demarcated by class, religion, and race—with the Republicans tending to hold the allegiance of more affluent and Protestant voters, as well as the city's small but growing African American population.[22] And while the Democrats were hardly inconspicuous in their production of roguish party leaders, among the most notorious figures in the city's pre-Depression period was three-time Republican mayor William Hale Thompson.[23]

In a movement that coincided with shifts in the national polity, Chicago's Democrats asserted themselves as the city's dominant party organization during the 1930s, with Mayor Edward Kelly presiding over a unified party and government apparatus that had been forged by his predecessor, Anton Cermak.[24] A nearly city-wide network of local ward organizations contacted residents and recruited voters, distributed government-derived favors, and bred new party activists. During the 1930s a considerable share of the local Democrats' agenda derived from the Roosevelt administration's New Deal, though by the end of World War II Mayor Kelly's personal prestige had eroded, and—as in other U.S. cities—the party's parochialism and corruption were under fire. Following an eight-year hiatus during which a nominally reformist Democrat, Martin Kennelly, held the mayoralty, in 1955 Cook County Democratic Party chair Richard J. Daley won election as Chicago's chief executive. In the next decade Daley rebuilt the Democratic machine, but as political scientist Theodore Lowi noted in the 1960s, Daley's was a "new machine."[25]

As a local campaigning apparatus, Daley's machine operated much like its predecessors—ward organizations tending their neighborhood flocks, party activists rewarded via a sliding scale of patronage jobs, access to policymakers, and ultimately, public office. But at its apex, the Daley machine was easily distinguishable from the party of the late 1940s and early 1950s. On the one hand, Daley was a modernizer, wishing to give city government a more forward-looking character, and like his counterparts in other major U.S. cities, feeling pressure to rebuild his city's downtown, neighborhoods, and public infrastructure. In order to accomplish these latter objectives, Daley assiduously courted the federal government in pursuit of fiscal support, upgraded the city's administrative capacity, and in sharp contrast to Edward Kelly, cultivated a congenial relationship with Chicago's business and civic leadership. And because Daley did not have a grand design for reshaping the city—his contribution to this era's policy-making environment seeming to be the intuition that something had to be done—his administration tended to cooperate with the emerging redevelopment schemes of prominent local developers, corporations, and other private institutions.[26]

The high-water mark of the Daley machine was the mid-1960s, a point in time when municipal finances were reasonably secure, in part because federal largesse continued to underwrite the city government, and also a time of relative political calm. Until the mid-1960s, Mayor Daley had successfully negotiated the gauntlet of maintaining the allegiance both of white working- and lower-middle-class constituents (via access to patronage, favorable city contracting practices, and unchallenged hegemony at the upper reaches of the Democratic Party hierarchy) and the city's growing African American population (via access to patronage and selective cooptation of prospective political leaders). The decade from 1966 until his death in December 1976 was Daley's slippery slope. The Chicago public schools' glacial response to desegregation pressures and Daley's hesitant welcome of Martin Luther King's open housing crusade of 1966 set the tone for a decade of mounting racial tension.[27] The city's fiscal health also began to decline, and a series of aggressive police actions—Daley's "shoot to kill" order in the wake of the King assassination and rioting of April 1968, the August 1968 police–youth conflict during the national Democratic Party convention, and the 1969 State's Attorney officers' shootings of two Black Panther leaders—earned Daley the reputation of unyielding autocrat.[28] In the mayoral election of 1975 (his sixth and final run for this office), Daley encountered his first Democratic primary challengers since 1955.[29]

Daley's sudden death produced a mad scramble to make rank within a new leadership cadre and shore up the Democratic Party.[30] The result, from 1977 until the election as mayor of his son, Richard M. Daley, in 1989, was for Chicago a period of unusual political volatility. One measure of this instability was rotation in the mayor's office. Following a 44-year period during which three men governed Chicago, in the next twelve years four mayors (including the city's first female and African American mayors) occupied City Hall's fifth-floor executive suite. The most notable of these inter-Daley mayors was Harold Washington, whose run for office was built on the city's rising tide of racial minority voters (by 1980 the U.S. Census reported a combined African American and Latino population proportion of 54 percent) and a movement-like reprise of the previous generation's civil rights campaigns.[31] In office, Washington recruited an administrative team that included far more political outsiders than had been typical—including civil rights veterans, non-organizational Democrats, liberal business figures, and neighborhood activists—and articulated an economic development model that eschewed major downtown and grand public works initiatives in favor of industrial retention, neighborhood-oriented development, and small business support.[32]

A half-year after winning reelection in 1987, Washington succumbed to a heart attack; and following the shaky two-year term of his successor, Eugene Sawyer, Chicago returned to its version of "normalcy" with the election of Richard M. Daley as mayor. The younger Daley's preparation for office included stints in the Illinois state legislature and as a local prosecutor, Cook County State's Attorney; his nearly seven-year administration has been characterized by the pursuit of large-scale development projects such as might have enthralled his father (for instance, a new metropolitan airport, a riverside casino complex on the city's near South Side, two stadium development proposals) and a business-like attention to internal management matters and cost containment. Among U.S. big city mayors, Richard M. Daley is one of the more vocal advocates of privatization as a means of improving service delivery and fiscal discipline.[33] If one thinks of mayors Washington and the younger Daley in tandem, it is fair to characterize them as responding to many of the same municipal problems—the decline of the city's industrial economy, serious neighborhood decay on the South and West Sides, near-total breakdowns of the city's public schools and public housing agency, and intense municipal budget pressure—with policy agendas that borrow from radically different public philosophies. Washington derived his vision from the egalitarianism of the New Deal, much of his program from the neighborhoodist agenda espoused by writers such as Harry C. Boyte. Richard M. Daley seems to have completed the party leader-business magnate convergence initiated by his father. As such, the younger Daley appears to dream of a Chicago in which economic well-being is widespread and for the most part structured and delivered by the city's private sector.

III

Uptown, whose southern margin is five miles north of Chicago's downtown "Loop," began to receive substantial settlement in the 1880s. A recollection of the area before its absorption by the growing city describes it as "a welcoming wilderness" whose "sand dunes were very picturesque and wild."[34] Indeed, as Chicago's development pushed north at the turn of the century, the eastern portion of the neighborhood adjoining Lake Michigan was dotted with hotels catering to vacationing beach-seekers. Uptown's growth was further accelerated by the extension of Chicago's elevated rail system (the "el"), whose northern terminus reached Wilson Avenue in 1900. At approximately this time Uptown won its name, which was derived from a local department store's. From the outset, Uptown's physical character was extremely varied. On its northern end, the Edgewater area was advertised as "one of the most beautiful suburbs in Chicago." To the south and along the lake, high-density hotel and apartment development predominated. Away from the lake, single-family homes and small-scale rental structures (mainly "two-" and "three-flats") were the typical building types. Nor was it just the neighborhood's varied physical character that contributed to early Uptown's rakish reputation. For a time, the Essanay Film Studios on West Argyle Street employed silent

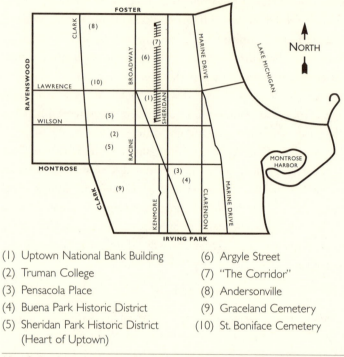

(1) Uptown National Bank Building   (6) Argyle Street
(2) Truman College   (7) "The Corridor"
(3) Pensacola Place   (8) Andersonville
(4) Buena Park Historic District   (9) Graceland Cemetery
(5) Sheridan Park Historic District   (10) St. Boniface Cemetery
     (Heart of Uptown)

Map 2–1 • Uptown

film luminaries Charlie Chaplin, Gloria Swanson, and Mary Pickford.[35]
More mundanely, the area's many small apartments made Uptown "…a
most desirable place of residence for the many young people who come to
Chicago to seek their fortune." However, alongside film stars and aspiring
youth, Uptown also sported numerous taverns and nightclubs, leading one
local merchant to describe Wilson Avenue of the 1920s as "notorious."

Thanks to the "community area" mapping of the city by University
of Chicago sociologists in the 1920s, Uptown's identity and boundaries
are of long standing (Map 2-1).[36] The area's southern and northern borders are two major east-west streets, Montrose and Foster Avenues. On
the east, Uptown is bounded by Chicago's lakefront park system. It is to
the west that Uptown's border is more complicated—on the southern
end following narrow but bustling Clark Street, then pulling farther
west to parallel the path of the Chicago and Northwestern rail line. This

dogleg to the west tends to confuse people: Clark Street is a more evident seam in the city's fabric, and some status-conscious residents of the area west of Clark (but still within the Uptown community area) refer to their locale by the presumably more refined name of East Ravenswood.

In part reflecting its original pattern of development but also resulting from subsequent redevelopment, "interior" Uptown is not easily characterized. However, by keeping in mind the two principal north-south streets that slice through Uptown—Sheridan Road and Broadway—we can make some basic distinctions among the neighborhood's "subareas." East of Sheridan Road and running toward the lakefront there is much high-rise residential development, including buildings erected both preceding and in the aftermath of World War II. In the past two decades a number of these structures have been converted from rental properties to condominiums. In the southeast corner of Uptown are two of the most affluent census tracts in Chicago, but farther north several of the high-rise buildings remain rental properties and cater to distinctly non-affluent populations. Sheridan Road and Broadway are both faded commercial boulevards, including some concentrations of thriving enterprise such as the Asian restaurant district along Argyle Street, but many vacant storefronts and open lots as well. Between Broadway and Sheridan is a physically mixed, generally dilapidated residential area of three-flat, six-flat, "courtyard," and post-World War II "four-plus-one" buildings.[37] Though the expression seems to be losing favor, long-term Uptowners—reflecting a measure of dread—still refer to this area as "the Corridor." West of Broadway, Uptown's topography pitches upward very gradually, and for the most part one finds rows of neatly maintained single-family and three-flat residential buildings. Other than the lakefront condominium belt, this is Uptown's principal area of homeownership.

As recently as the 1960s central Uptown was one of Chicago's most prominent neighborhood commercial districts. The core of this area is the intersection of Broadway and Lawrence Avenue, which is anchored by the imposing Uptown Bank Building and was once a thriving hub of insurance offices, retailers, and theatres. Many of the structures that

Storefront church, new construction, and federally subsidized apartment building on Winthrop Avenue

housed these enterprises remain, but most are in disrepair and only partially occupied. There are times when the Broadway/Lawrence intersection has the disquieting feel of a 1920s-era ghost town.

Uptown is like many Chicago neighborhoods in that one means of interpreting its history is to scan, as if counting tree rings, the traces of its various ethnic populations. At the end of the nineteenth century, Scandinavians and Germans were the area's most numerous residents, the former group leaving one local place name—Andersonville—which designates a stretch of Clark Street (and a few adjoining residential blocks) on Uptown's northwestern fringe. Again, like many other Chicago neighborhoods, Uptown's population turnover was quick. In part this was due to the larger city's dynamism; it was also because Uptown was experiencing reconstruction even in the 1920s. The neighborhood's heyday as a pastoral refuge for the affluent was long past, and between the world wars developers routinely replaced houses with higher-density apartment buildings, or if less ambitious, carved sprawling single-family dwellings into complexes of cramped "kitchenette" apartments. In the inter-war years Uptown, particularly nearer the lake, attracted a substantial Jewish population.

Though Uptown, from its very origins, was a neighborhood in transition, its future became a matter of concern only in the 1950s and 1960s. Suburban development was drawing residents from the neighborhood's pockets of affluence, as well as undermining the Broadway/Lawrence commercial district. Yet the neighborhood did continue to draw newcomers, but for established neighborhood leaders, this was precisely the problem. During these two decades thousands of poor southerners arrived from the coal-mining regions of Kentucky, Tennessee, and West Virginia. This hillbilly diaspora brought new residents to neighborhoods across Chicago, but in popular memory, Uptown was a special place: offering cheap housing and only a small and, as such, non-threatening African American population. With the arrival of the Appalachians, whose appearance, dialect, and communal habits released the anthropological imagination of dozens of Chicago newspaper reporters, Uptown achieved a new distinction—as a white slum. (The 1960 U.S. Census tallied Uptown's population as 94.8 percent white.) As one account put it: "Entire blocks in Uptown are inhabited by the former residents of a single Alabama or West Virginia county. Apartment buildings are filled with members of a single mountain clan, and the same names keep popping up everywhere."[38]

It was at the height of the Appalachian immigration that Uptown's urban renewal plan took shape. Little did its proponents realize that their neighborhood's post-World War II resettlement had only begun. In the 1960s there was a marked increase in Uptown's Latino population, and after 1970 the neighborhood's African American population also jumped. In 1975 a consortium of Chinese American business figures purchased a block of property along Argyle Street and announced plans to develop a "Chinatown North."[39] In the next few years their scheme proceeded very slowly, but with the late 1970s and the arrival of hundreds of Vietnamese, Laotian, Cambodian, and Hmong refugees on the city's North Side, the Argyle Street area evolved into a thriving Asian commercial strip. Thus, as Table 2-2 demonstrates (yet also underestimates—Uptown also providing residence to a few hundred Native Americans and recent influxes of eastern European, African, and Caribbean immigrants),

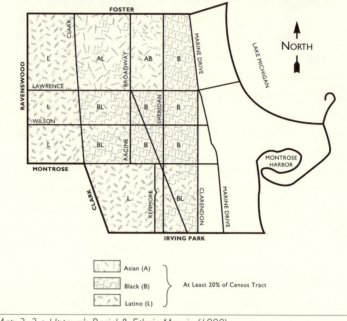

Map 2–2 • *Uptown's Racial & Ethnic Mosaic (1990)*

Uptown has become one of Chicago's most ethnically heterogeneous neighborhoods. Throughout this period its magnetic features have been constant: relatively inexpensive housing, good public transportation (particularly via the North Side "el"), and due to its lakefront location—attractive and accessible recreational areas.

TABLE 2-2
UPTOWN POPULATION

TOTAL POPULATION

1970	74,838
1980	64,414
1990	63,839

RACIAL/ETHNIC COMPOSITION (%)

	Asian	Black	Latino	White
1970	*	4.1	13.3	74.4
1980	10.7	15.1	23.3	51.0
1990	14.5	24.6	22.6	38.3

* "Other Nonwhites" comprised 8.2%

Sources: *1980 Local Community Fact Book Chicago Metropolitan Area,* 1990 U.S. Census.

Argyle Street

TABLE 2-3
UPTOWN HOUSING

	Total No. Housing Units	Percentage Vacant	Percentage Owner-Occupied
1970	36,864	10.2	4.9
1980	33,714	16.3	11.1
1990	31,956	12.3	13.5

Sources: *1980 Local Community Fact Book Chicago Metropolitan Area*, 1990 U.S. Census.

Asian produce garden

Within Uptown, there is a measure of geographic ordering to its social class, racial, and ethnic heterogeneity (Map 2-2). The neighborhood's "gold coast" is the southeasterly lakefront area, running as far north as Montrose Avenue. There are additional pockets of affluence farther north along the lakefront and in the gentrifying areas of Buena Park and Heart of Uptown/Sheridan Park (just east of Clark Street and north of Montrose Avenue). Much of Uptown's African American population resides in the Corridor between Broadway and Sheridan, as well as in westerly and easterly spurs at its southern end, that is, Heart of Uptown/Sheridan Park and to the east between Wilson and Montrose Avenues. Along Argyle Street (yes, directly crossing "the Corridor") there is a concentration of Asian residents, as there is in the residential area just west of Broadway. Uptown's less-prosperous Latinos live in the southern end of the neighborhood away from the lakefront; on the western side of Uptown working- and lower middle-class Latinos own many of that area's modest single-family homes.

Uptown's extremely disparate population is thus segmented without being altogether separated. In part, this is a reflection of the neighborhood's volatile history. It is also an indication of ongoing change, as new patterns of settlement, residential investment, and other economic development

For-purchase housing sponsored by an Uptown non-profit organization, Voice of the People

emerge. Efforts to give Uptown greater coherence as a community can be dated to the mid-1950s when the Uptown Chicago Commission (UCC), an alliance of local civic and business figures, formed and proceeded to propose a series of schemes for local rejuvenation. In Chapter 3 I detail the course of the political debate that grew out of the UCC's initiatives. During the 1960s and 1970s a considerable portion of Uptown's housing stock was lost, initially through abandonment and redevelopment-related clearance (Table 2-3). Then in the 1970s a wave of arson struck the neighborhood, particularly in the Heart of Uptown/Sheridan Park area.[40]

The degree of political strife that resulted from the urban renewal program undoubtedly disheartened Uptown's civic leadership. It is also certain that the State of Illinois' decision, in the early 1970s, to "de-institutionalize" thousands of patients previously residing in state mental facilities further eroded the faith of the neighborhood's institutional leaders.[41] Uptown, already holding a variety of social service agencies as well as thousands of small apartment units, received a sizable share of the state's former wards. Since the 1970s the living conditions of the de-institutionalized population—and maybe more immediately, their often-erratic street behavior—have been persistent sources of local tension. By the late 1970s Uptown's reputation had sunk to the point that residents of its northerly portion, including the old Edgewater area, convinced the city government to uncouple them from Uptown. With the city government's compliance, Uptown achieved the dubious honor of being the first (and to this point, the only) of Chicago's original 75 community areas to experience a secession movement. Since 1980 various City of Chicago documents identify "Edgewater" as Chicago's Community Area 77.[42]

In spite of Uptown's unruly history and persistent economic malaise (from 1969 to 1989 Uptown's median family income fell from 83 percent to 73 percent of the city-wide median), during the 1980s residential developers invested millions of dollars in housing renovations and new construction, and there was a noticeable upturn in local homeownership (Table 2-3).[43] In the mid-1980s local residents and real estate interests also won historic district status for the Buena Park and Heart of Uptown/Sheridan Park (the Sheridan Park Historic District) areas. Along sections of Argyle Street (the Asian commercial district) and in the

Andersonville section of Clark Street there were visible commercial revivals. As such, Uptown was, in no one's view, a neighborhood locked in an unbreakable spiral of disinvestment and population loss. Nonetheless, the implications of these signs of life were matters of dispute, and in 1987 the 46th ward—the Chicago City Council district that overlays most of Uptown—elected a controversial alderperson, Helen Shiller, who was opposed by virtually all of the local realtors and most homeowners, and who in the subsequent decade has been a persistent critic of the city administration and focus of local controversy. As in the past, Uptown's future is uncertain, and to a remarkable degree its every neighborhood feature—emerging demographic patterns, housing trends, and commercial investments—seems to feed into an unending chain of political discord.

IV

Accounts of the Sheffield region locate, by the Middle Ages, a network of villages in the vicinity of the modern city. Already in this early period the precursors of Sheffield's later industrial economy were evident. Taking advantage of a series of streams running down from the Pennine Mountains to converge in the valley of the Don River, small shops, their mill wheels set in the Rivelin, Porter, Sheaf, and Loxley Rivers, produced various kinds of metal tools. The local availability of iron ore and millstone grit gave impetus to these pre-industrial operations.[44]

With the coming of the Industrial Revolution, Sheffield's population and economic prominence began to grow at a considerable pace. By the early eighteenth century the city's environs had assumed the forbidding physical character that has impressed so many subsequent observers. Visiting Sheffield on his tour of Great Britain in the mid-1720s, Daniel Defoe described the city in this way: "This town of Sheffield is very populous and large, the streets narrow and the houses dark and black, occasioned by the continued smoke of forges, which are always at work."[45] At the time of Defoe's visit, the population of the town of Sheffield probably approached 10,000.[46]

During the early decades of the nineteenth century, Sheffield did not experience the kind of explosive growth that characterized the textile cities to the west in Lancashire. Isolated by the Pennines from Manchester and the network of cities surrounding "Cottonopolis," Sheffield grew steadily but less dramatically (Table 2-4). Until the mid-1800s the city could better be described as a belt of adjacent, economically interdependent villages. In the wake of Britain's reform of parliamentary representation in the early 1830s, Sheffield received a Town Charter in 1843. The new town was a municipal contemporary of such northern communities as Manchester and Bradford, which were granted charters in 1838 and 1847, respectively.[47]

TABLE 2-4
SHEFFIELD POPULATION

1801	45,755	1901	409,070
1811	53,231	1911	454,632
1821	63,375	1921	482,798
1831	91,692	1931	511,757
1841	110,891	1951	512,834
1851	135,310	1961	494,344
1861	185,172	1971	520,327
1871	239,946	1981	537,557
1881	284,408	1991	501,202
1891	324,291		

Sources: Sheffield City Libraries, Dept. of Local History and Archives, "Population in Sheffield, 1086-1967," Local History Leaflets, No. 2, 1967; Clyde Binfield et al., *The History of Sheffield* 1843-1993, Vol. II, *Society* (Sheffield, S. Yorkshire: Sheffield Academic Press, 1993), p. 483; Central Policy Unit, Sheffield City Council, "The Detailed Results for Sheffield," Sheffield 1991 Census Report 3, January 1993, p. 1.

Sheffield was the home of "little mesters," small-scale cutlers and metal fabricators whose operations were regulated by a guild-like system of interpersonal and production relationships. The scale of individual shops was small; employees were paid on a piecework basis. Some proportion of work was "put out" to independent artisans, and within the shops workers devoted part of their work time to jobs they had contracted independently of the "mester."[48] From the material standpoint, this decentralized economy probably did not greatly benefit the bulk of the population. Just as in the Lancashire heartland of the Industrial Revolution, the housing, nutritional, medical, and overall living conditions of the Sheffield workforce and its families were grim.[49] Sheffield's comparatively backward system of production did have unique political ramifications. The class of cutlers bridged the city's abject poor and its growing commercial and professional groups, tending to deflect the social antagonisms characteristic of Lancashire's "two class" urban economies. It was indeed plausible for the employees of the city's numerous small shops to aspire to the status of shop-directing cutlers. Further, the exploitation of workers via the despised factory system was not so evident in Sheffield. To the degree that workingmen did turn to violent expression in nineteenth-century Sheffield, their characteristic mode of action is instructive. Periodically, cutlers who were perceived as unscrupulous employers were subject to "outrages," which usually took the form of workingmen invading their shops and destroying the machinery.[50]

Yet as a rule, the cutlers were a progressive force in local social and political matters. Before the granting of manhood suffrage, Sheffield was among the English cities with the largest proportion of electors—many of its artisans meeting the contemporary property-holding requirements for admission to the voting lists.[51] In E.P. Thompson's account of working-class politics at the outset of the Industrial Revolution, *The Making of the English Working Class,* Sheffield was one of the centers of republican agitation in the North.[52] For a short period of time in the 1840s, Chartists held a large block of seats on Sheffield's newly founded Town Council.[53]

By the middle of the nineteenth century the Sheffield of "little mesters" was giving way to the Sheffield of steel magnates. A number of Sheffield's pioneering steelmakers had begun their working lives in the metals crafts. The turning point in Sheffield's shift to heavy industrial production can probably be set in 1859 when Henry Bessemer opened his steel works. Bessemer's facility introduced a new production process by which air was injected to molten pig iron to remove impurities, an innovation that revolutionized how steel was manufactured. For the next several decades Sheffield produced the bulk of Great Britain's steel, and the city's many steelworks developed an array of new technologies and products, notably stainless steel.[54] Coincidentally, in the second half of the nineteenth century, the city's population exploded to more than 400,000. Sheffield further centered an extensive industrial region including the nearby cities of Barnsley, Rotherham, and Doncaster. During this era, the latter city's railway workshops were major consumers of Sheffield steel. [55] The local steel industry's hub—in the Don

Valley lowlands on Sheffield's "East End"—meant that the city added a sprawling industrial complex without substantially affecting previously settled areas in the city centre and to the west and south of central Sheffield.[56] In 1893 Parliament awarded Sheffield an expanded city charter, and just a few years later, in 1897, the city dedicated its new Gothic Revival Town Hall. Queen Victoria attended the dedication ceremony on May 27, but the elderly monarch, evidently unimpressed by the steel capital of the North, did not vacate her carriage during her three-hour visit.

The rise of big steel, Sheffield's "second Industrial Revolution," also had a marked impact on the city's working population and politics. In the early years of this second Industrial Revolution, leadership within the working-class population remained in the hands of the small tradesmen based in cutlery. The politics of this relatively well-off group were reformist rather than revolutionary, and regularly cooperating with the Liberal Party in Sheffield, they participated in what has been called a "Lib-Lab" coalition. However, as the scale of the steel industry outstripped the older metal trades, a more class-conscious unionization emerged. Initially, the older and newer wings of labour usually managed to find common ground, but from 1908 separate councils spoke for the older craft trades and the newer industrial workers, respectively.[57] After the First World War this division was closed by the rise of the Labour Party, and in 1926 Sheffield became the first major English city to elect a Labour majority to the City Council. Since its rise to power in Sheffield, Labour has lost control of the local council only in 1932-33 and 1968-69.[58]

In the two-thirds of a century that the Labour Party has controlled Sheffield's municipal administration, the city's political leadership has in many respects epitomized the ethic of "gas and water socialism." The local Labour Party's brand of socialism has centered on using the municipal administration as the lever to provide a wide array of services to the city's working-class population. Coinciding with this ideological stance has been a down-to-earth pragmatism that has assumed that the city's Labour administration can find solutions for the city's problems. In no area has this philosophy of activist local government been more

evident than in city planning and the development of municipal housing; and yet, quite interestingly, Sheffield was a pioneer in this field well
before Labour controlled the local council. By the turn of the century—
that is, almost a generation in advance of the Labour Party ascen-
dancy—Sheffield was involved in ambitious slum clearance and
municipal housing schemes. Historian Enid Gauldie observes that in
this period "Sheffield showed more enthusiasm for housing reform
among its voters than almost any other town."[59] Once Labour took control of city government, municipal housing initiatives accelerated.
Between the First and Second World Wars, the Sheffield authority built
28,000 units of housing, a figure that exceeded private sector construction by several thousand.[60]

In addition to its far-reaching housing schemes, the Sheffield municipal authority has prided itself in a progressive approach to city planning
matters. In 1924 the noted city planner, Patrick Abercrombie—who
would prepare the London regional plan in the closing years of World
War II—issued the city's first master plan. In 1931 Abercrombie followed
his city plan with a regional plan for Sheffield and the surrounding area.
By the end of the 1930s the council had approved a Green Belt to girdle
the developed portions of Sheffield. Later still, in the mid-1950s the
authority enacted strict environmental pollution controls that did much to
improve the quality of Sheffield's air.[61] Moreover, in both the pre- and
post-World War II periods Sheffield's council built housing meeting the
most advanced design standards. In the 1920s and 1930s Garden City-
style developments were built on the edge of the city. After the Second
World War Sheffield pioneered in the new enterprise of constructing
multi-level, inner-city housing blocks.[62]

Ironically, the Sheffield Labour Party's greatest crisis during the
post-World War II period grew out of its housing program. From the
mid-1950s the central government had pressured local authorities
across Britain to reduce unnecessary subsidies to the tenants of their
extensive council housing operations. The Sheffield City Council at first
resisted central government directives to scale rents to tenant incomes.
However in 1967, and facing a growing housing expense deficit, the
council adopted a plan that mandated an across-the-board increase in

council flat rents, offset by rebates to various categories of tenants. One of the plan's provisions also applied a surcharge to the rents of tenants whose households included working "adult occupiers," such as teenage children who had left school to enter the workforce. This measure, in particular, enraged many council tenants, and across Sheffield a vigorous grassroots movement emerged with the aim of blocking the new rent scheme. Coupled with the declining popularity of Harold Wilson's national Labour government, the 1968 municipal elections were a disaster for the local party, resulting in the first Conservative-majority City Council since the Great Depression.[63] However, the Conservatives did not seize the opportunity to take hold of the local authority. In the following year's municipal election the Labour Party regained control of the council, which it has held during the subsequent quarter century.

Of greater consequence than the Conservative Party's brief control of the Sheffield council was the housing controversy's effect on the Labour Party. An older group of Labour councillors who had run the city for most of the post-World War II period stepped down during the latter years of the 1960s and the early 1970s. As we shall see, the post-war Labour leadership's program of inner-city rebuilding and highway upgrading was beginning to generate popular discontent, and the late 1960s electoral setbacks experienced by Labour, in effect, drew the curtain on this era of the city's politics. During the 1970s a new generation of Labour activists assumed power in the party and City Council. A number of these new Labour Party leaders had ties to the city's emerging community organization movement. By the 1980s this group would attempt to forge a new version of "local socialism" in its efforts to cope with Sheffield's dramatically changed economic fortunes.

The 1921 national census set Sheffield's population at 482,798, a figure that has not changed substantially in the ensuing three-quarters of a century. The city's subsequent population increases have been due, for the most part, to a series of boundary expansions. Over the course of the century Sheffield's economy has boomed during the two world wars, when the city's industrial capacity has been turned to armaments production. The quarter century following the end of the Second World War also represented good, if not always boom years in Sheffield.

Conversely, the city's economy experienced a long drought during the 1920s and 1930s. At the present time the city is struggling with its most serious economic crisis since the Great Depression.

As recently as 1979 unemployment in Sheffield was below 5 percent of the workforce, a figure that was substantially lower than the national unemployment figure and reflective—so Sheffielders thought—of the city's unbreachable status as a good place for labor. In the decade and a half since the late 1970s, this view of the local economy has vanished. Unemployment climbed steadily during the 1980s, reaching a peak of 16 percent in 1986. In the closing years of the decade this figure declined, but since the early 1980s Sheffield's unemployment rate has invariably exceeded the national figure.[64]

The sources of economic hard times in Sheffield are easily ascertained. For decades the city's older metal-working trades have declined, undercut by international competition, and according to some accounts, as a result of their own declining standards of production. Nonetheless, until the 1970s Sheffield's heavy industry—steel and a wide array of related engineering works—prospered, but with the national recession of the 1970s Sheffield's industrial economy began to wither. Between 1971 and 1986 locally held jobs in steel and related manufacturing operations declined by more than half, from 82,000 to 40,000.[65] In 1985 novelist and Sheffield native Margaret Drabble, after an absence of several years, returned to her hometown to record these observations:

> All along the Lower Don Valley, buildings stand empty and machinery rusts. More than 1,000 acres lie derelict....There is an eerie silence, a sense of emptiness, a deathly calm. The scale of decay is daunting: the buildings look hopelessly dilapidated and, indeed, many are over a century old—historic, with touches of architectural beauty mingled in the rubble. This is no modern industrial quarter of gleaming factories with automated carparks: it is ancient, unplanned, accumulated, a maze of accidental growths. In its time it worked, but that time is over.[66]

Drabble's portrait touches on the core of Sheffield's particular sources of decline. All of the vertical links in the East Midlands industrial economy have eroded. The coal mining belt in surrounding Yorkshire and Derbyshire, once the source of power for Sheffield's steel mills, is experiencing its death throes as British Coal closes most pits and prepares to sell its handful of profitable mines to private operators.[67] Sheffield's steel manufacturers, located in the English city that is farthest from coastal ports and beset with obsolete private and public infrastructure, are hard pressed to compete in international markets. Domestic steel customers, such as the Doncaster railway workshops, have themselves reduced their operations.[68] Nor is the northern industrial collapse confined to Sheffield and its environs. To the west in the English Midlands, cities such as Manchester and Liverpool have also lost core industries, experienced substantial inner-city decay, and presently confront serious social problems.[69]

In Sheffield, the council's response to industrial decline has been structured by political conflict as much as by economic constraint. By the early 1980s, when the generation of Labour activists who emerged from the conflicts of the 1960s had assumed control of the city government, they found—in the regime of Conservative Prime Minister Margaret Thatcher—a hostile central government. The tone of Thatcher government-Sheffield Council relations is captured in this remark by Sheffield's principal municipal official, Council Leader David Blunkett in 1981:

> The Council has declared itself wholeheartedly against the Conservative Government's social and industrial policy. It believes that the millions of pounds cut from public spending in this City, the high interest rates which hit industry and Council alike, soaring energy costs and appalling levels of unemployment are disastrous for Sheffield and for the nation.[70]

In the years to follow, Sheffield was among the group of Labour-held local councils that contested the Thatcher government's efforts to restrain local government spending. In the central government's view, the lavish service expenditures of many municipal governments undermined the competitiveness of their local economies. According to the leaders of the "Socialist Republic of South Yorkshire" and their allies in other industrial centers, the central government's passion for scaling down the welfare state and privatizing nationalized industry necessitated an increasingly activist local state. Accordingly, in the early 1980s the Sheffield council explored means of rebuilding the city's industrial economy, guided by the assumption that municipal initiatives could contribute to generating new industrial jobs, firms, and technologies.[71]

In 1981 the Sheffield council formed a new Employment Department with the mandate to oversee its economic development projects. The Employment Department monitored trends in local heavy industry, supported retraining programs for those laid off by steel and engineering firms, and sponsored innovative economic development ventures such as the formation of workers' cooperatives. At the edge of the old cutler's quarter near the Sheffield city centre, the council founded the Sheffield Science Park to house technology-based firms. The council declared an adjacent area the Cultural Industries Quarter and helped underwrite the construction of a recording studio to serve local musical performers and offer job training in audio recording techniques. The council also reconfirmed its commitment to the high level of service provision that had always been the hallmark of Sheffield Labour administrations. In so doing, local property taxation—the "rates"—were pushed up substantially. [72]

Beyond the details of urban policymaking, the City of Sheffield's opposition to the Thatcher government was highlighted in more public ways. Throughout the early 1980s the region surrounding Sheffield was a center of anti-Thatcher labor agitation, and typically, prominent Sheffield political figures lent their support to the striking mine and steel workers.[73] Surely the high-water mark of Sheffield's prominence as municipal thorn in Margaret Thatcher's side was the Cutlers' Feast of April 28, 1983. The Cutlers' Feast is an old Sheffield civic event, bringing together business leaders to celebrate their city and hear a speech by a visiting dignitary. In 1983 the prime minister was invited to address the assembled civic elite. Unwilling to pass up the opportunity to confront the prime minister, local union and Labour Party leaders organized a rally to "welcome" Thatcher outside the Cutlers' Hall. Several thousand attended the rally, which became overtly hostile upon the appearance of the prime minister's motorcade: "When Mrs. Thatcher arrived just before 7 PM shouts and chants reached a crescendo and eggs and bags of flour were thrown at her car. None found their target."[74]

Prime Minister Thatcher's Conservative central government devoted great energy to deflating the rhetorical and programmatic flourishes of the Labour-dominated councils in Sheffield and other northern industrial cities. Among the central government's most powerful tools in this effort was its oversight of municipal finances, which by the mid-1980s the Thatcher government used to impose "rate-capping" (that is, to set ceilings on property levies) on local councils. At first, the Labour-dominated big city councils sought to resist rate-capping, but by 1985 their alliance was broken, and local councils across England had to accommodate themselves to reduced locally derived revenues as well as cuts in direct aid from the central government.[75] The rate-capping defeat, combined with the fairly meager accomplishments produced by its Employment Department, by the latter 1980s forced on the Sheffield council what political scientist Patrick Seyd has described as a "new realism." Its most visible sign was the council's sudden willingness to consider the kinds of real estate and commercial development schemes that were favored by the Thatcher government. Relatedly, the leadership of the council and the heads of locally based corporations began to discuss the prospects for "public-private partnerships" as the vehicle for economic development.

The fruits of Sheffield's new realism have been, at best, bittersweet. On the site of what was once one of Sheffield's leading steelworks, Hadfield's, has arisen Meadowhall, a huge regional shopping complex. Dozens of retailers have located in Meadowhall, and on certain weekends the volume of auto traffic spilling from the M 1 motorway and into the shopping mall's mammoth, multi-level parking area is extraordinary, but Meadowhall—located in the heart of the old East End steel belt—also appears to have drawn customers from Sheffield's increasingly forlorn city centre.[76] In 1991 Sheffield played host to the World Student Games, having won the event by committing itself to an ambitious program of sports facilities development. In order to finance construction of a new outdoor sports stadium, an indoor arena, a huge swimming complex, and other smaller sporting facilities, Sheffield's council assumed debt approaching £150 million, which has further strained its fiscal situation.[77] Since 1991 the city's quest for recognition as a sporting centre does not seem to have produced substantial increases in tourism or other forms of sporting event-derived economic growth. However, servicing the city's greatly increased debt has pinched resources available for day-to-day service delivery. Indeed, among Sheffield residents it is not unusual to hear slighting references to the "World Stupid Games."

Another manifestation of Sheffield's new realism is the local council's cooperation with the Thatcher government-mandated Lower Don Valley Development Authority, which was formed in 1987 to oversee regeneration of some of the most derelict sections of the East End. [78] Like the Urban Development Corporations (UDCs) in other British cities, the Lower Don Valley Authority pursued a program of office, residential, and tourist-oriented development, but after several years of defining and publicizing its agenda, the UDC experienced slow going in its quest to attract private investment. Whether or not there is any realistic prospect of such a rebirth of Sheffield's old manufacturing heartland remains an open question. At present, Sheffield's public and private leaders struggle to find a new economic niche for their city amidst a most trying array of circumstances: industrial decline, forbidding levels of local unemployment, a citizenry alienated by harsh economic circumstances and the perception of ineffective political leadership.

V

The Sharrow section of Sheffield lies just to the south of the city centre, and indeed, until the 1970s residents of Sharrow routinely viewed themselves as residents of the city's core. Sharrow's principal shopping street, London Road, entered central Sheffield at The Moor, a major market area. Furthermore, their proximity to central Sheffield

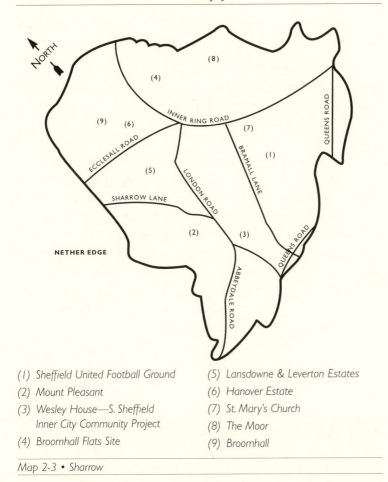

(1) Sheffield United Football Ground

(2) Mount Pleasant

(3) Wesley House—S. Sheffield
    Inner City Community Project

(4) Broomhall Flats Site

(5) Lansdowne & Leverton Estates

(6) Hanover Estate

(7) St. Mary's Church

(8) The Moor

(9) Broomhall

Map 2-3 • Sharrow

meant that Sharrow residents typically walked when they did business at the Town Hall or elsewhere in the centre city. It is thus rather startling to realize that Sharrow was not developed as a residential area until the second half of the nineteenth century. Up to this time the hillier parts of Sharrow lying away from central Sheffield were still open fields. A few large country houses and farm buildings dotted this landscape. Closer to the city centre and on lower ground adjoining the Porter and Sheaf Rivers, cutlers and other metal fabricators had their establishments. But in the 1870s and 1880s as Sheffield's population swelled, Sharrow's open areas were subdivided, and this section of the city was filled in with a dense, somewhat chaotic arrangement of housing, small merchants, and manufacturers.[79]

Although Sharrow was never the sort of self-contained neighborhood—such as portions of Sheffield's East End, or Chicago districts such as the stockyards-centered Back of the Yards—in which the concentration of housing, employment centers, and social institutions made for an enclave-like isolation from the surrounding city, the neighborhood that formed in the late nineteenth century was virtually a microcosm of Sheffield (Map 2-3). The sections of Sharrow closest to the city centre included numerous cutlers' establishments. Most of these shops have closed, leaving behind an industrial ghost town in which one does still find a few cutlers surviving on the last trickle of the once-healthy demand for their products. Roughly approximating Sharrow's eastern and western margins, the narrow beds of the Sheaf and Porter Rivers radiate from central Sheffield, and along each of these rivers bands of metal-working establishments and other industries developed in the nineteenth century. Again, much of this older industrial economy has vanished. In recent years the inner section of the corridor bounded by the Porter and Ecclesall Road has been the site of the following development: a Safeway Supermarket, an auto-

London Road

Corner shop and terrace houses near the Sheffield United Football Ground

mobile dealership, an office park, and a second auto dealer. Interrupting this sequence of projects is a single holdover, the Wards Brewery, saved when its local owners were bought out by a national beer producer.

Linking the Porter and Sheaf basins is London Road, which runs out from Sheffield city centre and across "lower" Sharrow to connect with Chesterfield Road, a main artery between Sheffield and the region to the south and east. London Road is a lively commercial strip—featuring Italian, Indian-Pakistani, and Chinese restaurants, second-hand and antique stores, many other small retailers, and implausibly enough, one surf shop. Yet contemporary residents complain of the decline in London Road retailers. A generation ago London Road ran directly up to The Moor, a major commercial area. But with the conversion of The Moor to a pedestrian precinct, and the erection of a large office building at its foot—thus cutting off London Road from The Moor—the higher-quality merchantry abandoned Sharrow. And maybe more to the point of local resident discontent, their section of Sheffield was no longer so tangibly a part of the city centre.

On the city centre side of London Road is a mixed area of small industry and nineteenth-century terrace housing. The single most prominent physical feature of this section of Sharrow is the Sheffield United Football Club ground on Bramall Lane, which approximately once per week for most of the year brings large crowds of soccer fans into Sharrow. Up from London Road, that is, on the right and following a decided rise in the ground, is a mixture of leftover terrace housing and council estates from the 1960s and 1970s. At the upper reaches of this rise, toward the adjoining neighborhood of Nether Edge, is one of Sharrow's two areas of affluence. On this and the other side of Ecclesall Road and rising above the remaining sections of Sharrow, meandering tree-lined streets reveal beautifully intact Victorian villas. Here resides Sharrow's middle class.

For much of this century, life in Sharrow followed the relatively placid rhythms of life characterizing many inner-city English neighborhoods. Although most Sharrow residents were far from prosperous, local employment opportunities for the men—both within the community as well as in other portions of Sheffield—were good. The neighborhood's social network—centered on churches, which were mainly non-Anglican Protestant, pubs, and extended families—anchored social life. Although more affluent merchants and professionals lived up the hill in the direction of Nether Edge, social tensions between classes seem to have been muted. One of my older contacts in Sharrow recalls a considerable Jewish population in upper Sharrow and Nether Edge in the 1930s. When asked if this group was the object of any envy or hostility, Arthur Fellows responded quite to the contrary. Indeed, as a tradesperson doing house-painting and other interior decorating work, his livelihood—as well as that of many other local artisans—was in part dependent on this more affluent population.[80]

A snapshot of Sharrow's mid-twentieth-century social and physical character is provided by a survey from the 1950s. At that time the physical condition of Sharrow was becoming a source of concern for its local churches. Most of Sharrow's housing dated from before 1900, and from the start, the neighborhood's concentration of "back-to-back" houses was a problem. These two- or three-story buildings—usually twelve feet wide, covering about 150 square feet on the ground, sporting one window opening per four walls, with a second row of structures built directly behind the rows facing onto the street—made for very incommodious living conditions. Indeed, the back-to-backs made Sharrow's terrace houses—in this instance rows of mainly two-story dwellings, but with rear "courts" usually housing the privy—seem positively opulent. But the fact of the matter was, much of Sharrow's terrace housing was also in bad condition, and even when well maintained, lacking in many up-to-date household amenities. In 1956 the four churches (two Methodist and two Anglican) constituting The Moor and Lower Sharrow Council of Churches, commissioned a University of Sheffield sociologist to survey the community.

Professor Peter H. Mann's report was based on door-to-door interviewing of 300 local households, approximately a 7 percent sample of the survey area. The survey area was the belt of Sharrow running roughly parallel to London Road. In reference to the contemporary Sharrow ward, Mann's survey area "shaved" some of the poorest areas near the central city as well as the more affluent uplands toward Nether Edge and Broomhill.[81] Nevertheless, a number of Mann's findings shed light on the general conditions of the neighborhood. Sharrow was, in the mid-1950s, an extremely settled community. Only 13 percent of Mann's respondents had lived in Sharrow fewer than five years. Indeed, only 22 percent of the respondents had lived in their house for fewer than five years. Conversely, over three-fifths had lived in their house for a least ten years; over three-quarters had lived in Sharrow for that length of time. Given this degree of residential fixity, it is not especially surprising that some of Mann's expert informants noted that Sharrow was a neighborhood with a high proportion of older residents.[82]

According to the Mann survey, a considerable part of Sharrow's housing was, by modern standards, substandard. Of the 300 households contacted by Mann, 279 lacked indoor lavatories. Nonetheless, Mann's Sharrow respondents were not terribly dissatisfied with their accommodations. Over 70 percent (217) reported no plans to move from the area. Indeed, aside from old housing, Sharrow residents seemed to find little that was terribly wrong with their community. At the local schools, recreation space was in short supply. Also, many of the mothers in these economically pressed working-class families seemed to have too many

Lansdowne Estate

responsibilities—that is, managing the children, keeping house, sometimes working outside the home to supplement family income. But, even taking into account this gendered economic pressure, Sharrow was not a community revealing severe social problems. Probably the most portentous comment offered by Professor Mann pertained to the number of local pubs: "Economically, the area is over-supplied with these amenities."[83]

Rather prophetically, a substantial number of Mann's respondents identified traffic conditions as a major local problem.[84] Due to its proximity to the offices, shopping places, and other attractions of the city centre, even in the 1950s Sharrow was becoming a neighborhood through which commuters sped on their way into and out of central Sheffield. In subsequent decades the perilousness of Sharrow's streets increased and became a major point of contention dividing neighborhood activists and the local authority. Finally, the Mann survey is interesting for one rather surprising oversight. Mann's interviewers seem not to have inquired about their informants' race or ethnicity. One is left to infer that few blacks or East Asians lived in Sharrow at that time. Certainly, in the 1950s Sheffield remained a very insular, homogeneous city.[85] Nor do any of my contemporary Sharrow informants recall a local minority population in the 1950s.

In the years immediately following World War II Sharrow probably did appear to be much the same community it had been before the war, but by the end of the 1950s a variety of forces were reshaping the neighborhood. As one of the principal industrial centers of the English North, Sheffield, whose population traditionally was drawn from a very narrow geographic realm, began to experience a considerable demographic diversification. Drawn by the lure of plentiful factory jobs, immigrants from well beyond the Yorkshire/Derbyshire hinterland arrived in Sheffield. Sharrow became a point of settlement for immigrants from Italy and Poland, as well Jamaica and other former British colonies in the Caribbean. The 1961 census found among Sharrow ward's 15,249 residents, 214 immigrants from former British territories in Asia, Africa, or the Caribbean. By 1971 more than 10 percent of the ward's population was born in or descended from two parents born in these "New Commonwealth" countries.[86]

During the 1960s Sharrow's physical character also began to change. Before World War II the Sheffield council had concentrated most of its house building on the city's periphery. Land was available away from the city centre, and the Garden City-style development favored by the Labour leadership, which was not just building hous-

Renovated ("enveloped") terrace houses in the Sharrow Street area

ing but good housing for its constituents, was best suited to such semi-pastoral settings. By the 1950s the council turned to inner-city housing development. In the vicinity of Sharrow the large Broomhall, Hanover, Lansdowne, and Leverton Estates were erected between the mid-1960s and early 1970s. As a consequence, by 1971 Sharrow's housing stock included 1,203 units of council housing, or a little more than one in five local residences.[87] During the 1960s Sharrow's traffic problems also increased, and the council began to consider means of speeding the flow of traffic into and out of central Sheffield. As we shall see, these plans provoked considerable disquiet among Sharrow residents.

Yet, even with the social changes and physical disruptions affecting Sharrow during the 1960s, a considerable portion of its local population seems to have retained a strong loyalty to their community. In 1970 and 1971 members of the Sharrow Action Group, the grassroots organization seeking to modify council-sponsored redevelopment plans in the community, surveyed residents of several smaller areas within Sharrow. Although reactions to the prospect of the council's condemning and demolishing their houses were mixed (for instance, in the Bedale Road area a majority of respondents were willing to give up their residences), most of the surveyed residents wished to remain in Sharrow.[88] Typically, their assessments of Sharrow's virtues were prosaic—access to the city centre, access to local shopping, availability of bus services, even the simple fact of having lived in the community for many years—but, nevertheless, out of such mundane amenities powerful attachments can develop.

The economic crisis that struck Sheffield in the late 1970s left clear marks in Sharrow. Dozens of workshops closed in the neighborhood's industrial precincts. By 1981 the unemployment rate among Sharrow residents was 18.1 percent, well above the citywide figure of 11.0 percent. Nor did economic opportunities in Sharrow improve noticeably over the course of the most recent decade. The 1991 census reported a Sheffield unemployment rate of 12.4 percent, but within Sharrow unemployment stood at 23 percent.[89]

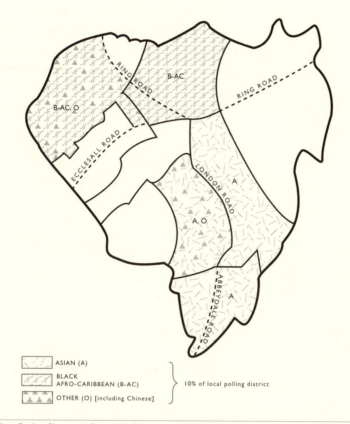

ASIAN (A)

BLACK
AFRO-CARIBBEAN (B-AC)

OTHER (O) [including Chinese]

} 10% of local polling district

Map 2–4 • *Sharrow's Racial & Ethnic Mosaic (1991)*

TABLE 2-5
SHARROW POPULATION AND HOUSING

	Total Population	Racial/Ethnic Minority %
1981	15,551	15.5*
1991	13,504	22.9

	Total Number of Housing Units	% Owner-Occupied	% Council-Owned
1981	6,396	34.8	34.9
1991	5,964	37.5	29.3

* "New Commonwealth"

Sources: Corporate Management Unit, "Summary Ward Profiles," Sheffield 1981 Census Report 7, n.d.; Corporate Management Unit, "Key Indicators for the Sheffield Wards," Sheffield 1981 Census Report 5, n.d.; Central Policy Unit, Sheffield City Council, "Summary Ward Profiles for Sheffield," Sheffield 1991 Census Report 4, January 1993; Central Policy Unit, Sheffield City Council, "Key Indicators for Sheffield Wards," February 1993, appendix.

In the last generation Sharrow has become one of the most ethnically diverse areas in Sheffield. In 1991 members of ethnic minority population groups constituted 22.9 percent of the local population. The citywide figure at that time was 5.0 percent, and Sharrow's minority population percentage was the second highest among Sheffield wards.[90] Sharrow's largest minority group are immigrants and their descendants from the Indian subcontinent. Afro-Caribbeans, who were Sharrow's first substantial minority population, have, according to my informants, decreased in number. However, in the Broomhall section of Sharrow there remains a substantial Afro-Caribbean presence. Sharrow is also home to a Chinese community, and since the late 1980s at least several hundred Somali refugees have settled in the neighborhood. By most accounts, local interethnic relations are civil. Nevertheless, in the context of Sheffield's declining economic fortunes, members of ethnic minority populations sometimes sense a degree of hostility that is bred, in part, by their presumed impact on local job opportunities. In some instances, whites in Sharrow also resent what they perceive as special treatment accorded to minorities. For example, I have spoken with numerous white Sharrow residents who feel that Somalis have been unjustifiably moved up the waiting list and assigned flats in the Lansdowne Estate.

Within Sharrow there is a clear geographic patterning of ethnic minority settlement (Map 2-4). The Indian-Pakistani ("Asian") population is concentrated in areas adjoining London Road, in particular Highfield and South View. In addition to South View's large Indian and Pakistani population, this area is also home for smaller numbers of Afro-Caribbeans and Chinese (included in the "Other" category of Map 2-4). On the western side of Ecclesall Road in Broomhall, the population is very mixed, including Afro-Caribbeans, Chinese, and some Indians and Pakistanis. Conversely, Sharrow's minority population is smallest in the area near the city centre adjoining the Bramall Lane football ground and "uphill" toward Nether Edge and Broomhill.[91]

Interestingly, and certainly quite at variance with Uptown's experience, as Sharrow's demography has shifted in the last two decades, its physical character remained relatively fixed. In the late 1960s the Sheffield City Council had planned to begin an ambitious program of housing clearance and road improvements in Sharrow. In the face of well-organized community resistance, these plans were considerably curtailed. While various sections of Sharrow did receive the attentions of the wrecking ball during the mid-1970s, a substantial portion of the community's terrace housing was saved. Subsequently, smaller low-density council housing estates were built on some of the cleared sites, and rehabilitation schemes upgraded the older housing in five subareas within Sharrow. Nor did the council succeed in implementing most of its planned road improvements. The result is that, with the exception of the Inner Ring Road cutting through the foot of Sharrow adjoining the city centre, contemporary Sharrow's street system is little changed from a generation ago. Unfortunately, from the standpoint of many Sharrow residents, this is a mixed blessing as these streets carry much larger volumes of traffic. In "upper" Sharrow there are some signs of gentrification as younger families rehabilitate the handsome Victorian villas along streets such as Priory Road, but this is a trend of very modest scale. In particular, one observes very few instances of rehabbers at work on the less imposing terrace houses of old working-class Sharrow.

VI

Chicago, the comet, and Sheffield, the hearth flame, are cities that rose to prominence within comparable political-economic contexts: nations that industrialized in the nineteenth century, whose courses of economic development were shaped in no small part by the workers, entrepreneurs, and capitalists based in their major cities. During the twentieth century, each city has experienced mixed fortune, though again there are points of evident comparability in their recent stories. These include the decline of industrial production in economically mature nations, the decentralization of urban development in the United States and Britain, and in the last generation, the reduced support for local municipalities provided by their national governments. As we shall soon see, these shifts in national policy have trickled down to the neighborhood level, and over the course of the last generation have, in each city, played a substantial role in structuring grassroots political activity.

At first glance, Uptown, the cauldron, and Sharrow, the cup of tea, might seem to be quite disparate neighborhoods. The former's history is a sequence of disruptions as real estate interests and new settlers repeatedly uproot an area that was never, in the first place, very fixed. In contrast, Sharrow—after rapidly filling at the turn of the century—settled into a half-century's stability which has been shaken only in the last 25 years. However, within their respective cities, Uptown's and Sharrow's situations are more evidently comparable. Each is a "middling" neighborhood, neither having an especially distinguished past, neither having "fallen" to the point of becoming a major source of civic concern. Neither was first, or even near the head of the line, for redevelopment within its respective city. This, indeed, probably offers a hint as to why each community was able to mobilize in response to late-1960s/early-1970s redevelopment proposals. Their residents had the time to observe the effects of redevelopment in other areas. Though this point of comparison may be more or less coincidental, both Uptown and Sharrow have become among their cities' most racially and ethnically diverse areas, a matter of some importance in thinking about the capacity of local movements to forge "communities" out of neighborhoods. Ultimately, while no two neighborhoods divided by city, nation, and even continent can be perfect "matches," there are enough intriguing points of comparison between Uptown and Sharrow to suggest an array of provocative research questions.

As I have already outlined my main research concerns, let us conclude our introduction to the comet and hearth flame, cauldron and cup of tea, by noting some evident points of contrast that have bearing on the narratives to follow. To begin with our two cities, Sheffield's jousting with the Conservative national government during the 1980s underlines the more closely intertwined circumstances of local and central government in Britain. Not only does the British central government exercise more direct control over the finances of municipalities, but over the course of the past 15 years, Tory national administrations—in particular during Margaret Thatcher's three terms as prime minister—have sought to restructure domestic public policy by, among other means, intervening in the day-to-day practices of local municipal authorities. In the United States, the Reagan administration of 1981 through 1988 sought to reorient public policy in an analogous way, but the federal government's impacts on local municipalities were far more indirect.[92]

To take another step backward in time, there is a particular sense in which Chicago's and Sheffield's programs of redevelopment may be contrasted. In the former instance, urban rebuilding was initiated in reaction to the widespread perception of urban decline. Following World War II, Chicago's population—for the first time—began to diminish as suburban development drew residents and businesses from the city. Moreover, the process of decline, notably the build-up of minority and low-income residents in central city neighborhoods, caused considerable apprehension among the city's civic and municipal leaders. For them, redevelopment was a desperately needed remedy. In the corresponding period, roughly the quarter century from the end of World War II until 1970, Sheffield's local leadership did not imagine their city to be in decline. Indeed, the governing Labour Party viewed its program of slum removal as a mopping-up operation through which a new Sheffield was being perfected. This contrasting attitude toward municipal fortunes and the imperative of urban rebuilding probably made little difference in terms of redevelopment advocates' response to criticism: in neither city did they like it. However, it is equally true that Sheffield's leadership adopted a less hard-edged attitude toward the neighborhoods whose rebuilding would be their handiwork.

In Uptown, a central impetus for the planning effort that resulted in that neighborhood's urban renewal program was demographic change. In the 1950s, as thousands upon thousands of economic refugees from Appalachia arrived in Uptown, the neighborhood's civic and institution-based leadership determined that their local area needed shoring up. In contrast, population change had little to do with the targeting of Sharrow for redevelopment. Although the neighborhood's proportion of ethnic minority residents was on the upswing by the late 1960s, there was no local call for physical redevelopment, nor did the Sheffield municipal government take particular interest in the neighborhood because of its racial/ethnic diversity. Quite unlike Uptown, in Sharrow conflict has not tended to grow out of tensions over who lives in the neighborhood.

Finally, and relatedly, neighborhood debates over redevelopment in Uptown—both in the late 1960s and in the subsequent 25 years—have typically spilled over into the political sphere. Since the late 1970s, 46th ward elections have been extremely fractious affairs, and for politically active local residents, this has come to be expected. Most such people presently think of Uptown as an inherently conflictual neighborhood. In Sharrow, redevelopment conflict was initially more muted, and in the long run—even as the neighborhood has experienced significant demographic change in tandem with nasty economic reversals—the relative calm of Sharrow ward politics has persisted.

I have highlighted this last set of points, because, even as one observes the broad areas of comparability between Chicago and Sheffield, as well as Uptown and Sharrow, it is evident that parallel circumstances may still have disparate consequences. In the next four chapters we look at Uptown and Sharrow in considerable detail, from which we will emerge with the insights to make more conclusive generalizations about what links and divides the experiences of these two neighborhoods.

NOTES

1. William Cronon, *Nature's Metropolis: Chicago and the Great West* (New York: Norton, 1991), pp. 23-93.

2. Daniel J. Boorstin, "The Businessman as an American Institution," in Alexander B. Callow, Jr., ed., *American Urban History* (New York: Oxford University Press, 1969), pp. 137-139.

3. Robert A. Slayton, *Back of the Yards: The Making of a Local Democracy* (Chicago: University of Chicago Press, 1986), pp. 15-38; Cronon, *Nature's Metropolis*, pp. 207-259.

4. Stanley Buder, *Pullman: An Experiment in Industrial Order and Community Planning 1880-1930* (New York: Oxford University Press, 1970), pp. 15-27; Harold M. Mayer and Richard C. Wade, *Chicago: Growth of a Metropolis* (Chicago: University of Chicago Press, 1969), pp. 186-192; Sam Bass Warner, Jr., *The Urban Wilderness: A History of the American City* (New York: Harper & Row, 1972), pp. 85-112.

5. Cronon, *Nature's Metropolis*, pp. 97-147.

6. James Gilbert, *Perfect Cities: Chicago's Utopias of 1893* (Chicago: University of Chicago Press, 1991), pp. 75-130; Robert W. Rydell, *World of Fairs: The Century-of-Progress Expositions* (Chicago: University of Chicago Press, 1993).

7. Paul Avrich, *The Haymarket Tragedy* (Princeton, N.J.: Princeton University Press, 1984).

8. Buder, *Pullman*, pp. 147-201.

9. Slayton, *Back of the Yards*, pp. 92-95; Allan H. Spear, *Black Chicago: The Making of a Negro Ghetto 1890-1920* (Chicago: University of Chicago Press, 1967), pp. 159-164.

10. St. Clair Drake and Horace R. Cayton, *Black Metropolis: A Study of Negro Life in a Northern City* (Chicago: University of Chicago Press, 1993), pp. 65-76; Spear, *Black Chicago*, pp. 214-222.

11. Slayton, *Back of the Yards*, pp. 117-118.

12. Kipling is quoted in Asa Briggs, *Victorian Cities* (New York: Penguin, 1980), p. 56. Historian Briggs' assessment of Chicago in this era is also clear enough. It is his "shock city" of the 1890s.

13. Rivka Shpak Lissak, *Pluralism and Progressives: Hull House and the New Immigrants, 1890-1919* (Chicago: University of Chicago Press, 1989); Jane Addams, *Twenty Years at Hull House* (New York: Signet, 1981).

14. Dennis R. Judd and Todd Swanstrom, *City Politics: Private Power & Public Policy* (New York: HarperCollins, 1994), p. 34.

15. Thomas S. Hines, *Burnham of Chicago: Architect and Planner* (Chicago: University of Chicago Press, 1979), pp. 73-138; Mel Scott, *American City Planning Since 1890* (Berkeley: University of California Press, 1971), pp. 31-109.

16. Burnham is quoted in Hines, *Burnham of Chicago*, p. 315.

17. Thomas Lee Philpott, *The Slum and the Ghetto: Neighborhood Deterioration and Middle-Class Reform, Chicago, 1880-1930* (New York: Oxford University Press, 1978), pp. 229-243.

18. Arnold R. Hirsch, *Making the Second Ghetto: Race and Housing in Chicago, 1940-1960* (New York: Cambridge University Press, 1983), pp. 100-134.

19. Hirsch, *Making the Second Ghetto*, pp. 135-170; Larry Bennett, "Postwar Redevelopment in Chicago: The Declining Politics of Party and the Rise of Neighborhood Politics, in Gregory D. Squires, ed., *Unequal Partnerships: The Political Economy of Urban Redevelopment in Postwar America* (New Brunswick, N.J.: Rutgers University Press, 1989), pp. 167-171; Bennett, *Fragments of Cities: The New American Downtowns and Neighborhoods* (Columbus: Ohio State University Press, 1990), pp. 57-69.

20. Robert A. Caro, *The Power Broker: Robert Moses and the Fall of New York* (New York: Vintage, 1975). Logue and Herman are discussed in John H. Mollenkopf, *The Contested City* (Princeton, N.J.: Princeton University Press, 1983), pp. 162-169.

21. Steven P. Erie, *Rainbow's End: Irish-Americans and the Dilemmas of Urban Machine Politics, 1840-1985* (Berkeley: University of California Press, 1988), xii.

22. Paul Kleppner, *Chicago Divided: The Making of a Black Mayor* (DeKalb: Northern Illinois University Press, 1985), pp. 15-31.

23. Harold F. Gosnell, *Machine Politics Chicago Model* (Chicago: University of Chicago Press, 1977), pp. 10-12; Ira Katznelson, *Black Men, White*

Cities: Race, Politics, and Migration in the United States, 1900-1930, and Britain, 1948-1968 (Chicago: University of Chicago Press, 1976), pp. 89-102.

24. Gosnell, *Machine Politics Chicago Model,* pp. 27-90; Roger Biles, *Big City Boss in Depression and War: Mayor Edward J. Kelly of Chicago* (DeKalb: Northern Illinois University Press, 1984).

25. Theodore J. Lowi, "Gosnell's Chicago Revisited Via Lindsay's New York," foreword to the second edition of Gosnell, *Machine Politics Chicago Model,* pp. v-xviii.

26. Milton Rakove, *Don't Make No Waves Don't Back No Losers: An Insider's Analysis of the Daley Machine* (Bloomington: Indiana University Press, 1975), pp. 43-89; David Halberstam, "Daley of Chicago," *Harper's Magazine,* August 1968, pp. 25-35; Roger Biles, *Richard J. Daley: Politics, Race, and the Governing of Chicago* (DeKalb: Northern Illinois University Press, 1995), pp. 46-52; Bennett, "Postwar Redevelopment in Chicago," pp. 165-167.

27. Alan B. Anderson and George W. Pickering, *Confronting the Color Line: The Broken Promise of the Civil Rights Movement in Chicago* (Athens: University of Georgia Press, 1986); David J. Garrow, *Bearing the Cross: Martin Luther King Jr. and the Southern Christian Leadership Council* (New York: Vintage, 1988), pp. 431-525; Nicholas Lemann, *The Promised Land: The Great Migration and How It Changed America* (New York: Vintage, 1992), pp. 234-240.

28. Mike Royko, *Boss: Richard J. Daley of Chicago* (New York: Signet, 1971).

29. Kleppner, *Chicago Divided,* pp. 78-90.

30. Sanford J. Ungar, "Chicago: A.D. (After Daley)," *The Atlantic Monthly,* March 1977, pp. 4-18

31. Kleppner, *Chicago Divided,* pp. 134-239; Abdul Alkalimat and Doug Gills, *Harold Washington and the Crisis of Black Power in Chicago* (Chicago: Twenty-First Century Books, 1989); Gary Rivlin, *Fire on the Prairie: Chicago's Harold Washington and the Politics of Race* (New York: Henry Holt, 1993).

32. Larry Bennett, "Harold Washington and the Black Urban Regime," *Urban Affairs Quarterly* 28 (March 1993): 423-440; Pierre Clavel and Wim Wiewel, eds., *Harold Washington and the Neighborhoods: Progressive City Government in Chicago, 1983-1987* (New Brunswick, N.J.: Rutgers University Press, 1991).

33. William J. Grimshaw, *Bitter Fruit: Black Politics and the Chicago Machine, 1931-1991* (Chicago: University of Chicago Press, 1992), pp. 197-224; Greg Hinz, "The Pothole Mayor," *Chicago,* February 1995, pp. 104-109, 122-127.

34. This and subsequent quoted descriptions of early Uptown are drawn from "Documents: History of the Uptown Community, Chicago," prepared for the Chicago Historical Society and Local Community Research Committee, University of Chicago (n.d.). The Chicago Historical Society holds this file, whose narratives were collected in the 1920s.

35. Sheila Gribben, "Uptown: City's Defiant Former Playground," *Crain's Chicago Business*, April 25, 1983; Marjorie DeVault, "Uptown," pp. 6-7 in Chicago Fact Book Consortium, eds., *Local Community Fact Book Chicago Metropolitan Area* (Chicago: Chicago Review Press, 1984).

36. Gerald D. Suttles, *The Man-Made City: The Land Use Confidence Game in Chicago* (Chicago: University of Chicago Press, 1990), p. 83.

37. Three- and six-flat buildings are three-floor structures with a single or two residential units on each level. Courtyard buildings are larger structures, arranged on site in a roughly horseshoe configuration with the open end facing the street. "Four-plus-ones" are post-World War II apartment buildings with four residential levels set atop pillars and an open-air parking area.

38. Clarus Backes, "We Call Them Hillbillies," *Chicago Tribune Magazine*, September 22, 1968, pp. 26-27.

39. Lester Jacobson, "Sweet and Sour Views Divide 'New Chinatown'," *Uptown News*, February 4, 1975; Richard Phillips, "Chinatown North: Can It Revive Area?," *Chicago Tribune*, December 12, 1976.

40. Leonard Aronson, "Fires Plaguing Uptown Area," *Chicago Today*, June 9, 1971; Brian J. Kelly, "Series of Uptown Fires Yields Group $560,000," *Chicago Sun-Times*, February 8, 1980.

41. Carolyn Toll, "Halfway Houses 'Invade' Uptown," *Chicago Tribune*, February 21, 1971; Jerome Watson, "Uptown...Halfway to Nowhere," *Chicago Sun-Times*, March 14, 1972.

42. Ed Marciniak, *Reversing Urban Decline: The Winthrop-Kenmore Corridor in the Uptown Communities of Chicago* (Washington, D.C.: National Center for Urban Ethnic Affairs, 1981), pp. 26-49. The territory around O'Hare Airport, annexed by the City in the 1950s, became Chicago's 76th community area.

43. *Focusing In: Indicators of Economic Change in Chicago's Neighborhoods* (Chicago: Woodstock Institute, 1994), p. 16.

44. Mary Walton, *Sheffield: Its Story and Its Achievements* (Otley, U.K.: Amethyst Press, 1984), pp. 35-45; Bryan E. Coates, "The Geography of the Industrialization and Urbanization of South Yorkshire, 18th Century to 20th Century," in Sidney Pollard and Colin Holmes, eds., *Essays in the Economic and Social History of South Yorkshire* (Sheffield: S. Yorkshire County Council, 1976), pp. 16-18.

45. Daniel Defoe, *A Tour Through the Whole of Great Britain*, Vol. 2 (New York: Dutton, 1966), p. 183.

46. Sidney Pollard, "The Growth of Population," in D.L. Linton, ed., *Sheffield and Its Region* (Sheffield: British Association for the Advancement of Sciences, 1956), p. 172.

47. Briggs, Victorian Cities, p. 89; Derek Fraser, *Power and Authority in the Victorian City* (New York: St. Martin's Press, 1979), p. 134.

48. Sidney Pollard, *A History of Labour in Sheffield* (Liverpool: Liverpool University Press, 1959), pp. 50-59; Nigel Thrift, "Introduction: The Geography of Nineteenth-Century Class Formation," in Nigel Thrift

and Peter Williams, eds., *Class and Space: The Making of Urban Society* (London: Routledge & Kegan Paul, 1987), pp. 31-41.

49. Pollard, *A History of Labour in Sheffield*, pp. 8-17; Fraser, *Power and Authority*, p. 140; E.P. Thompson, *The Making of the English Working Class* (New York: Vintage Books, 1966), pp. 321-331.

50. Sidney Pollard, "The Trade Unions," in Linton, *Sheffield*, pp. 192-193.

51. Pollard, *A History of Labour in Sheffield*, p. 121.

52. Thompson, *The Making of the English Working Class*, pp. 472-521; also see F.K. Donnelly and John L. Baxter, "Sheffield and the English Revolutionary Tradition, 1991-1820," pp. 90-117 in Pollard and Holmes, *Essays.*

53. Fraser, *Power and Authority*, pp. 139-148.

54. Geoffrey Tweedale, "The Business and Technology of Sheffield Steelmaking," pp. 142-193 in Clyde Binford, Richard Childs, Roger Harper, David Hey, David Martin, and Geoffrey Tweedale, eds., *The History of the City of Sheffield 1843-1993*, Vol. II: *Society* (Sheffield: Sheffield Academic Press, 1993); G.P. Jones, "Industrial Evolution," pp. 155-160 in Linton, *Sheffield*; Pollard, *A History of Labour*, pp. 159-175.

55. Coates, "The Geography of the Industrialization and Urbanization of South Yorkshire," p. 19.

56. A.J. Hunt, "The Morphology and Growth of Sheffield," in Linton, *Sheffield*, p. 234.

57. Pollard, "The Trade Unions," pp. 193-194.

58. Andrew Thorpe, "The Consolidation of a Labour Stronghold 1926-1951," pp. 85-118, and William Hampton, "Optimism and Growth 1951-1973," pp. 119-149 in Binford et al., *The History of the City of Sheffield*, Vol. I: *Politics.*

59. Enid Gauldie, *Cruel Habitations: A History of Working-Class Housing 1780-1918* (London: George Allen & Unwin, 1974), p. 299.

60. Peter Dickens, Simon Duncan, Mark Goodwin, and Fred Gray, *Housing, States, and Localities* (London: Methuen, 1985), p. 166. "Council flats" are roughly the equivalent of "public housing" in the United States. However, in British cities a far larger proportion of the population lives in council "estates," and until very recently, residence in council housing did not bear anything like the social stigma characteristic of public housing in the United States.

61. Hampton, "Optimism and Growth," pp. 129-131.

62. Sheffield Town Planning Committee, *Sheffield Replanned*, 1945; Dickens et al., *Housing, States, and Localities*, pp. 164-166, 170-173; Anthony R. Sutcliffe, "Planning the British Steel Metropolis: Sheffield Since World War II," pp. 183-199 in Joel A. Tarr, ed., *Pittsburgh-Sheffield Sister Cities* (Pittsburgh: Carnegie Mellon University Press, 1986); R.J. Marshall, "Town Planning in Sheffield," pp. 17-32 in Binford et al., *The History of the City of Sheffield*, Vol. II.

63. William Hampton, *Democracy and Community: A Study of Politics in*

Sheffield (New York: Oxford University Press, 1970), pp. 246-277; Stuart Lowe, *Urban Social Movements: The City After Castells* (London: Macmillan, 1986), pp. 94-97.

64. Sheffield City Liaison Group, "The Way Ahead: Plans for the Regeneration of Sheffield," April 1994, p. 31.

65. Paul Lawless, "Regeneration in Sheffield: From Radical Intervention to Partnership," in Dennis Judd and Michael Parkinson, eds., *Leadership and Urban Regeneration* (Newbury Park, Calif.: Sage Publications, 1990), p. 134.

66. Margaret Drabble, "A Novelist in a Derelict City," *New York Times Magazine*, April 14, 1985, pp. 76-81.

67. William Schmidt, "In Village Under Ax, British Miners Feel Betrayed," *New York Times*, October 25, 1992, p. 3; Celia Weston, "Outlook for Britain's Collieries Grows Gloomier," *The Guardian*, August 14, 1993, p. 31.

68. P.D. Foley and D.H. Green, "Yorkshire and Humberside: The Strategic Framework for Change in a Declining Industrial Region," University of Sheffield, Department of Town and Regional Planning Occasional Paper #58, May 1985; P. Gibbon, "Recession, Restructuring, and 'Regeneration' in Sheffield During the 1980s," Sheffield City Polytechnic, Centre for Regional and Social Research, September 1989.

69. A.G. Champion and A.R. Townsend, *Contemporary Britain: A Geographical Perspective* (London: Edward Arnold, 1990), pp. 69-97, 207-232.

70. David Blunkett, "Message from the Leader of the Sheffield City Council," March 1981. In British cities the Lord Mayor is an honorific position. The chief local official, who functions something like a municipal prime minister, is the Council Leader. The Council Leader is selected by the majority party on the City Council.

71. David Blunkett and Geoff Green, "Building from the Bottom: The Sheffield Experience," London: Fabian Tract 491, October 1983, pp. 7-20; Paul Lawless, "Regeneration in Sheffield," pp. 137-141; Patrick Seyd, "The Political Management of Decline 1973-1993," in Binford et al., *A History of the City of Sheffield*, Vol. I, pp. 159-167.

72. Patrick Seyd, "The Political Management of Decline," p. 166.

73. David Waddington, Karen Jones, and Charles Critcher, *Flashpoints: Studies in Public Disorder* (London: Routledge, 1989), pp. 32-39, 71-88.

74. "Barrage of Protest," *Sheffield Morning Telegraph*, April 29, 1983.

75. Stewart Lansley, Sue Goss, and Christian Wolmar, *Councils in Conflict: The Rise and Fall of the Municipal Left* (London: Macmillan, 1989), pp. 34-46.

76. Wendy Battersby, "Worst Fears Coming True for Hard-Hit City Centre Stores," *Sheffield Telegraph*, July 26, 1991; "Ideas in Store to Breathe Life Back into City Centre," *Sheffield Telegraph*, July 2, 1993.

77. Seyd, "The Political Management of Decline," p. 177.

78. Lawless, "Regeneration in Sheffield," pp. 141-146; Seyd, "The Political Management of Decline," pp. 167-183; Sheffield Development Corporation, "A Vision of the Lower Don Valley: A Planning Framework for Discussion," October 1989.

79. "They Lived in Sharrow and Nether Edge," (Nether Edge Neighbourhood Group, Local History Section, 1988), pp. 4-5; Sheffield Housing Department, "Sharrow Renewal Area," February 1992, pp. 6-7; Pollard, *A History of Labour in Sheffield*, p. 185.

80. Interview with Arthur Fellows, Lansdowne Residents Association, August 7, 1993.

81. My benchmark in discussing contemporary Sharrow is the Sharrow ward as redistricted in the late 1970s. As such, Sharrow's boundaries remained constant for the 1981 and 1991 censuses. For previous cen-suses, Sharrow ward included areas to the east presently lying within Heeley ward. The 1970s redistricting added areas west of Ecclesall Road to Sharrow ward. Of course, in residents' and outsiders' minds, Sharrow's geographic reach has surely been even more fluid—at least beyond its core along London Road—than in these relatively arbitrary political-jurisdictional definitions. P.N. Mann's Sharrow is demarcated in "The Moor and Sharrow Social Survey," n.d., p. 1.

82. "The Moor and Sharrow Social Survey," pp. 2-3.

83. "The Moor and Sharrow Social Survey," p. 2

84. "The Moor and Sharrow Social Survey," p. 7.

85. Pollard, "The Growth of Population," p. 179.

86. Census files, Sheffield Central Library, Local Studies Library.

87. Census files, Sheffield Central Library, Local Studies Library.

88. *Views of Sharrow*, (Sharrow Community Development Project, December 1972), pp. 44-49.

89. Corporate Management Unit, "Summary Ward Profile: Sharrow," Sheffield 1981 Census Report 7, n.d.; Central Policy Unit, Sheffield City Council, "Summary Ward Profiles for Sheffield," Sheffield 1991 Census Report 4, January, 1993; Central Policy Unit, Sheffield City Council, "The Detailed Results for Sheffield," Sheffield 1991 Census Report 3, January 1993, p. 4.

90. Central Policy Unit, Sheffield City Council, "Key Indicators for Sheffield Wards," Sheffield 1991 Census Report 6, February 1993, appendix, p. 1.

91. Central Policy Unit, "Summary Profiles for Central Constituency: Wards and Polling Districts," Sheffield 1991 Census Report 7, March 1993, pp. 55-64.

92. Robin Hambleton, *Urban Government in the 1990s: Lessons from the USA* (University of Bristol, School of Advanced Urban Studies, Occasional Paper 35, 1990), pp. 88-89.

CHAPTER THREE
URBAN RENEWAL IN UPTOWN

The roots of political conflict in contemporary Uptown are to be found in the 1960s. During that decade demographic changes that had been underway since the 1950s came to a head, with urban renewal the issue that kindled previously latent hostilities. The urban renewal debate spawned a degree of local mobilization and opened up a pattern of neighborhood cleavages that continue to influence Uptown's politics. Furthermore, the physical consequences of urban renewal are a principal source of contemporary Uptown's seemingly perpetual merry-go-round of residential decay, real estate speculation, and grassroots resistance to efforts at neighborhood upgrading.

II

Although the Great Depression was cruel to Uptown, as it was to communities across the United States, on the eve of World War II Uptown remained, in many respects, a desirable neighborhood. A compendious report on the city's housing, published by the Chicago Plan Commission in 1940 and carried out under the direction of the federal Works Progress Administration, reported that a higher percentage of Uptown's housing units were in good condition (85 percent) than in the city at large (80 percent) and that Uptown's median monthly rent was 31 percent greater than the city figure. At the same time, the neighborhood's fragmented socio-economic and geographic structure was already visible. North of Wilson Avenue along the "el" tracks in the Kenmore-Winthrop corridor, as well as west of the "el" in Heart of Uptown/Sheridan Park, overcrowded residential quarters without sanitary facilities were prevalent.[1]

In the decade following World War II Chicago was beset by an acute housing shortage, and in Uptown the demand for housing was especially intense. The 1950 census reported that fewer than 3 percent of the residential units in Uptown were unoccupied, and nearly 20 percent of the population was squeezed into quarters housing more than one person per room.[2] In the same year a survey of Uptown published by the Young Men's Jewish Association commented that "...it appears now that during the past decade changes have taken place which make the area no longer a desirable place for family residence."[3] In the years to follow, the population composition of Uptown changed dramatically as the flood of uprooted Appalachian whites began to arrive and indeed, over the course of the 1950s Uptowners' median educational attainment actually declined by half a year.[4]

In 1955 local business, political, and civic leaders formed the Uptown Chicago Commission (UCC), the organization that took the lead in promoting urban renewal in the subsequent decade and a half. In its early days the UCC fancied itself speaking for "a city within a city," and befitting such an identity, quite an impressive array of business and civic figures supported its activities. Executives from three local financial institutions, the Uptown National Bank, Bank of Chicago, and Uptown Federal Savings and Loan, served on the UCC Board. Two insurance companies with headquarters in Uptown, Kemper and Combined Insurance, also supported UCC initiatives, and a number of real estate firms were affiliated with the group. Also serving on the UCC Board was the wife of one of the Daley administration's leading city planners, Ira Bach. The Bachs were Uptown residents. One of the UCC's advisors was James C. Downs, Jr., head of the Real Estate Research Corporation and another important advisor to Mayor Daley.

From its genesis the UCC devoted itself to promoting an urban renewal program for Uptown, and in August of 1957, having worked for over a year with the staff of the city's urban renewal agency, the Community Conservation Board, the UCC released a proposal for a 10-year General Urban Renewal Plan. The proposal's cover letter described the neighborhood in the following terms:

The area has been afflicted by a growth of delin-
quency, an increase in housing and zoning code viola-
tions and an abnormal exodus of families. There is
dilapidation, obsolescence, deterioration, illegal uses,
lack of physical maintenance and an intense density
of population and overuse of community facilities. All
of this has created a blighted situation which in the
last few years has spread rapidly.[5]

Substantively, the proposal advocated a detailed study of the neigh-
borhood and action to prop up the business core around the
Broadway/Lawrence axis and to improve traffic flow in various parts of
Uptown. The document also anticipated "spot clearance" along the
Corridor and in Heart of Uptown/Sheridan Park. Yet despite the
UCC's portrait of neighborhood decline, and the Community
Conservation Board staff's participation in preparing the UCC proposal, in 1957 no urban renewal designation for Uptown was forthcoming. The UCC, in turn, continued to publicize the need for urban
renewal in Uptown while formulating a series of more limited measures
aimed at upgrading portions of the neighborhood.

On the public relations front, the UCC's annual meeting became a
forum for the group to articulate its vision of the community and discuss
practical initiatives to achieve its goals. Among the UCC's models was the
ongoing redevelopment of the South Side Hyde Park neighborhood,
which was directed by the University of Chicago and a planning body
closely associated with the university, the South East Chicago
Commission (SECC). Speaking to the 1960 UCC meeting, the SECC's
director, Julian Levi, suggested cooperation between the two groups, possibly anticipating that the UCC's efforts in Uptown would evoke the kind
of controversy emerging in Hyde Park: "We've got to work together. Your
problem is to develop economic and social forces that work toward community betterment. The time will come when your motives and reason
will be challenged. You must withstand criticism."[6] Three years later,
nationally renowned comedian Danny Thomas, whose first nightclub
engagement had been at the 5100 Club on Broadway, advocated urban
renewal more soothingly: "Make it pretty. It deserves to be. Get your

schools and streets maintained and teach your kids to run to the police, not from them."[7] Thomas backed up his commitment to the UCC and its efforts with a contribution of $1,000.

However, as the late 1950s wore into the early 1960s, and in spite of UCC's continued prodding the Community Conservation Board still did not designate Uptown for urban renewal, some UCC leaders expressed a more confrontational attitude toward the community and its ailments. In May 1963 at a citywide conference on neighborhood conservation, Jerome Pugh of Combined Insurance commented: "There are many people living in Uptown who don't belong there." Asked where these people, if displaced, might go, Pugh responded, "That's their problem."[8]

The first of UCC's self-help measures was a proposal, released late in 1958, to speed up building rehabilitation in the neighborhood through a combination of stricter code enforcement, targeted housing investment financed from a pool of funds set aside by UCC-affiliated lending institutions, and the provision of federal mortgage insurance for investors. The UCC's proposal suggested that this effort would be focused on a "pilot area" within the community, but the document did not specify the location of the pilot area.[9]

By the spring of 1960 the UCC committed itself to sponsor a full-fledged community study. The consulting firm hired to prepare the Uptown report was headed by Jack Meltzer, former head of the South East Chicago Commission's Planning Unit. *Uptown: A Planning Report*, which was usually referred to as the Meltzer Report, appeared in May 1962.[10] Echoing the UCC's half decade of urban renewal advocacy, the Meltzer Report proposed that all of Uptown constitute a conservation area, in which building rehabilitation and some clearance would be employed to upgrade dwellings and businesses. Within the conservation area the central spine of Uptown would be subject to more thorough-going urban renewal clearance. The proposed urban renewal area ran from the south end of Uptown up to Foster Avenue, and from a block or two west of Broadway over to the lakefront parks. As such, the urban renewal area included the Corridor, Heart of Uptown/Sheridan Park, and the deteriorated residential blocks along Clarendon Avenue.

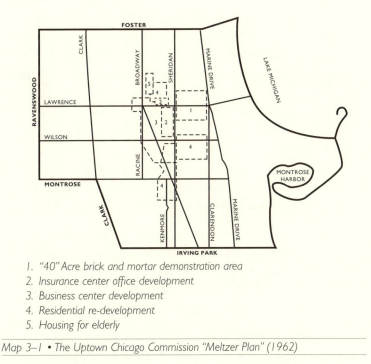

1. *"40" Acre brick and mortar demonstration area*
2. *Insurance center office development*
3. *Business center development*
4. *Residential re-development*
5. *Housing for elderly*

Map 3–1 • The Uptown Chicago Commission "Meltzer Plan" (1962)

The UCC's "city within a city" vision of Uptown pervades the Meltzer Report (Map 3-1). The principal ingredients of its urban renewal/conservation plan were upgrading the Broadway/Lawrence shopping district, reserving the area just to the east (surrounding the Kemper offices) as an "Insurance Center Office Development," rerouting Broadway to ease traffic congestion in the commercial core, and residential redevelopment along the Corridor-Heart of Uptown/Sheridan Park spine and to the east. The residential redevelopment would aim to decrease population densities by "deconverting" apartment buildings in which larger units had previously been cut up into more numerous, smaller units. On the ground small parks and pedestrian walkways would replace several streets. In short, the commercial heart of the neighborhood would be restored, while physical upgrading would enhance the surrounding residential areas. Except for its smaller scale, the Meltzer Plan's physical components duplicate the strategies characteristic of downtown planning documents of the same era.[11]

The Meltzer Report also carried through the UCC's earlier proposal to identify a target area in which intensive rehabilitation measures
would be concentrated. This "40" Acre Brick and Mortar
Demonstration Area covered four long blocks east of Sheridan Road,
running over to Margate Park and bounded by Castlewood Terrace on
the north and Lakeside Place on the south. In the aftermath of the
Meltzer Report's release, the city still failed to sponsor an urban renewal
plan for Uptown. However, the Department of Urban Renewal (the
Community Conservation Board's successor agency) did agree to purchase property in the "40" Acre Demonstration Area for rehabilitation
and sale to new private landlords.[12]

This city-sponsored rehabilitation project, which was managed by
a new unit called the Chicago Dwellings Association, was joined by one
of Uptown's principal financial institutions, Uptown Federal Savings
and Loan, in 1965. In the same Clarendon Park site of the "40" Acre
Demonstration Area, Uptown Federal initiated Operation Pride:

> ...a team of ten loan officers and appraisers were
> assigned...to contact every building in the Quadrant
> and to urge participation in an extensive exterior
> clean-up drive. Emphasis in this effort was not on
> achieving deconversion but rather on steam-cleaning
> and painting of exteriors, landscaping and general
> improvement of the environment of the block. Cash
> prizes were offered for each block and for the three
> best buildings in the larger area.[13]

However, after nearly a decade of failed efforts to win urban
renewal designation for Uptown, some of the UCC's core supporters
began to waver. Most notably, in 1964 Kemper Insurance commissioned a study to examine its locational options, the study advising
the firm to consider relocating its Uptown offices. Ironically, the
Kemper study was prepared by the Real Estate Research
Corporation, whose head, James Downs, was also a principal in
efforts to promote Uptown urban renewal. When queried by some of
his Uptown business associates about his firm's advice to Kemper,

Downs "assured the committee that his report to Kemper Insurance was an analysis of the best alternatives to meet the company's particular needs, not an expression of general lack of confidence in the Uptown community."[14] In retrospect, Downs seems to have been making a fine distinction. By the end of 1971 Kemper Insurance relocated its offices to suburban Long Grove, Illinois.

In fact, even as the resolve of some of Uptown's business leaders was flagging, the UCC's efforts were on the verge of success. In May 1965 the Chicago City Council authorized the Department of Urban Renewal to prepare a survey of Uptown, and by the fall of 1966 Uptown was approved for urban renewal. However, the city did scale down the ambitious plans of the UCC. Unlike the UCC's proposals, the approved Uptown conservation area did not include the portions of the neighborhood north of Argyle Street and south of Montrose Avenue. Within the conservation area, a "Project I" urban renewal zone was carved out of the portion of Uptown east of Sheridan Road, the area UCC had been targeting for intensive code enforcement and rehabilitation (Map 3-2).[15]

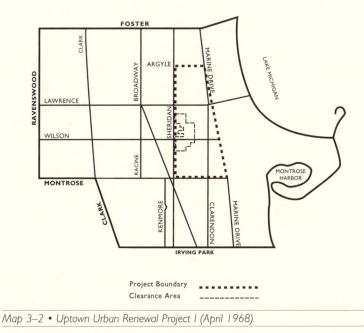

Map 3–2 • Uptown Urban Renewal Project I (April 1968)

In 1966 Department of Urban Renewal staff began to prepare detailed plans for the Uptown project, and in June of 1967 Mayor Daley appointed the local citizens council mandated to oversee urban renewal implementation. Of eleven appointees to the Uptown Conservation Community Council (CCC), eight were members of the UCC.[16] This concentration of UCC representation undoubtedly seemed wholly appropriate to the mayor, as well as to the Uptown leaders who had been advocating urban renewal for the past decade, but within weeks of its formation the CCC was under fire. Indeed, since the middle of the decade Uptown's political and organizational character had begun to shift, at first so subtly as to probably escape the notice of the neighborhood's established leadership. Part of this political change is attributable to the neighborhood's evolving demographic character. Part of the change must be attributed to the New Left's serendipitous appearance in Uptown.

In 1963 the Students for a Democratic Society (SDS) had initiated its Economic Research and Action Project (ERAP), an effort to push the student movement beyond university campuses and to build ties with the urban working class.[17] In Chicago, the ERAP organizers dubbed themselves Jobs or Income Now (JOIN), rented space next to an unemployment office on North Kedzie Avenue, and among other activities aimed at publicizing local unemployment, sold apples in the Loop. However, as these efforts seemed neither to generate much public attention nor lead to contacts with local labor-based organizations, JOIN rechristened itself JOIN-Community Union and determined to move its office to a neighborhood setting. Uptown was chosen as JOIN's new base of operations.[18]

JOIN's leaders, who included SDS notables Rennie Davis and Todd Gitlin, fixed on Uptown because of its Appalachian population, which they viewed as a potential ally for the civil rights and student movements. With the move to Uptown the group also shifted its agenda from publicizing broadscale social problems to meeting the more immediate needs of neighborhood "constituents." For example, in the spring of 1966 JOIN pressured a local landlord into accepting it as the "collective bargaining" agent for his tenants.[19] JOIN had considerable influence on Uptown's younger population, spinning off organizations such as the Goodfellows and the Young Patriots, groups of young men variously characterized as gangs or politically active teenagers. By the fall of 1966 JOIN was prominent enough to draw the attention of the Chicago Police Department, which raided its Uptown office.[20]

Certainly JOIN made its presence known at the first public meeting of the CCC on July 26, 1967. One of the group's members, Diane Fager, objected to the composition of the conservation council, observing that neither Appalachian whites nor Puerto Ricans were represented. Fager suggested that additional appointments to the council should represent these groups. Defending the predominance of UCCers on the CCC, Chairperson Urania Damofle responded that "...the commission has been an active community group working on community problems for 15 years, and never once has JOIN offered to work with us on those problems."[21] In spite of Damofle's efforts to dismiss JOIN, this meeting was the start of a furious controversy, in which all aspects of the urban renewal process and program content would be disputed.

As was typically the case of this era's urban renewal proposals, the Uptown project's planners foresaw a massive physical reconstruction of the neighborhood. The Uptown Conservation Plan, presented to the neighborhood in February 1968, anticipated the concentration of clearance activities (estimated to take from 20 to 30 percent of Uptown's housing units), predictably enough, in a "redevelopment" zone ("...areas that are to be potentially subject to general, but not necessarily 100 percent clearance") running north/south through the spine of the neighborhood. In effect, the Corridor and Heart of Uptown/Sheridan Park would bear the brunt of the clearance. Ironically, given the UCC's longstanding advocacy of building deconversion and the reduction of Uptown's population density, the conservation plan also proposed that the population of the redevelopment area increase from 38,000 to 47,000.[22]

The tentative land use map included in the February 1968 planning document also identified two alternative sites for a new Chicago City Colleges campus. One of the potential sites was between Wilson Avenue and Lawrence Avenue just to the southeast of the neighborhood business core. The second site was south of Wilson and just west of the "el" tracks, that is, the eastern section of Heart of Uptown/Sheridan Park. Within months the proposal to raze this area to provide space for the community college emerged as the urban renewal plan's most controversial element.

The UCC strongly supported the location of the community college campus in Uptown, although just how the college would benefit the neighborhood was a matter of some uncertainty. On the one hand, some proponents of the college claimed that it would serve the neighborhood's undereducated and economically marginal population. Others, seemingly thinking of the community college in terms of a traditional four-year institution, presumed that the student body would provide a needed economic stimulus for Uptown's merchants. However, the president of Uptown Federal may have offered the most candid rationale for siting the college in Heart of Uptown/Sheridan Park: "There are a lot of cheap hotels that have been there for years, the core when the decline of Uptown started. The storefronts were available, the hotels were available, the bars were available. The college would eliminate that problem."[23] In any event, by July 1968 the CCC had approved the Heart of Uptown/Sheridan Park site for the community college campus.

Throughout 1968 and 1969 the CCC encountered criticism, and on several occasions disruptive interruptions of its meetings, by a shifting array of hastily formed organizations, including the United People, the Voice of the Poor (soon renamed the Voice of the People), and the Uptown Area People's Planning Coalition. At the center of the opposition's concern with the CCC's plans was residential dislocation, with the urban renewal opponents claiming that the community college site alone would unhouse from 1,700 to as many as 6,000 residents. Contemporary accounts of the urban renewal debate present an ambiguous portrait of the people represented in these opposition organizations. For instance, although Uptown's Appalachians comprised the community's largest low-income population group, and many resided in the Heart of Uptown/Sheridan Park area slated to make way for the community college, bringing the Appalachians to meetings, much less solidifying their ranks into a mobilized political force, was difficult.[24]

Nonetheless, some indigenous Appalachian leaders did emerge to lead the opposition to urban renewal. By 1968 the student leadership of JOIN had been replaced by local residents. In effect, the anti-urban renewal coalition seems to have been a polyglot of the community's relatively new and disenfranchised residents—white, black, and Latino—initially leavened by some leadership from SDS students and later sustained by local community activists and social service workers.

The most visible urban renewal opponent was Chuck Geary, a native of Horsebranch, Kentucky, who directed a local employment service. Using what a journalist called a "stomp-on-the-tables and grab-the-microphone" approach to political debate, Geary had extensive ties among the Uptown Appalachian population.[25] By his own account he had helped 50 families relocate from Kentucky to Uptown, and from time to time Geary augmented his social service work with pentecostal preaching.[26] Geary's stance toward the Uptown urban renewal plan is captured in this excerpt from the newsletter of the Uptown Area People's Planning Coalition:

> Why do we have to keep reminding people in Uptown that the Poor People are human and have a mind to think with as well as the ones who say we cannot sit on their Advisory Councils and M.A.P.C. and C.C.C., etc. [sic] As for the people who do not want us here we know you have set out to make Uptown a Gold Coast and ship our families back to the farms—Puerto Rico—Africa, etc. But don't you know if we all go there will be no one to pay your taxes, there will be no one to work in your factorys [sic], to produce your goods, no one to live in your apartments or to pay you rent.[27]

In fact, quick on the heels of the city's authorization of Uptown urban renewal planning was an explosion of real estate speculation in the Project I urban renewal zone. By June 1968 the United People complained of more than a dozen building demolitions in this area.[28] Thus, in addition to their lack of representation on the CCC, urban renewal opponents such as Geary were observing the start of a dislocation process preceding the approval of a local urban renewal plan. In the face of these sudden developments, the urban renewal opposition inaugurated its own planning process in tandem with its efforts to impede CCC action.

Geary and other urban renewal opponents joined forces with a pair of architects, Rodney and Sidney Wright, who, even as the city's urban renewal planners were making their case to the community, were themselves meeting with block and tenant groups around the neighborhood. Focusing on the Heart of Uptown/Sheridan Park site, Wright, Geary, and their community supporters developed an alternative plan that would preserve most of the existing housing, introduce social service facilities and some commercial development, and retain affordable rents. As a physical plan, the village would retain the comparatively small scale of Heart of Uptown/Sheridan Park's extant architecture, reduce automobile traffic by closing streets, and ultimately, in the words of Chuck Geary, "give the people something that belongs to them." In an evocation of the southeast Piedmont roots of so many of Heart of Uptown/Sheridan Park's incumbent residents, the Geary, Wright et al. alternative plan was called Hank Williams Village.[29]

By the fall of 1968 plans for Hank Williams Village were sufficiently detailed for presentation to the CCC. In the meantime, the urban renewal opposition staged a series of marches and confrontational community meetings aimed at highlighting their objections to the CCC's tentative urban renewal plan. Indeed, in March of 1969 urban renewal opponents had one of their wishes granted as Mayor Daley appointed additional members to the CCC, filling it out to its maximum statutory membership of fifteen. Nonetheless, the new appointments did not especially satisfy the opposition. Commented Chuck Geary: "It's Dewey Couch against the world."[30]

Still, in May 1969 Urania Damofle and the CCC promised to reconsider the community college/Heart of Uptown/Sheridan Park site if Geary and his allies could demonstrate that there was financial backing for the Hank Williams Village proposal. In the following weeks the

Uptown Area People's Planning Coalition won financial commitments from a number of businesses and foundations; but ultimately, after a series of rancorous meetings with the CCC, failed to convince the council that its plan was economically viable. On July 21, 1969 the CCC subcommittee reviewing the coalition plan voted to reject Hank Williams Village. On July 29 a plurality of the CCC membership (voting 7-2) gave final endorsement to the community college proposal.[31]

For a time following the CCC's decision to reserve the Heart of Uptown/Sheridan Park site for the community college, the resolution of the conflict seemed to remain unsettled. To the surprise of both urban renewal proponents and opponents in Uptown, in September 1969 Oscar Shabat, chancellor of the Chicago City Colleges, announced that the community college system was reconsidering sites for its new northside campus.[32] On the one hand, the Uptown site might not be assembled for several years. On the other hand, another desirable site to the southwest of Uptown, land formerly occupied by the Riverview Amusement Park, was available. The City Colleges' change of mind appeared to give new life to the Hank Williams Village proposal, but in fact, Chancellor Shabat was engaged in a diversionary tactic intended to ease the city colleges' acquisition of the Heart of Uptown/Sheridan Park site. Even as debate over Uptown urban renewal quieted, Shabat engaged three local landlords to buy properties in the Uptown area proposed for the community college. Freed from the scrutiny that had accompanied urban renewal discussions and given the time to systematically pick up properties in the disputed site, by early 1970 Shabat "reconsidered" the Heart of Uptown/Sheridan Park site.[33] On September 10, 1970, the Chicago City Colleges administration committed itself to building a new campus in Uptown.

In a seeming concession to the urban renewal opposition, the community college site was to be shifted a bit to the east, that is, straddling the "el" structure and requiring less residential demolition.[34] In fact, the community college—which was named Harry S Truman College—never occupied any of the property east of the "el." Quite to the contrary, the expansion of Truman College that did follow the construction of the original college buildings pushed to the south and west, into the residential core of Heart of Uptown/Sheridan Park.

With the approval of the Truman College site the Uptown urban renewal battle was effectively concluded. Until the mid-1970s local organizations continued to tangle with Truman College's administration, but these arguments over issues such as the participation of minority contractors in erecting the college's physical facilities were grounded in the assumption that the college was a reality.[35] The CCC drifted into oblivion, as the city itself ceased to extend or amend the planning documents developed in 1968 and 1969. Chuck Geary remained in Uptown for a few more years, but his prominence as a community advocate had passed. In the early 1990s the UCC continues to play a role in Uptown affairs, but even by the mid-1970s its resemblance to the corporate-driven urban renewal advocate of the late 1950s and early 1960s was slight.

On the streets of Uptown, as chaotically self-defeating as the urban renewal battle had seemed to be, there was indeed a striking set of impacts. In the early 1970s a wave of fires struck Heart of Uptown/Sheridan Park in the vicinity of the Truman College site.[36] It is difficult not to accept the widely held opinion that property owners in the line of community college development were torching their buildings to collect on their insurance before selling out. Yet even with the construction of Truman College the "low-down" character of Heart of Uptown/Sheridan Park persisted. The campus did not cover the entire area, and to the campus' south, west, and north physical deterioration, if anything, expanded in the subsequent years. In the Project I area developers put up a series of federally subsidized apartment towers, the number of units ultimately reaching over 2,000. Nevertheless, after 1970 more housing units were lost than added in this area, and its resulting physical character—a handful of apartment towers rising amid acres of rubble-strewn vacant lots and clusters of smaller, older, and often deteriorated structures—bears scant resemblance to the pastoral residential enclave originally envisioned by the city planners and UCC leaders.

III

To this day there is a considerable number of Uptown organizational activists who retain bitter memories of the urban renewal controversy. And even among politically active Uptowners who only arrived after the early 1970s, one often encounters surprisingly sharp opinions regarding whose plans would have better served the neighborhood or whose participation in the urban renewal controversy was essentially misguided. One of the constants of Uptown politics since the 1960s has been its division into mutually hostile pro- and anti-development camps.

An evident contributor to the persistence of the development cleavage is the endurance of several of the organizations that participated in the urban renewal controversy. On the pro-development side, the Uptown Chicago Commission has more or less consistently supported initiatives to increase Uptown's stock of upscale housing. At the same time the UCC regularly weighs in against local proposals to produce subsidized housing or to open new social service agencies. Ironically, the UCC's consistent advocacy of neighborhood upgrading has been accompanied by a substantial transformation of the group's leadership and organizational character.

On the anti-development side, two of Uptown's most important organizations, the Organization of the NorthEast (ONE) and Voice of the People (VOP)—as well as the activists aligned with the neighborhood's most controversial figure, organizer Slim Coleman—trace roots back to the urban renewal era. Interestingly, and for different reasons, by the early 1990s each of these groups envisioned itself less as an anti-development force than was the case in the early 1970s. Moreover, over the years these groups have often been, at best, wary allies. Nonetheless, most Uptown activists recognize these groups as components of a reasonably powerful local movement that once fought urban renewal and that has, in subsequent years, worked to block or at least limit the gentrification of the neighborhood.

In short, two decades following the cessation of direct hostilities in Uptown's war of urban renewal, the principal political division defining that conflict—whether or not to make a concerted effort to physically, and as a consequence, socially upgrade the neighborhood—remains the central feature of the neighborhood's public affairs. As I have noted, the longstanding organizations that date from the urban renewal era, to a degree, sustain this cleavage, but in fact, the agendas and composition of these groups have been relatively fluid. Apart from the longevity of these organizations, something else has fundamentally changed in Uptown since the 1960s. For all of the neighborhood's notoriety before the 1960s, political division was not among its evident traits. Since the 1960s, and even as local activists and their organizations have often evolved quite markedly, the pro-development/anti-development split has remained.

The fact that so many of Uptown's organizations date back to the urban renewal conflict camouflages a fundamental discontinuity in the neighborhood's public affairs, a discontinuity, which, if anything, is a more powerful ingredient in understanding the persistence of Uptown's development cleavage. In the decade preceding the city government's authorization of urban renewal, the local planning and lobbying that prepared the way for this major initiative was dominated by a narrowly recruited, tightly integrated network of community leaders and activists. Uptown's business elite, which included two national insurance companies as well a number of substantial banks and realtors, was, by the standards of most big city neighborhoods, a potent spearhead for the drive to redevelop the local area. This business leadership team worked with a group of local politicians and planning consultants having significant ties to the city administration and what was at the time the city's model urban renewal initiative, the University of Chicago-sponsored redevelopment of Hyde Park. This planning elite did not achieve the quick action that it sought in the late 1950s, but nonetheless, it had a fairly explicit vision for rebuilding Uptown and, at least for a number of years, the resources and will to sustain its program for the neighborhood.

As the UCC sought to pave the way for urban renewal in the late 1950s and early 1960s, there was little or no criticism of its agenda. The portion of the neighborhood's population that paid any attention to matters like neighborhood redevelopment, for the most part, acceded to the leadership of the prominent men who were formulating Uptown's new game plan. Moreover, even as Uptown's low-income population grew and urban renewal's dire implications for them became evident, the likelihood of any kind of sustained dialogue on urban renewal, much less mobilized resistance to UCC- and city-sponsored plans, seemed slight. As late as 1967, local activist and urban renewal opponent George Morey lamented to a journalist, "Our people won't fight."[37]

In fact, Morey's people did fight, although the origin of the grassroots politics that generated the opposition to urban renewal—as well as the sustained grassroots activism that has persisted in Uptown since the 1960s—is the subject of much local disagreement. Clearly the arrival of JOIN had a major effect on Uptown politics. Before the young SDSers located in Uptown, the neighborhood's low-income population was quiescent. Since the mid-1960s this has seldom been the case. Indeed, even JOIN's critics acknowledged as much, for instance, a UCC publication from the early 1970s obliquely commenting: "People come here from other countries, or sections of our country, where race riots abound, but once in Uptown feel safe to live without prejudice, so stir up no dissent themselves, and although of late a few radical groups have made some abortive attempts to change this, so far, people remain just people—in Uptown."[38]

Aside from noting the dissent that had become a major force in affecting the direction of the urban renewal debate, the UCC newsletter commentary also reveals the view of grassroots mobilization that even now is regularly expressed by Uptown's development proponents. This is that opposition to their initiatives has been stimulated by the efforts of outside agitators; that left to their own devices, Uptown's poor would have little to say about the future of the community. This theme, often raised during the Uptown urban renewal fight, was repeated in the 1980s by critics of local anti-gentrification activists such as Slim Coleman and Helen Shiller.

Yet the most powerful evidence of the opening up of Uptown politics comes not from the ranks of the development opposition, but rather from the forces tending to support development. The leadership of the UCC in the 1980s and early 1990s comes not from the boardrooms of Kemper Insurance (long relocated from Uptown) or Uptown Federal (absorbed in a corporate merger in the 1980s), but from the

ranks of the middle-class homeowners whose block clubs dot the neighborhood's more desirable sections. Some of these activists are longtime
Uptowners with direct recollections of the urban renewal fight. Some
are recently arrived gentrifiers. In neither case are they, typically, representatives of the local business elite, which no longer is as powerful or
unified as in the 1950s. Uptown in the 1950s was a politically quiet
neighborhood in which a cadre of institutional leaders attempted to
direct its affairs. Uptown in the 1990s is an activated neighborhood with
an array of grassroots organizations pursuing a disparate range of particular agendas. Overlaying this seemingly confusing jumble of organizations is a longstanding and generally recognized conflict over how to
best shape the future of the neighborhood.

A final element in understanding the political divisions characterizing Uptown in the 1990s is the physical legacy of urban renewal. Judged
by its own criteria, urban renewal failed Uptown. Urban renewal neither
upgraded nor stabilized the eastern end of the neighborhood, especially
along the Corridor. Moreover, the incoherent redevelopment of this area
and Heart of Uptown/Sheridan Park exacerbated their physical deterioration, which in turn has produced subsequent spurts of real estate speculation and flurries of controversy over residential dislocation.

In the early 1960s the UCC envisioned an Uptown with a busy
shopping and business district at the Broadway/Lawrence intersection
and running to the east. North of this commercial area was to be a local
government center. To the west smaller apartment buildings would be
mixed with single-family homes. East of the business core would be a
more concentrated but "pastoralized" residential area of renovated six-
flats, courtyard apartments, and a few taller buildings. Further east
along the parkfront would stand Uptown's Gold Coast of high-rise towers overlooking Lake Michigan. The UCC sought to make Uptown,
truly, a city within a city whose commercial and governmental complexes anchored a clearly demarcated hierarchy of residential areas.

In fact, the city planners who laid out Uptown's urban renewal program, from the start, violated the UCC's vision. The entire area east of
the Corridor was zoned for high-rise development, and with the desig-

nation of Uptown for urban renewal, developers intending to put up subsidized apartment complexes rushed to assemble sites. Ironically, at the very time urban renewal opponents began to complain of the rash of building demolitions east of the Corridor, the CCC was beginning to recognize that its urban renewal efforts were spinning out of control. For instance, in March 1968 Urania Damofle of the CCC, concerned about overdevelopment in the Project I area, criticized a local developer for not "acting in behalf of the community in his support of high rise moderate income building construction."[39]

By the early 1970s developers receiving assistance under the terms of the federal government's Section 221(d)3 subsidy program had erected ten high-rise towers in or adjoining the Project I urban renewal zone. This "sawtoothing" of Uptown's eastern end—new high-rises standing amid vacant lots—in no way corresponded with the UCC's desire to renovate existing buildings, reduce traffic, and deconcentrate the population. Over the subsequent two decades building maintenance of several of these "subsidy" buildings declined appreciably, and particular structures such as Winthrop Towers at 4848 N. Winthrop Avenue became home to the kind of intensive social pathology usually associated with public housing.

Across from Winthrop Towers is a desolate half-block on which stands a single old building enclosed by a fence. Given Winthrop Towers' notoriety throughout Uptown and this evidently desolate stretch of streetscape, local pedestrians go to great pains to avoid the area. The gang graffiti, abandoned cars, and piles of rubbish that punctuate the Winthrop Towers area further mark it as a no-man's land. Winthrop Towers rises above the kind of physically desolate urban moonscape that provides the ideal staging area for various anti-social or positively illegal activities. Urban renewal produced a dozen or so of these "zones" along the Corridor and on Uptown's eastern side.

However, this ragged cityscape of often-decayed residential complexes towering above hinterlands of devastation, or Heart of Uptown/Sheridan Park's near-equivalent—fine old six-flat apartments surrounded by acres of emptiness—does not prevent real estate speculation. Since the late 1970s developers have sought to extend the Uptown Gold Coast inward toward the Corridor, or by establishing defensible beachheads in Heart of Uptown/Sheridan Park. Assembling enough parcels to form an autonomous island of affluence, or renovating a six-flat into a posh stockade of opulence amid the devastation, is a recurring practice. And usually some degree of low-income housing dislocation accompanies this process. Not always, but frequently, a political battle follows the threat or realization of this dislocation. This is the most subtle sequence of effects produced by Uptown's urban renewal, as subsequent real estate speculation further destablizes particular buildings or blocks, aggravating the longstanding distrust between developers and residential incumbents, and generating another battle—large or small—over development.

NOTES

1. Chicago Plan Commission, *Housing in Chicago Communities: Community Area 3,* 1940, pp. 7, 11.

2. Chicago Fact Book Consortium, *Local Community Fact Book: Chicago Metro Area* (Chicago: Chicago Review Press, 1984), p. 7.

3. Erich Rosenthal, "The 1950 Survey of Rogers Park, West Ridge (West Rogers Park), and Uptown," (Young Men's Jewish Council, August 1950), p. 26.

4. Chicago Fact Book Consortium, *Local Community Fact Book,* p. 7.

5. Letter to General Richard Smykal, Community Conservation Board, from Eugene Votaw, Exec. Director, Uptown Chicago Commission, August 30, 1957, Chicago Municipal Reference Library (MRL) Files.

6. Donald Kirk, "Mammoth Urban Renewal Project Seen for Uptown," *Chicago Tribune,* June 12, 1960.

7. "Uptown Unit Leader Cites Renewal Need," *Chicago Tribune,* June 27, 1963.

8. Suzanne Avery, "Uptown Asks for Funds, Told to Show Good Investment Potential," *Chicago Tribune,* May 9, 1963.

9. Uptown Chicago Commission, "Rehabilitation and Code Enforcement," November 1958, MRL.

10. *Uptown: A Planning Report,* prepared for the Uptown Chicago Commission by Jack Meltzer Associates, May 1962.

11. For example, see the discussion of the Minneapolis downtown plan in Alan A. Altshuler, *The City Planning Process* (Ithaca, N.Y.: Cornell University Press, 1965), pp. 229-267. Also, City of Chicago, Department of City Planning, *Development Plan for the Central Area of Chicago,* August 1958.

12. Ruth Moore, "Meeting to Hear Drastic Plans for Uptown Revival," *Chicago Sun-Times*, September 12, 1966.

13. Eugene Matanky and Associates, "A Pilot Rehab Program for the Uptown Community," 1966, p. 15, MRL.

14. Matanky and Associates, "A Pilot Rehab Program," p. 21.

15. "Uptown Gets Green Light for Renewal," *Chicago Tribune*, October 14, 1966; City of Chicago, Department of Urban Renewal, "Uptown Conservation Area Staff Report," August 1966.

16. "Name Uptown Council for Urban Renewal," *Chicago Tribune*, June 15, 1967.

17. James Miller, *Democracy Is in the Streets* (New York: Simon and Schuster, 1987), pp. 184-196.

18. Richard Rothstein, "Evolution of the ERAP Organizers," pp. 272-288 in Priscilla Long, ed., *The New Left: A Collection of Essays* (Boston: Porter Sargent, 1969); Todd Gitlin, "The Radical Potential of the Poor," pp. 136-149 in Massimo Teodori, ed., *The New Left: A Documentary History* (New York: Bobbs-Merrill, 1969).

19. Ruth Moore, "Tenant Union Signs Building Contract, Believed City's First," *Chicago Sun-Times*, May 26, 1966.

20. Clarus Backes, "Poor People's Power in Uptown," *Chicago Tribune Magazine*, September 29, 1968, p. 50.

21. "Uptown Council Leader to Talk with Dissidents over Membership," *Chicago Tribune*, August 3, 1967.

22. Barbara Amazaki, "DUR Tells Proposals for Uptown Land Use," *Chicago Tribune*, February 18, 1968; City of Chicago, Department of Urban Renewal, "Uptown Conservation Plan," February 1968, p. 6.

23. Thomas Gray, "Uptown Poor—Are They the Victims of Urban Renewal?" *Chicago Sun-Times*, October 5, 1970.

24. Backes, "Poor People's Power in Uptown," pp. 46-56; Jeffrey R. Henig, *Neighborhood Mobilization: Redevelopment and Response* (New Brunswick, N.J.: Rutgers University Press, 1982), pp. 105-116.

25. Gray, "Uptown Poor."

26. Neal Amidei, "The Agony of Uptown," *Omnibus Chicago*, July 1968, p. 37.

27. Chuck Geary, "Freedom or Death," *Uptown Light*, May 28, 1969, Chicago Historical Society (CHS) Uptown Files.

28. *What's New? Que Pasa*, June 15, 1968, CHS.

29. Alice Graber, "Hank Williams 'Lives' in Uptown," *North Town*, October 1, 1968; Rodney Wright and Associates, "Neighborhood and Community Planning," 1971, CHS.

30. Roger Flaherty, "Renewal Board Appoints 9 New Members," *North Town*, March 23, 1969.

31. Roger Flaherty, "Uptown's Village Plan—To Oblivion and Back Again," *North Town*, September 16, 1969.

32. Flaherty, "Uptown's Village Plan."

33. Flora Johnson, "In Order to Save It," *Chicago,* December 1976, pp. 184-185.

34. Harry Golden, Jr., "Uptown Junior College Compromise Site Chosen," *Chicago Sun-Times,* September 11, 1970.

35. Robert McClory, "Alinsky Lives!" *The Reader,* April 3, 1981.

36. Leonard Aronson, "Fires Plaguing Uptown Area," *Chicago Today,* June 9, 1971.

37. Amidei, "The Agony of Uptown," p. 38.

38. Uptown Chicago Commission, "Annual Report," 1972, CHS.

39. Robert Svejcara, "Seeks Uptown High Rise O.K.," *Chicago Tribune,* March 14, 1968.

CHAPTER FOUR
SHEFFIELD COMES TO SHARROW

Neighborhood controversy over redevelopment proposals emerged in Sharrow very soon after urban renewal divided Uptown. However, in Sharrow the emergence of political conflict followed a decidedly different course than in Uptown, and also unlike Uptown, debate over housing demolition, the provision of support services for residents, and the probable impacts of highway improvements did not divide the community against itself. As a consequence, the era of debate over redevelopment in Sharrow did not as a rule produce the fist-clenching confrontations characteristic of Uptown. Indeed, by the end of the 1970s Sharrow seems to have emerged as a more self-conscious and cohesive community than it had been a decade previously. Most of the controversy in Sharrow followed from individual residents, or community groups, confronting the Sheffield City Council and its administrators. Unlike Uptown's locally generated urban renewal battle, 1960s and 1970s development controversies were brought to Sharrow by the municipal government.

II

Since the turn of the century the city of Sheffield had been demolishing inner city-residential slums, and from the 1920s housing construction had been a principal emphasis of local council policy. At the national level, the British government sought to rehouse returning veterans of the Great War in accommodations "fit for heroes," that is, better quarters than the urban slums from which so many had been drafted.[1] In Sheffield, the Labour Party took control of the municipal administration in the mid-1920s and dedicated itself to following the lead of the national government in constructing "council housing." For the most part, during the 1920s and 1930s the city of Sheffield built housing on the edge of the city—beyond the industrial East End on estates such as Shire Green, to the southeast in the hills overlooking central Sheffield at Manor.[2] This strategy offered the double advantage of not only meeting contemporary expectations for airy, Garden City-style accommodations, but also locating much of the housing in proximity to the workplaces that employed such a large share of Sheffield's working class.

In the years immediately following World War II, as the council once more began to build working-class housing, its siting of estates such as New Parson Cross and Gleadless followed the prewar fashion. However, land available for future council housing on Sheffield's margins was fast becoming scarce, which in a few years led to a shift in the council housing program. In part, the land scarcity resulted from the establishment of the city's greenbelt in the late 1930s. In the early 1950s the city sought to expand its physical boundaries, but it was unable to win necessary parliamentary approval.[3] As a result, by the mid-1950s the authority began to build inner-city council estates, residential complexes that would be erected in areas whose older back-to-back and terrace housing had been cleared. And, as in the period between the wars, local policy was partially shaped by national policy. From the mid-1950s the national government shifted its fiscal support for local authority housing construction: providing aid for the construction of larger flats only in slum clearance areas, and providing greater subsidies for units in high-rise apartment towers. Across urban Britain, and including Sheffield, the decade of the 1960s was a time of intense high-rise council flat development.[4]

Sheffield executed this shift in its housing program with some gusto, commissioning modernist designs and adopting industrialized construction techniques. In the late 1950s and early 1960s the council proceeded with the construction of the huge Park Hill and Hyde Park estates on a hilly site directly above the city centre. By 1962 the chair of the council Housing Committee, Harold Lambert could announce:

> Sheffield's housing development during the last few
> years has made its impact not only upon the people of

Sheffield but upon the country as a whole. Visitors to
our schemes from other parts of the British Isles are
frequent and visitors to Britain from foreign lands,
anxious to study British housing, are more and more
frequently advised to include Sheffield on their
tour....The reason for the interest now shown in
Sheffield's housing is not, I think, difficult to explain.
Briefly, it is that we have envisaged each scheme, be it
new development on virgin territory or the redevelopment of a slum area, as a piece of civic design to be
carefully integrated with the whole Town Plan....The
careful exploitation of this topography—the building
up of hill-top architectural compositions—is gradually producing something of the fascination of the
Italian hill towns.[5]

In short, for leaders of Sheffield's city government the clearance of
old housing and its replacement with new, cutting-edge apartment
complexes was becoming a municipal hallmark.

During the 1960s the Sheffield Council not only prided itself in the
architectural quality of its new housing estates, it also dedicated itself to
finally ridding central Sheffield of its nineteenth-century housing legacy.
Each year the council planned to raze more than two thousand units of
housing, a program of slum clearance that it sought to implement with
iron-willed determination. At the end of the decade Councillor Lambert
observed that "each and every year the Corporation rehouses about 2,400
families."[6] With the Council pursuing demolition and new estate construction at this pace, it was only a matter of time before Sharrow would
draw the attention of the municipal administration. Indeed, from approximately the mid-1960s, word circulated in Sharrow that the council would
be clearing a substantial amount of local housing. However, at this time
the council's policy was not to provide detailed information on its clearance agenda, and, quite unlike Uptown, slum clearance did not enter the
local public agenda in the context of a neighborhood planning exercise.
Indeed, in early 1971 when the city announced its slum clearance program for the coming five years, which mandated the demolition of several

thousand units of housing in various portions of Sharrow, there was no local plan prepared for the community.[7]

At the end of the 1960s Sheffield's highway planners were, in their turn, formulating roadway improvements that would affect Sharrow (Map 4-1). In their efforts to cope with the increased use of the automobile in and around the city, the local government's traffic engineers proposed the development of three "ring roads," limited access highways that would cut across the older street system. These three ring roads would be a Civic Circle linking principal office and commercial hubs in the city centre, an Inner Ring Road circling central Sheffield, and an Outer Ring Road skirting the outlying portions of the city. The Inner Ring cut through Sharrow's northern edge, or "lower" Sharrow, the portion of the neighborhood nearest the city centre, and would create major new junctions at Bramall Lane and Moore Street (providing access to

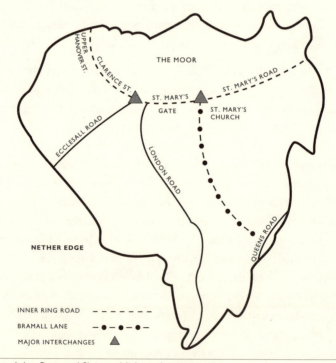

Map 4-1 • Proposed Sharrow Highway Improvements

Ecclesall Road). For Sharrow residents, the Inner Ring Road's cutting off the neighborhood from the city centre was, of itself, a cause for alarm, but this was not the end of the highway plans that would reshape the neighborhood. The city also wished to ameliorate the movement of cars into and out of Sheffield from the south. The development of new housing in northern Derbyshire on Sheffield's southern flank was giving significant impetus to auto-based commutation to central Sheffield. The city's plan was to direct traffic off Chesterfield Road/London Road to the east of Sharrow and run it directly through Sharrow on a widened Bramall Lane. The effect of this proposal, which came to be known as the Heeley Bypass, would be to split lower from upper Sharrow and to create a major interchange at the meeting of Bramall Lane and the Inner Ring Road.[8]

III

In 1966, as rumors of the municipal government's plans to clear much of Sharrow began to circulate, a new minister named John Peaden arrived to serve the local Methodist congregations of Brunswick Trinity and Sharrow St. John's churches. These were two of the four congregations comprising the Moor and Lower Sharrow Council of Churches, which had commissioned Peter Mann's survey of the neighborhood in the mid-1950s. In addition to performing the usual functions of a Methodist minister, Peaden's mandate included working with grassroots organizations as a means to making his churches a larger part of the general social life of the community.

Soon after assuming his post in Sharrow, Peaden visited the Sheffield Town Hall and asked to view maps presenting the authority's plans for highway improvements in the vicinity of his churches. In reference to Brunswick Trinity, Peaden recalled to a journalist a number of years later, "if the road plans went ahead, an elevated highway would pass within 40 feet of the church which would stand in splendid isolation with 125 acres of empty land around it."[9] For Peaden, this was the first of several discouraging encounters with local council members and administrators as he attempted to collect additional information on the council's plans for Sharrow. In retrospect, Peaden describes his reaction to these circumstances as that of an "angry vicar" who did not really know how to deal with the authority's unwillingness to communicate its plans with the community.[10] Nonetheless, in the next several years he was a principal agent in organizing community meetings to discuss authority plans and begin the effort to formulate a community response to the municipal government.

In addition to calling community meetings, such as the October 9, 1969 event at Cemetery Road Baptist Church with the evocative title "The Shape of Things to Come," Peaden was a founding member of the Sharrow and Heeley Neighbourhood Association (SHNA) in early 1970. Heeley lies just to the east and across the Sheaf River from Sharrow, most of the neighborhood rolling up the farther hillside. Like Sharrow, Heeley was becoming the home of an increasing ethnic minority population, and Heeley Bottom—along the Sheaf River—was also affected by the roadway improvements that would bisect Sharrow. Initially, SHNA focused its efforts on local race relations and initiated a series of projects aimed at smoothing the transition experienced by ethnic minorities settling in Sheffield. These programs included seminars on "the running of democracy in Britain," the organizing of multi-racial social events and children's play groups, and English-language training.[11] However, by late 1970 SHNA's organizers identified redevelopment as a principal "tension point" in Sharrow and Heeley.[12]

In February 1971, the city of Sheffield announced its housing demolition program for the coming five years, which included the razing of nearly 4,000 residences in Sharrow. Within a month SHNA called a meeting to discuss the city's plans. About 200 hundred local residents attended the meeting at Sharrow Lane Junior School, at which the Sharrow Action Group (SAG) was formed. Its chair was one of Sharrow ward's three local councillors, Ethel Evans; John Peaden was named "convenor" of the group.[13] SAG was not Sheffield's first "action group." Two years previously residents of Walkley, another central Sheffield neighborhood, had organized the Walkley Action Group to fight authority-sponsored demolition plans.[14] One of the Walkley Action Group's leaders, Geoff Green, spoke at the inaugural meeting of SAG. For the next several years SAG, with John Peaden as its guiding figure, was the principal grassroots organization representing Sharrow's case before city officials.

SAG came into being for two reasons. A considerable number of Sharrow's population did not wish to lose their homes; and as activists such as John Peaden attempted to discover the details of the authority's plans for the community, they met with indifference or at times, out-right resistance. Thus, one of SAG's first actions was to call for the authority's opening an "Advice and Information Centre" to provide information to individuals who would be affected by local redevelop-ment. The authority dismissed this idea, and its reaction to SAG's ini-tiative, as reported in a local newspaper gives some sense of the mindset that at that time prevailed among many of Sheffield's officials: "The Council's Policy Committee has turned it (the advice centre) down because it feels information will be given adequately by existing Town Hall facilities, and the service to be provided by a permanent advice cen-tre and mobile information unit planned by the Housing Committee."[15] Members of Sheffield's City Council did not appreciate neighborhood residents telling them how to mind their house.

By the summer of 1971 SAG took the lead in organizing local hearings to discuss clearance plans in the area just above London Road along Sharrow Lane. The council was pressing ahead in this part of Sharrow because of overcrowding in the local school, a problem that was complicated by the school's proximity to a historical building. The Sheffield Council's Education Committee claimed that its preference was to demolish the old manor house, Mount Pleasant, to permit expansion of the school. However, because Mount Pleasant was a "listed" structure, national Department of the Environment regulations protected it from clearance. Consequently, the authority had adopted an alternative plan to raze a number of private dwellings to make way for the school expansion. SAG sponsored meetings to familiarize local res-idents with the Mount Pleasant situation, and the new organization took on the role of advocating the perspective of the residents of the Mount Pleasant area.[16] Ultimately the authority did proceed with most of the Mount Pleasant demolitions, but SAG derived from this experi-ence its model for future organizing in Sharrow. Peaden and his cohorts in SAG focused on small sections of the neighborhood—usually hand-fuls of street blocks numbering no more than a few hundred residences, and typically areas that were slated for clearance. By the summer of 1972 SAG put in motion its first significant success. Working with local residents and representatives of various city departments, SAG man-aged (in 1975) to qualify the Fentonville area—just a few hundred yards from Mount Pleasant—as a Housing Action Area (HAA), a central government-sponsored program that provided assistance to owners for rehabilitating their buildings.[17] Over the next several years SAG orga-nized nine of these small neighborhood groups, and subsequently, five HAAs and GIAs (or General Improvement Area, another national pro-gram financing building rehabilitation) were mandated in Sharrow. Within these five clusters of blocks approximately 1,500 units of hous-ing were saved from demolition.[18]

During its years of peak activity, in the early to mid-1970s, SAG devoted much of its energy to surveying the residents of its nine target "subneighborhoods." SAG worked with the Sheffield Planning Department, which assigned a graduate planning student-intern to han-dle the technical work involved in the design, administration, and tabu-lation of these surveys. SAG activists contacted local residents and conducted interviews. In December 1972 SAG produced *Views of Sharrow,* a report that presented the action group's general appraisal of the community and assessed the impacts that authority-sponsored devel-opment was already producing. Lengthy portions of the report discussed specific transportation and housing issues. *Views of Sharrow* concluded with breakdowns of SAG's first three surveys, of the Mount Pleasant, Bedale Road, and Langdon Street/Fentonville Street areas. Although a considerable number of SAG activists contributed to *Views of Sharrow,* John Peaden was principally responsible for the document's analysis.

Views of Sharrow, true to its title, provides a series of cross-cutting perspectives on the neighborhood. The report discusses the social net-works and institutions linking residents, while also noting how the area's physical characteristics and location contribute to its social life. In par-ticular, one reads in this report a very clear-sighted account of how a pre-sumably on-the-skids neighborhood such as Sharrow functioned as a working-class and immigrant community, whose proximity to the city centre was among its greatest virtues. Even as Peaden, in a fashion quite characteristic of neighborhood activists, makes note of the social networks that gave shape to Sharrow as a community, he observes that there are other more material factors that structure residents' attachments: "There is an appreciation of the value that is provided by living in a central area, both from the point of view of cheaper travel and greater shopping choice. Thus before even mentioning more emotional arguments about 'liking the area' and feelings of belonging, there are straightforward economic arguments for this choice."[19] Moreover, the report quite convincingly discusses how authority clearance planning, by designating neighborhoods and particular units of housing for clearance years in advance of actually initiating action to remove dwellings, contributed to neighborhood decay. In the report this process is called "planning blight," which grew out of the authority's relentless commitment to razing two thousand units of housing per year coupled with its relatively haphazard methods of specifying particular units of housing that required demolition.[20] In effect, planning blight represented a self-fulfilling prophecy of neighborhood decay. As local tenants and property-owners became aware that their dwellings would be taken by the city, even if this might not come for ten years, they began to defer maintenance and look for other places to live or invest. Furthermore, the council's acquiring particular structures and boarding them up to wait for demolition often was the precipitator of other private owners' losing interest in property upkeep. The result was to speed the physical decay of a community, and no less significantly, to destablize local social networks.

As the chronicle of a neighborhood in jeopardy, *Views of Sharrow* is both poignant and persuasive. In its capturing the sense of vitality in an inconspicuous inner city neighborhood—from the residents' standpoint, that is—it is quite remarkable. *Views of Sharrow* is also, when compared to documents and public statements produced in Uptown at about the same time, remarkably moderate in its tone. Only occasionally does one encounter outright criticism of the Sheffield Council and its administrators. However, on these occasions Peaden makes his point without flinching: "...there is a deep and widespread feeling of alienation from the City Council and its departments. A recurring theme in meeting after meeting has been the suspicion of the Council's sincerity in relation to the Study and a belief that little account will be taken of their views."[21] In fact, SAG was already working quite a substantial transformation in the municipal administration's approach to neighborhood planning, and although the action group was formed out of vigorous antagonism for authority plans and planning processes, SAG was beginning to forge a mutually beneficial working relationship with the city's planners.

IV

At the very time that Sharrow was organizing in response to the city's redevelopment agenda, the Sheffield municipal government was reorganizing how it redeveloped the city. Until the late 1960s the council and the city's administrative officers viewed the rebuilding of Sheffield as a straightforward question of physical reconstruction. In the 1950s, when the city uprooted the old district that would be redeveloped as Park Hill, an estate comprised of interconnected mid-rise apartment blocks, the council assumed that the radically transformed physical environment merely represented the replacement of the older pattern of terrace house blocks by "streets in the sky."[22] One of the Sheffield Council's great prides during this era was the share of new construction carried out "in house" by the city's Public Works Department.[23] In this city local socialism meant the municipal authority directly providing high-quality housing. Presumably, private contractors would not be so reliable in the delivery of their product. As for city planning, until the early 1970s this function was left up to the Engineer's Department. However, by the late 1960s the increasingly truculent response of inner-city neighborhoods to the council's plans was producing a transformation in its thinking about neighborhood planning. In Sharrow, this change in authority attitude was welcome, if a bit tardy. In June of 1971 the City of Sheffield announced a community planning effort in Sharrow and adjoining "uphill" Nether Edge— that is, about four months after presenting its big clearance program for 1971 through 1976.

In announcing the Sharrow-Nether Edge planning exercise, Roland Adamson of the newly formed Department of Planning and Architecture described the neighborhood consultation process as "something quite new."[24] Indeed, for the authority's planners the process was sufficiently new that they managed to cause a great deal of consternation in their first efforts to explain what they were doing. Intending to persuade people that the authority did not harbor some secret plan for Sharrow and Nether Edge, the planners adopted what they called the "blank canvas" approach. That is, at a number of initial public meetings, the planning department representative displayed a blank map of Sharrow and Nether Edge, only demarcated by a thick black line along the perimeter. The planners' thinking was that the blank canvas would invite those in attendance to begin filling in the map with their ideas for the community. Unfortunately, "most people...were mystified by this approach, and many interpreted the black line to be a ring road encircling the Study Area."[25] At this time, a principal anxiety in Sharrow concerned the impact of the Inner Ring Road cutting across Bramall Lane and London Road.

In spite of the planners' good intentions, their initial efforts to work with residents in Sharrow were, at best, uneven. There were a number of reasons for local uncertainty over the planning process. For a start, the authority did not speak with one voice. The Engineering Department remained firmly committed to its plan to upgrade the roadway network running through Sharrow. In August 1972, the engineers displayed models for the new Inner Ring Road-Bramall Lane intersection. The Inner Ring Road would "fly over" Bramall Lane via an expressway-like overpass, with a "roundabout" or traffic circle underneath the overpass and girdling a submerged pedestrian passageway. This rather elaborate interchange would also slice a large corner from the historic St. Mary's churchyard.[26] The Engineering Department also continued to push for the widening of Bramall Lane. In contrast to SAG's fairly low-keyed approach to authority housing demolition/redevelopment proposals, the action group opposed road widening much more strenuously, committing itself "to fight everything connected with the plan to widen Bramall Lane."[27]

Yet if the authority did not speak with one voice, Sharrow was also turning out to have multiple perspectives. For instance, in its surveying of local areas SAG discovered that resistance to housing demolition was not universal. In the Bedale Road, Pembroke Street/Pomona Street, and Shoreham Street areas, many residents were willing to give up their old and deteriorating homes if they could count on the provision of decent replacement housing.[28] However, the very same people who had little or no attachment to their homes quite frequently did wish to remain in the neighborhood.

The authority's amalgamating largely working-class Sharrow with the more affluent Nether Edge area also tended to complicate the formation of a single local perspective on planning issues. Nether Edge's population included a much larger share of professionals and other white-collar workers. Much of its housing was comprised of handsome Victorian era villas. As one might expect, there emerged from Nether Edge a more characteristically preservationist approach to planning proposals. Indeed, by early 1973 SAG was in substantial conflict with certain groups representing Nether Edge. For example, The Conservation Society, a national preservationist group with a local chapter and membership in Sheffield, had called a meeting—which it billed as a joint effort with SAG—at which "generalized critical remarks" were made about city officials. Moreover, speakers at the meeting objected to demolition plans in one of the Sharrow subareas where SAG surveying had, in fact, found much support for clearance. Yet at this meeting only a handful of Sharrow residents were present. SAG, in a letter disavowing any role in this event, chastised its organizers for their "ham-fisted intrusion" in the local planning effort.[29]

Nonetheless, from the early months of the Sharrow-Nether Edge planning process SAG and the Sheffield Department of Planning and Architecture built and sustained a working understanding. The planners depended on SAG, via its surveying and public discussions, to generate information on local attitudes; SAG came to see the planners as a cooperative, if not always politically efficacious ally in the municipal government. On September 22, 1973, the various parties to the planning process—councillors from Sharrow and Nether Edge, authority administrators, and local organizations—held a planning seminar at Sheffield Town Hall. The participants were so pleased with the exchange of viewpoints that they committed themselves to reconvening. Thus was formed the Joint Advisory Group, which met another dozen times through the winter of 1973-74. The first several sessions were devoted to traffic and highway issues, and by the end of January the advisory group had agreed on an overall traffic plan for Sharrow and Nether Edge. For the most part discussions were congenial, and by the end of this process in April 1974, councillors, municipal officers, and local activists had developed a fairly broad consensus regarding the immediate future of Sharrow and Nether Edge.[30]

It was not until February 1976 that the authority produced its "Sharrow-Nether Edge Draft District Plan," but for the most part this document confirmed the terms of agreement produced by the Joint Advisory Committee. Already, in May and October of 1975, the Fentonville Street and Wolseley Road sections of Sharrow were declared Housing Action Areas. Within these two districts nearly 600 houses were saved from demolition, and homeowners were eligible for grants to underwrite up to 90 percent of their rehabilitation expenses. The draft report also suggested that similar action might be taken in three other sections of the community. In all, by early 1976 approximately 1,200 units of housing had been removed from the clearance list of 1971. Even with these adjustments to the original clearance program Sharrow was still slated for considerable housing demolition, and across Sharrow and Nether Edge the draft plan anticipated a drop in population of approximately 6,000 (from an early 1970s base of 30,000) by the mid-1980s.[31] Nonetheless, one must bear in mind that in several sections of Sharrow many residents were willing to trade their old terrace houses for up-to-date dwellings.

The draft report's highway recommendations were more ambiguous. The construction of the Inner Ring Road was already moving ahead, but the engineer's more expansive dreams for this route had been scaled down. In particular, the Inner Ring Road cutting along Sharrow's northwest margin would be but a grade-level "dual carriageway," that is, a four-lane limited access highway without flyovers and other expressway-like features. The report also recommended measures to reduce the through-traffic that sought to save time by cutting across Sharrow and Nether Edge side streets. The draft report did not resolve the issue of the Heeley Bypass, and in turn whether or not Bramall Lane would be "dualed." These measures were, in fact, recommended, but the report also noted that final decisions awaited the results of the Sheffield and Rotherham Land Use Transportation Study.[32] This latter piece of transportation planning was caught up in the mid-1970s local government reorganization in Great Britain, which mandated the formation of a South Yorkshire County Council (including Sheffield and the adjoining areas of Barnsley, Doncaster, and Rotherham). Ultimately, the new South Yorkshire Council would determine which options would be pursued in improving traffic flow in central and southeastern Sheffield.

V

In the late 1970s discussion of the Heeley Bypass took on a considerably more volatile character than the relatively calm Sharrow-Nether Edge planning process of the middle years of the decade. This was due, in part, to the "zero-sum" debate that emerged between SAG and the Heeley Residents Association (HRA). In effect, activists on the opposite sides of the Sheaf River came to see themselves as having opposite interests in regard to the various highway proposals floated by the South Yorkshire Council. Moreover, having spent half a decade working with Sheffield planners, SAG was less inclined to confront the City Council or the South Yorkshire Council over this issue. Heeley activists clearly felt fewer inhibitions in this regard, and the debate over the Heeley Bypass was more "politicized" than previous redevelopment disputes in Sharrow.

The reality of Sharrow and Heeley geography certainly contributed to the split between the two neighborhoods. The Sheaf River has formed the traditional border between Sharrow and Heeley. Over time, a series of busy thoroughfares were pushed through this corridor, with Heeley Bottom, as this area became known, emerging as a significant shopping district for residents of Heeley (but less so for Sharrow residents, who favored London Road or the city centre). The authority's longstanding commitment to upgrade the Chesterfield Road/London Road link between central Sheffield and its southern suburbs necessitated right-of-way acquisitions that would bring down shops along these streets. This was not a popular measure in Heeley, but until the formulation of specific, alternative development proposals in the mid-1970s, SAG also opposed road improvements in Heeley Bottom. This was because the "dualing" of London Road—or one of the other Heeley Bottom streets—would inevitably be linked to the upgrading of Bramall Lane (a proposed street widening long approved by the Sheffield Council), thus connecting southern and southeastern Sheffield with the Inner Ring Road—and splitting lower and upper Sharrow. However, as

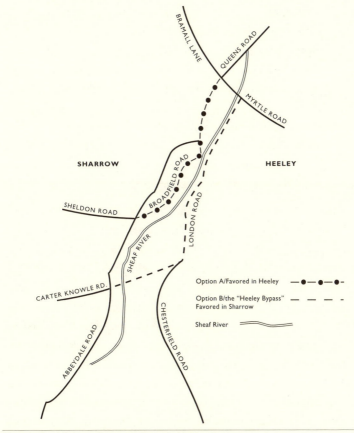

Map 4–2 • Highway Proposals Through Heeley Bottom

the mid-1970s metropolitan transportation planning exercise resulted
in (a) the apparent commitment to some sort of Heeley Bottom highway improvement, and (b) the examination of alternative means of
increasing traffic flow through this area, Sharrow and Heeley split. In
effect, SAG preferred Heeley Bottom road improvements on the eastern, that is, Heeley side of the Sheaf River (Map 4-2). The Heeley preference was for improvements in the direction of Sharrow.

In the fall of 1977 the South Yorkshire County circulated for public comment five alternative schemes for Heeley Bottom highway
improvements. The Heeley Residents Association response was quick
and furious:

> Heeley, Sharrow, and Highfields are areas which have
> suffered greatly (and still will for years to come) from
> "redevelopment." Communities have been split up,
> shops and businesses have been ruined and closed,
> meeting places have been lost, landmarks have been
> demolished. Long lost sons and daughters compare
> their childhood playgrounds to the bombed streets of
> Belfast and other disaster areas. The last thing such
> areas need is a dual carriageway road carrying some-
> body else's cars through its middle.[33]

Having noted that Heeley and Sharrow would both suffer as a result
of the construction of the Heeley Bypass, the HRA's newsletter then
observed that it was "militantly opposed" to Option 3, the alternative formally termed the Heeley Bypass, which would produce maximum clearance in Heeley. Conversely, HRA acknowledged Sharrow's dislike of
Option 1, which shifted roadwork toward that community.[34] In a similar
vein, minutes of the SAG meeting at which the South Yorkshire Council's
set of proposals were reviewed, observe: "there was some discussion as to
whether a common ground could be reached with the Heeley Residents
Association...and a conclusion was reached reluctantly that this was probably not possible at this time."[35] SAG found the proposal for new construction east of Chesterfield Road/London Road, that is, the Heeley
Bypass, the most satisfactory of the county council's set of options.

Beyond this organizational split, public discussion of the Heeley Bypass was more spirited than debate over previous redevelopment issues in Sharrow. For example, a January 19, 1978, public meeting was called off when over 100 people were unable to squeeze into the packed auditorium of the Lowfield School. A press account described the scene inside the hall before the meeting's cancellation: "South Yorkshire County Council officers were heckled by angry residents." Outside the meeting hall various groups distributed pamphlets laying out their particular positions on the bypass controversy.[36] A few weeks later, SAG's Secretary, Harry Kirk, criticized the "over emotional attitudes" of bypass opponents.[37] Nonetheless, HRA and its local allies were winning converts to their cause. Possibly sensing a countercurrent to Sheffield's predominant Labour winds, in February 1978, the Conservative Party candidate for the Heeley parliamentary seat announced his opposition to the Heeley Bypass.[38] Not to be outdone, almost coincidentally the Labour group in the City Council also joined the bypass opposition, committing itself to seek the bypass' cancellation by the County Council.[39]

In the face of boisterous community opposition and with the beginning of a revolt among some of its political allies in Sheffield, the Labour-dominated South Yorkshire Council backed away from the Heeley Bypass in the summer of 1978. Rather than press ahead immediately with any of the autumn 1977 bypass options, the County Council mandated an "interim traffic management" scheme to operate over the existing Sharrow/Heeley road system. This "tidal flow" proposal included the one-waying of certain streets, the coordination of traffic lights to speed morning in-bound and evening out-bound traffic, and the provision of restricted bus lanes. The County Council also proposed further examination of long-range options for Heeley Bottom, including the widening of London Road.[40] Nonetheless, opponents of the Heeley Bypass had sustained the status quo, while in Sharrow the seemingly foreordained "dualing" of Bramall Lane was also put off.

VI

By 1980 Sharrow was at the end of a decade-long period of uncertainty that had followed from the Sheffield Council's plans for redevelopment. In fact, by this time the storm over Sharrow had passed. Nationally, the recently elected Conservative government of Margaret Thatcher was just initiating its efforts to force local authority belt-tightening. Among the intentions of the central government was constraining municipal authorities, including Sheffield, from carrying on ambitious redevelopment/council housing construction schemes. Within a few years Sheffield Council housing development would be reduced to a trickle. And without funds to pursue new council flat construction, the local authority also scaled back its clearance program.

During the 1970s, SAG managed to remove well over 1,000 units of housing from demolition, but the council nonetheless cleared nearly 2,000 residences. Spot clearance occurred throughout Sharrow, including the five areas that were set aside for government-financed rehabilitation schemes. The areas of Sharrow that experienced the most concentrated clearance were adjoining its industrial corridors—especially the margins of the Porter and Sheaf Rivers. There was also considerable clearance "below" London Road running down toward Bramall Lane. In the early 1980s the council built new housing estates in this area and nearer the city centre along Lancing Road. With these new Thorp and Lancing Road estates, the council returned to an approximation of the Garden City model of housing. Groups of attached apartments and small single-family "bungalows" are grouped around open areas and along meandering walkways. Both estates represent a marked departure from the high-density projects built in the previous decade and a half, including Broomhall Flats, Hanover Estate, Leverton Towers, and Lansdowne Estate.

Sharrow escaped from the most devastating combination of council highway plans, but many local residents still argue that the community suffered from what was built. The scaled-down Inner Ring Road is a substantial barrier dividing Sharrow from the city centre along the community's entire northwestern flank. In addition, in the late 1970s the central government built the Manpower Services Commission complex at Moorfoot, that is, at the end of the city centre shopping corridor across the ring road from London Road. This building completed the segmentation of London Road from the city centre. Although Bramall

Lane was not "dualed," traffic on this road increased, and by the mid-1980s traffic congestion reemerged as a major issue in Sharrow.

In 1980, Sheffield, and Sharrow as well, were just beginning to enter the sharp economic depression that has brought so much hardship in the past decade. The severe local effects of these economic problems render the evaluation of redevelopment's impact on the community more difficult. Relative to two decades ago, unemployment is higher in Sharrow, and in many people's minds national government policy, economic recession, and local authority decisionmaking commingle as sources of their hardship. Moreover, economic decline has worked an independent effect on the local physical environment. Most people agree that London Road is scruffier than a generation ago. Similarly, despite much spending on terrace house rehabilitation after the mid-1970s, Sharrow's older housing continues to decline. However, if more local people had been working in the 1980s, this new cycle of housing deterioration might have been averted. Yet even in the context of these relatively dispiriting trends, Sharrow appears to have emerged from its decade of redevelopment relatively less damaged—physically and socially—than Uptown. Furthermore, one can trace a clearly different dynamic of planning, community mobilization, and redevelopment conflict in the two communities.

The clearest point of contrast between the Sharrow and Uptown experiences turns on how neighborhood activists sought to fight redevelopment. In Uptown, the opposition to urban renewal called meetings, circulated information, and demonstrated at public hearings of the Conservation Community Council (CCC). Although the Uptown Area People's Planning Coalition did work with architects to produce a plan for Hank Williams Village, this was a fairly schematic piece of urban design. The contrast with the Sharrow Action Group is vivid. SAG certainly called meetings and registered its protests at various authority actions, but the bulk of its energy in 1972 and thereafter was devoted to surveying subcommunities and formulating an alternative perspective on the community and redevelopment. The major product of this organizing and surveying was *Views of Sharrow.*

Looking back on this period, John Peaden suggests that when a mild-mannered clergyman leads a neighborhood movement, the prospect of outright conflict escalating from mere disagreement is reduced.[41] This is probably true, but other features of the Sharrow situation also contributed to its less confrontational redevelopment politics. Although Sharrow residents in 1971 or 1972 were sharply critical of council policy, they faced a municipal government that was not uniformly hostile. In particular, the staff of the planning department, though sometimes clumsy in its methods, was committed to real citizen participation in the Sharrow-Nether Edge planning process. This willingness to consult, in turn, seems to have strengthened the resolve of SAG's leaders to follow through in their efforts to tap local opinion on redevelopment, identify just where housing could be saved, and organize residents whose property might qualify for one or another of the government-sponsored rehabilitation programs.

Of course, other parts of Sheffield's municipal government were not so accommodating. The city's engineers, in their efforts to improve traffic flow through southern and eastern Sheffield, imagined themselves to be dealing with nothing more complicated than a series of surveying problems. More fundamentally, members of Sheffield's City Council found it very difficult to understand that they did not know, intuitively, what were the interests of Sharrow's working-class residents. Were they not, in fact, products of neighborhoods very much like Sharrow? This perspective was well-summarized by an anti-redevelopment activist: "To committee chairmen and officials, with many years of service behind them and a justified if somewhat paternalistic pride in the city's achievements, conceding any part of their power of decision to popular forces in the community does not come easy."[42] Yet in the early 1970s this attitude was already losing its force. One of Sharrow's ward councillors, Ethel Evans, was SAG's first chair, and although Councillor Evans' relations with the Labour leadership were strained by her taking this stand, within a few years many of Labour's old, paternalistic councillors retired. Indeed, one of the ironies of Sharrow ward politics is that the early 1970s marked the beginning of a long period of Labour Party domination. In what was once one of Sheffield's more competitive wards, the Conservative Party elected its last councillor in 1968.

The contrast with Uptown could not be more complete. Until some of the members of the CCC realized that developers of subsidized housing east of Sheridan Road were actually increasing the residential density of this area, there was no division among supporters of urban renewal. The local business elite, the Uptown Chicago Commission, and a large majority of CCC members accepted the model of neighborhood renewal first outlined in the 1962 Meltzer Report. Furthermore, with the city government's designation of Uptown as an urban renewal area, municipal officials fell into line with the local pro-urban renewal coalition. City planners played no independent role in formulating the urban renewal program for the community, and local alderpersons representing Chicago's 46th and 48th wards also refrained from criticizing either the urban renewal planning process or the substance of the evolving plans for Uptown.

The opponents of urban renewal in Uptown claimed that they were being pushed out of the neighborhood by a conspiratorial alliance of business leaders, real estate speculators, and politicians. This, in large part, accounts for the intemperate nature of their actions, which in turn contributed to the ferocity of their battles with the pro-urban renewal forces. In Sharrow, neither SAG nor any other local groups claimed that they were subject to any sort of conspiracy. Their harshest claims were that Sheffield Council leaders had lost touch with their constituents and that Sheffield administrative officers viewed planning and highway improvement issues from an overly technocratic perspective. In fact, the activists in each neighborhood were essentially correct in their analyses.

The points at which Sharrow redevelopment politics look most similar to Uptown's were when SAG jousted with the Nether Edge-oriented Conservation Society, and later with the Heeley Residents Association. In the case of the Heeley Bypass decision, two historically separate neighborhood areas with conflicting interests in the siting of the proposed highway fell behind different roadway options. Their conflict was probably unavoidable, even though both groups seem to have regretted finding themselves at odds. At first glance, the SAG/Conservation Society dispute exhibits more substantive similarities with intergroup battling in Uptown. Rather paradoxically, the preservationist bent of the middle-class Nether Edge activists ran counter to SAG's more pragmatic approach to Sharrow redevelopment. Whereas the Conservation Society argued for housing preservation as an ultimate value, SAG found that most Pembroke Street/Pomona Street residents simply desired better housing—even if this resulted in demolition of the terrace housing they currently occupied. Furthermore, this conflict reflected more than contradictory organizational perspectives growing out of contradictory constituent interests. In this early phase of redevelopment discussions in Sharrow and Nether Edge, the activists emerging in working-class Sharrow were put off by what they perceived as the arrogance of the middle-class Nether Edge activists, who presumed to speak for them before municipal officials.[43]

As such, the SAG/Conservation Society fight seems to reflect the convergence of local interest, social class, and organizational style-derived conflict that typified the urban renewal debate in Uptown. Yet in another way, one can discern an instructive divergence in these disputes. Although Sharrow and Nether Edge activists disagreed over the appropriate means to plan and redevelop south-central Sheffield, there is no evidence to suggest that Nether Edgers were engaged in a campaign to increase the middle-class presence in Sharrow or even to protect themselves from their poorer cousins "down the hill." Long-time Nether Edge Neighbourhood Group activist Joan Flett put the point quite bluntly: "There is no sense of threat from Sharrow."[44] In sharp contrast, the warring factions in Uptown really were fighting to determine who would control and occupy this section of Chicago.

The behavior of local politicians in Sharrow and Uptown also makes for an instructive contrast. By the late 1960s the Labour Party's control of the Sheffield authority extended back for a quarter of a century, although Sharrow, like a number of central Sheffield wards, was a reasonably competitive electoral ground. Sheffield is also a city, like most large English cities, in which the Labour and Conservative Parties exact a considerable degree of discipline on their members. It is one

thing to disagree in private with the local party leadership, even to communicate some degree of sympathy for party critics at community meetings, but when it comes to voting and speaking publicly on issues,
councillors, like other party members, are expected to follow the leadership. In their early dealings with the Sheffield Council, Sharrow's anti-
redevelopment activists certainly found these conditions to hold. Yet in
time SAG began to win over some of the local representatives.
Councillor Evans was SAG's first chair, athough she gave up this post
as it became evident that her association with anti-redevelopment
activists would undermine her relations with the council leadership.
Evans, nonetheless, continued to support SAG.[45] Ultimately, the work
of SAG and other Sheffield action groups swayed the thinking of the
council's Labour leadership, and by the 1980s the Sharrow ward Labour
organization included a number of community-oriented activists.

In the 1960s and 1970s Uptown straddled Chicago's 46th and 48th
wards, each dominated by Chicago's Democratic "machine," but neither
ward a powerhouse within the Democratic Party structure. At no point
during the urban renewal controversy was either the 46th or 48th ward
alderperson willing to stake an independent position. In effect, the will of
the local business leadership, combined with key personal ties between
neighborhood leaders and the Daley administration, defined the official
course of action on urban renewal, which was to work from the Meltzer
document. Without any sort of personal or otherwise independent organizational base, the locally elected officials were captives of the community's
recognized leadership. Democrats continued to hold the aldermanic positions in these two wards into the 1980s (although after the 1979 election
Uptown was principally within the bounds of the 46th ward), but in 1987
the 46th ward aldermanic election was finally won by an insurgent candidate with ties to the anti-urban renewal activists of the previous decade.
Interestingly, the party discipline of the later Daley machine seems to have
had greater force than the presumably iron-fisted leadership of Sheffield's
Labour Party leadership. Uptown's Democrats never gave up on urban
renewal; so that when gentrification emerged as a neighborhood issue a
decade later and consolidated various oppositional groups, the party and its
incumbent alderperson were ripe for a fall.

A principal legacy of urban renewal in Uptown was to fragment the community, producing antagonistic organizations that would continue their battling into the next decade. More broadly, a substantial part of the local population became convinced that Uptown "just isn't a single community." Sheffield's efforts to redevelop Sharrow had nearly the opposite effect. In a city in which local loyalties are very local, before the mid-1960s "Sharrow" was a term of uncertain meaning for many residents of south-central Sheffield. In most people's mental mapping, very circumscribed areas such as Highfield, Lowfield, or even Shoreham Street would have carried more weight than Sharrow. In fighting the Sheffield authority, and in particular by virtue of SAG's efforts to mobilize residents of various subareas within Sharrow, the larger community emerged as a comprehensible field of association and action. This was not the intention of the Sheffield Council, whose plans to rebuild housing and improve roadways reflected a very mechanical approach to restructuring its city. It also is not clear that consolidating Sharrow from Highfield, Lowfield, Shoreham Street, Lancing Road, Mount Pleasant, and so on was the intent of John Peaden and his fellow organizers. Nevertheless, this was the effect of their work, which in the subsequent, troubling decade probably gave to the residents of this part of Sheffield a tenacity they otherwise might not have mustered in the face of a devastating economic crisis.

NOTES

1. Mark Swenarton, *Homes Fit for Heroes: The Politics and Architecture of Early State Housing in Britain* (London: Heinemann, 1981).

2. Peter Dickens, Simon Duncan, Mark Goodwin, and Fred Gray, *Housing, States, and Localities* (London: Methuen, 1985), p. 166.

3. Dickens et al., *Housing,* p. 169.

4. Patrick Dunleavy, *The Politics of Mass Housing in Britain,* 1945-1975 (New York: Oxford University Press, 1981), pp. 37-41; Stephen Merrett, *State Housing in Britain* (London: Routledge & Kegan Paul, 1979), pp. 248-249.

5. Harold Lambert, "Foreword" to *Ten Years of Housing in Sheffield, 1953-1963* (Housing Development Committee of the Corporation of Sheffield, April 1962).

6. Harold Lambert, "A Review of Sheffield's Housing Policy," in Colin Fudge and Geoff Green, eds., *Sheffield's Grassroots* 2, 1971, p. 2.

7. "2,400 Homes to Go in City 12-Year Plan," *The Star,* February 5, 1971.

8. *Sheffield—The Emerging City* (Sheffield: City Engineer & Surveyor and Town Planning Officer, 1969), map, p. 28; p. 32.

9. *Sheffield Morning Telegraph,* March 31, 1982.

10. Interview with John Peaden, August 5, 1993.

11. "Sharrow and Heeley Neighbourhood Committee," n.d., South Sheffield Inner City Community Project (SSICCP) Files.

12. John Peaden, "Report on the Sharrow and Heeley Neighbourhood Association," September 22, 1971, SSICCP Files.

13. Robert Poulton, "Sharrow Residents to Set up Action Groups," *The Star,* March 19, 1971; Ralph Taylor with Jim Humberstone and John Peaden, "Participation in Practice Case Study 1: The Sharrow Experience," *Journal of the Royal Town Planning Institute* 59 (April 1973): 167-168.

14. Geoffrey Green, "People, Politics, and Planning," *Yorkshire Architect,* November-December, 1969, pp. 209-211.

15. "Advice Centre Turned Down," *Sheffield Morning Telegraph,* August 31, 1971 (author's parenthesis).

16. *Sheffield Morning Telegraph,* May 5, 1971; John Peaden, "The Sheffield Moor and Lower Sharrow Council of Churches Community Development Project," April 1973, SSICCP Files; John Peaden, "A Sheffield Action Group," in Roy Darke and Ray Walker, Jr., eds., *Local Government and the Public* (London: Leonard Hill, 1977), p. 149.

17. Peaden, "A Sheffield Action Group," pp. 151-155.

18. Department of Planning and Design, Sheffield City Council, *Sharrow - Nether Edge District Plan,* October 1980, pp. 4-5.

19. *Views of Sharrow* (Sharrow Community Development Project, December 1972), p. 23.

20. *Views of Sharrow,* pp. 21-22.

21. *Views of Sharrow,* p. 5.

22. Chris Bacon, "Park Hill in Its Social Context," (University of Sheffield Department of Town and Regional Planning Occasional Paper #63, December 1985), pp. 47-61.

23. Dickens et al., *Housing,* pp. 174-75.

24. *Sheffield Morning Telegraph,* June 18, 1971.

25. *Views of Sharrow,* p. 6; Peaden Interview, August 5, 1993; Interview with Joan Flett, Nether Edge Neighbourhood Group, August 17, 1993.

26. Mark Pickering, "Bitter Attack on Inner Ring Plan at Moorfoot," *Sheffield Morning Telegraph,* August 23, 1972.

27. "M-way Protest Begins," *Sheffield Morning Telegraph,* February 18, 1972.

28. *Views of Sharrow,* p. 46; Joan D. Naish, "Report to the Secretary of State for the Environment Regarding the Sheffield City Council Application for Confirmation of Pomona Street and Pembroke Street Compulsory Purchase Orders," hearing: March 20, 1973, report: June 1973, SSICCP

Files; "Activists Press for Better Housing," *Sheffield Morning Telegraph*, January 31, 1974; "Call for Parking Curbs by Bramall Lane Area Residents," *The Star*, January 31, 1974.

29. Sharrow Action Group Letter to Sheffield Councillors and Officers, March 20, 1973, SSICCP Files.

30. Peaden, "A Sheffield Action Group," pp. 150-151.

31. Sheffield Metropolitan District Council, *Sharrow-Nether Edge Draft District Plan*, February 1976, p. 55.

32. *Sharrow-Nether Edge Draft District Plan*, p. 56.

33. *Heeley Residents Association Voice*, Winter 1977/78, p. 1.

34. *Heeley Residents Association Voice*, Winter 1977/78, pp. 3-4.

35. Sharrow Action Group, "Record of Meeting—Tuesday 5th July 1977," p. 1, SSICCP Files.

36. Laura Seale, "Meeting Is Abandoned in Uproar," *Sheffield Morning Telegraph*, January 19, 1978.

37. "Anxiety over Link Road Scheme," *Sheffield Morning Telegraph*, February 11, 1978.

38. "Tory to Fight By-pass," *The Star*, February 16, 1978.

39. Philip Andrews, "By-pass Opponents May Win Labour Backing," *The Star*, February 15, 1978.

40. *Sharrow-Nether Edge District Plan*, pp. 13-14.

41. Peaden Interview, August 5, 1993.

42. Peter Hildrew, "Labour's Withering Grassroots," in Fudge and Green, *Sheffield's Grassroots* 2, p. 8.

43. Taylor, "Participation in Planning Case Study 1: The Sharrow Experience," p. 170.

44. Flett Interview, August 17, 1993.

45. Taylor, "Participation in Planning Case Study 1: The Sharrow Experience," p. 168.

CHAPTER FIVE

SHARROW IN THE 1980s: THE TRIALS OF COMMUNITY DEVELOPMENT

During the 1980s, Sharrow reeled from the same shocks that buffeted all of Sheffield. The decline of traditional industries throughout the English North struck Sheffield's cutlery, steel, and engineering enterprises, whose lay-offs pushed the neighborhood's unemployment figures far above previous levels. The Thatcher government's efforts to impose restraints on Sheffield Council spending not only brought large-scale redevelopment to a halt but also hampered the authority's day-to-day service delivery. As a result, Sharrow seemed to become a harsher, grimier place, as well as a poorer place. Within Sharrow the anti-redevelopment activism of the 1960s and 1970s was transformed. The watchword of 1980s activists became community development, a notion connoting local participation in setting policy, attention to the particular problems of the neighborhood, and a willingness to bring local resources to bear on local problems. However, in the face of changing central government-municipal authority relations and the resulting fiscal austerity forced on the Sheffield Authority, by the end of the decade community development was an endangered principle.

II

In 1971, just as the battle over Sharrow redevelopment was beginning in earnest, John Peaden made the transition from minister with a strong interest in community issues to full-time community worker. It was in this role, as principal staff person of the Sheffield Moor and Lower Sharrow Council of Churches Community Development Project, that Peaden contributed to the formation of organizations such as the Sharrow Action Group. By the mid-1970s, when the Sharrow planning process had shifted redevelopment conflict into the more comfortable domain of neighborhood-authority negotiation, Peaden, while remaining in Sharrow, went to work for Shelter, a nonprofit national housing organization, which in England was a prime agent seeking to respond to the emerging problem of homelessness. During this period, Peaden recalls a significant movement in his own sense of priorities. In the early stages of the Sharrow redevelopment debate his principal concern was the planning process, in particular the Sheffield Council's unwillingness to deal with Sharrow as a unique community and the councillors' paternalistic attitude toward Sharrow and its residents. By mid-decade Peaden began to see the plight of Sharrow in a broader context and grew convinced that larger forces such as industrial decline also played a major part in undercutting the quality of local life and residents' sense of community:

> It was like putting your hand in the machinery, and before you know it you've gone right through the whole thing. I hadn't been doing community development. Now I became more professionally oriented, but without wishing to impose my values on people.[1]

With these considerations in mind, Peaden, along with fellow local activists David Skinner of Broomhall and Richard Harrison of Heeley, began to conceptualize a new kind of community organization to serve Sharrow.

Peaden, Skinner, and Harrison were not the only Sheffield figures seeking to move beyond neighborhood-council confrontation and to reformulate neighborhood activism. By the late 1970s Sheffield's "New Urban Left" was making its mark on city politics. Councillors such as David Blunkett, Clive Betts, and Bill Michie—Michie having been an early proponent of the Sharrow-Nether Edge planning process—were seeking to move the Sheffield Labour Party in new directions. Among the precipitators of their own reconsideration of local Labour politics were the tenants and community movements that had emerged in the previous decade. Between 1976 and 1980 Blunkett chaired the council's Family and Community Services Committee. In the latter year he was elected Labour Group Leader on the council. Even as he maintained a fierce allegiance to socialist principles, Blunkett recognized that the bureaucratization of local socialism in Labour-dominated municipal councils had itself reduced the efficacy of governance in cities such as Sheffield. Once he became an influential voice on the Sheffield Council, Blunkett began exploring ways to reconnect the municipal administration with its constituents. As Council Leader, Blunkett articulated this agenda quite forcefully:

> The Council's aim, particularly in the last two years, has been to encourage the active involvement of inner city residents in shaping the future of their areas. Some councillors live in the priority areas, most of them in the wider inner city area. And many council officers spend much of their working day there. But they alone cannot sustain the vitality of each community. Helping the residents themselves to give expression to complex needs, supporting their aspirations, is an essential part in regenerating our city. It is not primarily a question of responding to individual grievances but of supporting their collective contribution to the life and well being of their neighbourhood.[2]

Out of Peaden's work in Sharrow and Blunkett's desire to reshape local socialism grew the South Sheffield Inner City Community Project (SSICCP), which, once Blunkett threw his support behind the proposal, was approved by the Sheffield Council in 1979 with the bulk of its funding provided by the central government Urban Programme. The Urban Programme, which had been authorized by Parliament in 1968, enabled local authorities to provide special social services in low-income areas. Urban Programme funding was also commonly used to support innovative projects, which was precisely what Peaden had in mind. The SSICCP's service area was defined as Heeley, Sharrow, and Broomhall, the latter neighborhood an economically and ethnically mixed area lying just across Ecclesall Road and the Porter River from Sharrow proper (and within the boundaries of Sharrow ward). Programmatically, the SSICCP aimed to build on and extend the grassroots activism that had appeared in

Sharrow and its environs in the early 1970s while also serving as an agent to redirect and improve authority-provided services. By 1981 SSICCP defined its agenda by reference to the following items: (1) advocacy of local interests, via units such as its Citizens Advice Bureau and "community lawyer"; (2) housing work, through staff assistance for local residents associations seeking General Improvement Area or Housing Action Area designation, or by work with resident associations responding to authority-sponsored or privately initiated redevelopment plans; (3) ethnic minority groups—including local Asian and Caribbean populations—which were promoted and assisted by SSICCP staff; (4) employment schemes, which were developed by SSICCP-affiliated groups; (5) education schemes, especially for "non-traditional" populations including adults and members of ethnic minority populations; and (6) informing public policy by way of the grassroots mobilization.[3]

From Blunkett's standpoint, the SSICCP provided a local institutional base to which authority personnel could be "outposted." Employees of municipal departments including Education, Family and Community Services, and Housing were assigned to SSICCP and devoted themselves, besides working on their more characteristic tasks, to building contacts with local residents and organizations. Working within the community in this fashion gave these authority officers more knowledge of the particular service delivery problems found in Heeley, Sharrow, and Broomhall. At the same time they were released from the bureaucratic atmosphere of their departments' Town Hall operations.[4]

SSICCP established its physical presence in Sharrow by acquiring Wesley House, Brunswick Trinity Church's former Sunday School building on Highfield Place. In addition to providing a base of operations for SSICCP staff, authority employees assigned to Sharrow, and SSICCP neighborhood volunteers, Wesley House served the surrounding community in a variety of other ways. Many local organizations held their meetings in Wesley House, and SSICCP's library and audio-visual equipment were available for use by local residents. The building also housed the Sharrow Citizens Advice Bureau, and later the Asian Welfare Association.

By the early 1980s SSICCP's programs touched a considerable portion of Sharrow's population. With the winding down of council-sponsored redevelopment and the conclusion of the Sharrow-Nether Edge planning process, the Sharrow Action Group disbanded. However, SAG's absence was barely noticed as John Peaden began convening the Sharrow Neighbourhood Groups Forum in early 1980. The Neighbourhood Groups Forum brought together representatives from Sharrow's various residents and tenants organizations to discuss issues of mutual concern. The Neighbourhood Groups Forum also allowed activists in Sharrow subareas to keep in touch and, when necessary, to mobilize for collective action such as the organizing and information-gathering required by the Sharrow Traffic Campaign at mid-decade. In the late 1980s the Sheffield Council instituted a Sharrow Community Forum to formalize councillor-administration-resident communication. For a short time at the turn of the decade the two forums convened on alternating months, the Sharrow residents not wanting to give up their "internal" meetings at which political figures and authority staff would not, as a rule, be present.[5]

In addition to sponsoring the Sharrow Neighbourhood Groups Forum, SSICCP hired a "community lawyer" to work with organizations and individuals throughout Sharrow. In many instances SSICCP's community solicitor, Bob Martin, provided counsel for individuals who would otherwise not have access to legal representation. For example, Martin handled the cases of recent arrivals to Sharrow who needed steering through the shoals of British immigration law. However, individuals were not alone in requiring legal help. In the early 1980s Martin worked with the tenants' organization in the Broomhall Flats as it sought to pressure the Sheffield Council into authorizing repairs for its residential complex. Similarly, when the Sheffield United Club sought planning permission to acquire and redevelop the area around its football ground, Martin advised the local neighborhood group that fought the United proposal.[6]

Among the most frequently used SSICCP services was the Citizens Advice Bureau located in Wesley House. In the early 1970s SAG had requested authority support for an advice service in Sharrow, presumably to concentrate on residents' questions growing out of the local redevelopment plans. The authority had not approved this proposal, but in the mid-1970s an independent Citizens Advice Bureau (funded by the national alliance of CABs) had opened in Sharrow. With the formation of SSICCP, the advice bureau joined the new program and moved into Wesley House. By the mid-1980s, the Sharrow CAB's professional staff and volunteers were handling up to 20,000 inquiries per year.[7] Many of the people visiting the CAB were from Sharrow's growing ethnic minority population, and, with the deepening of Sheffield's recession during the 1980s financial advice became the principal area of CAB service.[8]

A centerpiece of SSICCP work was outreach to and support for Sharrow's various ethnic minority communities. In the mid-1970s the Asian Welfare Association (AWA) began as an autonomous group serving Sharrow's growing Indian, Pakistani, and Bangladeshi populations. Members of these communities frequently encountered difficulties with British immigration statutes, and the AWA devoted much of its energy to advising and representing people in their dealings with the government. The AWA also sponsored an array of social and economic development initiatives. In the early 1980s, having received its own funding from the Urban Programme, the AWA joined with SSICCP in purchasing Wesley House, with the AWA then taking over a portion of the building.[9] SSICCP also supported the formation of the I and I Committee, a group of young Afro-Caribbeans, who opened a bookstore specializing in Third World literature. In addition to running their bookshop, the I and I Committee worked with local schools in developing special programs—again with a Third World emphasis—for Sharrow students. The I and I Committee was able to collaborate with the local schools by way of two "school community teachers," Paul Worrall and Janet McDermott, who were among the Sheffield authority workers assigned to SSICCP.[10] Throughout the 1980s the SSICCP also worked with Sharrow's Chinese, Italian, and Somalian immigrant communities.

By the early 1980s, SSICCP had established itself as a dynamic force within Sharrow. Its staff—SSICCP employees and authority personnel assigned to the project—numbered twelve, and the central government was supporting the project with an appropriation of nearly £70,000 annually.[11] Local volunteers contributed much to SSICCP programs, the advice bureau alone depending on the work of as many as 20 volunteers at any given time. When presented with the opportunity to purchase Wesley House in association with the AWA, SSICCP raised £17,000 from private sources to pay for building renovations.[12] Former SSICCP staff member Chris Hodgkinson recalls the organization in this period:

> When I started in 1982 it was absolutely buzzing. We had enormous staff meetings, which we held out in Derbyshire to get away from the phones ringing. And it wasn't just Wesley House people. We also had people based elsewhere, like Mount Pleasant.[13]

Given SSICCP's quick growth and variety of projects, it was surely inevitable that some community people would disapprove of one or another of the organization's operations. Some residents have objected to the project's programmatic emphasis, in particular, its catering to ethnic minority populations. It is also observed that John Peaden's determination to work on so many different projects, in fact, reduced the effectiveness of SSICCP. In this view, Peaden's multiple agenda prevented SSICCP from carrying specific initiatives through to completion. Finally, a few local observers have suggested that SSICCP, itself, became a victim of bureaucratization. Yet even taking into account such criticism, it is also clear that organizations and residents throughout Sharrow were touched by SSICCP. Moreover, as the following accounts emphasize, SSICCP did not simply carve out a role as local service provider. Just as John Peaden and David Blunkett had anticipated, SSICCP's presence and resources—meeting space, technical services, and staff support—aided a variety of initiatives whose chief architects were local residents.

III

Although neighborhood-authority conflict was not the rule during the 1980s, Sharrow still lives with the physical consequences of the

Sheffield Council's post-war building program. In the late 1970s the rise of the Broomhall Tenants Association was in response to circumstances set in motion by the Sheffield authority's rush to reconstruct the inner city during the previous decade. In this particular instance, a distinct irony of "community development" was that mobilization by the Broomhall Flats residents ultimately resulted in the demolition of their housing estate. Moreover, in order to gain the attention of councillors and authority officers, the tenants group was forced to pursue an aggressive course of political action.

The odyssey of the Broomhall Tenants Association began in 1962 when Sheffield's council joined with the municipal authorities of Nottingham, Leeds, and Hull in forming the Yorkshire Development Group (YDG). The YDG's mandate was to devise an industrialized housing system that could be adopted by all four cities in building council flats. The housing estate prototype subsequently developed by the YDG engineers included these basic design elements: covered-deck access walkways allowing "economical use of lifts," a variety of unit sizes, high residential densities in low-rise structures, and "standard components" intended to produce construction economies.[14] For their part, the four municipal authorities committed to ordering the construction of at least 4,500 units of housing built via the YDG model. The building system developed by YDG has been described in the following way: "The walls, floors and roofs consist of pre-cast concrete slabs which are built very much as a child would build a 'house' of dominoes. Slabs standing on edge form the walls, and other slabs laid horizontally form the floors and roofs."[15] The concrete dominoes were held in place by steel rods projecting from one slab and "threaded" around steel hoops set in adjoining slabs. In short, the YDG housing prototype used relatively inexpensive materials, concrete and steel, which in turn could be easily produced and deployed in various configurations. Further, the construction process itself was intended to require much less of the craft work associated with traditional building techniques.

In 1967 Sheffield's building contractor, Shepherd and Sons (based in York), began work on the Broomhall Flats. The estate was located on the city centre side of Sharrow and quite close to the old cutler's district. The 653-unit complex was comprised of nineteen separate, blockish concrete structures rising five to seven floors and grouped around courtyards. The "brutalist" simplicity of its architectural form discouraged most tenants of Broomhall Flats from feeling any strong affection for the complex, but former residents do recall its having some virtues. Its proximity to the city centre's shopping areas was advantageous for older residents and parents with young children. One of the leaders of the tenants association remembers the groves of trees gracing some of the courtyards. Adjoining the flats a new pub was built, and in a bow to the YDG's innovative design and construction methods, it was dubbed The Domino.

The Broomhall Flats were not completed until 1970, and the building of the complex did not proceed uneventfully. During construction four workers were killed, including three crushed by falling concrete slabs.[16] The flats' original design specified a gas heating system, but in May 1968, this feature had to be reconsidered. In London, the Ronan Point housing estate's gas heating system exploded, causing sections of this systems-built structure to collapse, resulting in the death of five persons. In the aftermath of the Ronan Point disaster, Sheffield officials decided to reconfigure the Broomhall Flats heating system, substituting a presumably safer electric system for the gas heaters.[17] Long after the completion of the estate, this decision cost tenants and the authority thousands of pounds due to the costliness of the electrically generated heat.

Even as the construction of Broomhall Flats fell behind schedule, the contractors, Shepherd and Sons, attempted to accelerate the work. Evidently, workers seeking to win pay bonuses for rapid completion of their tasks did not allow the poured slabs to "cure" for a sufficient time, resulting in weakened, "honeycombed" concrete. In addition, many of the steel connecting rods settled out of place, which prevented secure linking of the adjoining components.[18] In any event, very soon following the completion of Broomhall Flats in the spring of 1970, tenants began to complain to the Sheffield authority about persistent dampness within their apartments. Indeed, even before the completion of Broomhall Flats, the Sheffield Council had become disenchanted with

Broomhall Flats   **Source:** Sheffield Local Studies Library

the Yorkshire Development Group. Sheffield withdrew from the consortium in November 1968.

On several occasions during the 1970s the Sheffield Council attempted to correct Broomhall Flats' flawed design. Structural repairs cost £30,000 in 1977-78. In the next two years nearly £150,000 was spent, first adding insulation to the ceilings of apartments on the top floors of the estate, then placing external insulation on the roofs above these units. The council also considered taking legal action against Shepherd and Sons, but as a result of negotiations with the contractor, in September 1977 accepted a £20,000 cash settlement. In reaching this settlement with Shepherd and Sons, the council released the contractor from future liability for Broomhall Flats structural problems.[19]

During the 1970s residents of the estate were represented by the Broomhall Community Group, an organization that included homeowners and tenants from the larger Broomhall area. The neighborhood group was assisted by a community worker, Mandy Bryce, assigned by the Council to work in Broomhall and paid from Urban Programme funds. Bryce took a considerable interest in researching how the flats had been constructed, and as the residents of the estate became more concerted in their efforts to publicize their living conditions, Bryce played an important role in linking local residents with political allies beyond Broomhall. In early 1978 the Broomhall Community Group produced a report on the estate entitled "Living in Broomhall." Assisted by David Yeomans of the University of Liverpool School of Architecture, the residents' report discussed the estate's structural problems as well as the extraordinary expenditures tallied by tenants trying to keep their flats warm and dry.[20]

Although the Broomhall Community Group was making some progress in organizing tenants and bringing attention to the estate's problems, veterans of Broomhall Flats campaign identify Margaret Howard's joining the group in the late 1970s as a turning point in their efforts. Howard had moved into Broomhall Flats a few years earlier following her husband Leslie's disabling stroke. The Howards had lived in one of the large homes dotting Broomhall, but with her husband's disability, Margaret Howard quit her job at Town Hall (ironically, working for the Housing Department and advising tenants of council estates) and moved into the flats, whose single-floor layouts would permit her to tend to her husband more easily. The flooding of her apartment four days before Christmas in 1978 was the impetus for Howard's joining the Broomhall fray. Once she had identified the source of her flooding, two floors above her flat, Howard wrote the chair of the Sheffield Council's Housing Committee, Clive Betts, to complain. Betts did not reply to her letter, which led Howard to begin attending meetings of the community group. Howard was not at first impressed by the organization, but soon enough she was actively involved in its affairs, having been asked by Mandy Bryce to serve as secretary. Howard recalls that among her first initiatives was to help turn her fellow tenants into a "proper group."[21] In the spring of 1979 the Broomhall Flats Action Group evolved from the Broomhall Community Group. The new organization's mandate was to speak for residents of the housing estate, and it devoted itself unequivocally to pressuring the council to improve conditions in Broomhall Flats.

In the years to follow the action group—rechristened the Broomhall Tenants Association (BTA) in 1981—developed a complicated division of political labor. Mandy Bryce, university trained and

still in her 20s, investigated how the flats had been built, researched
national legislation that might serve the interest of the tenants, and
made contact with organizations outside of Broomhall, notably the tenants groups representing the residents of the other YDG-designed
estates in Hull, Leeds, and Nottingham. Later, as the tenants group
pursued action requiring legal assistance, they worked with the
SSICCP's community lawyer, Bob Martin. The core of the tenants
association included Margaret Howard, Madge Rule, Lawrence
Randell, and a handful of other older residents of the estate. One of the
group's allies, Sharrow councillor Tony Tigwell recalls that the tenants'
leadership "all seemed to be retired."[22] This was, in fact, the case, but
once again Mandy Bryce's role was crucial:

> I kept in touch with the younger residents of the flats.
> They often had kids. There were also many West
> Indians. They spent time at the advice centre, which
> is where I usually talked to them. Though they didn't
> participate in the core group, they could be counted
> on to attend the public meetings.[23]

In turn, members of the core group constituted BTA's presumptive
leadership at hearings and meetings with Sheffield officials. However, as
a result of personality conflicts that periodically split the group's core of
activists, the preponderance of the BTA's day-to-day political work—in
particular its complex round of communications with Sheffield officials,
representatives of the central government, and allies outside Sheffield—
fell on the shoulders of Margaret Howard.

The initial aim of the tenants association was to convince the
Sheffield Council that, even though it had poured hundreds of thousands of pounds into remedial work during the 1970s, living conditions
in Broomhall Flats remained intolerable. To that end the group invited
councillors to their meetings and routinely forwarded letters to the
authority. Bryce recalls that for a time, she and Howard virtually stalked
Clive Betts and Howard Knight (another of Sharrow's three councillors) at the Town Hall: "When they would see us they would head in the
other direction."[24] This frustrating period devoted to seeking acknowl-

edgment of their situation came to a head when the BTA wrote to the Sharrow Labour Party complaining of Knight's nonresponsiveness.[25] The local Labour group, which at the time was attempting to build closer ties with grassroots organizations in Sharrow ward, evidently persuaded Knight to give more attention to Broomhall Flats. In fact, in the coming years Knight took on this task so resolutely as to become a vocal advocate for the tenants.

As a member of the council's younger generation, Knight's initial hesitation to confront the Broomhall Flats problem reflected more than personal reluctance. In effect, the local government was caught between two unpleasant imperatives. On the one hand, planning catastrophes such as the flats were the handiwork of the early postwar Labour leadership in Sheffield, not the contemporary party. As such, Knight, Clive Betts, and other Labour Party figures resented having to mop up their predecessors' mess. Furthermore, by the time that the tenants of Broomhall were working themselves into an effective political force, the council had already spent quite a large sum seeking to rectify Broomhall Flats' faulty design and incompetent construction. Yet in spite of the council's recent efforts, the flats' residents persisted in their claim that their homes remained uninhabitable. On the other hand, the Thatcher government's squeezing of local finances was undermining the authority's fiscal latitude. Irrespective of who had produced the Broomhall Flats disaster, the contemporary council leadership could not easily raise the substantial additional funding necessary to remedy the estate's inept design. For a time it appears that those members of the local government familiar with the Broomhall situation simply wished that, somehow, the flats would repair themselves.

In the spring of 1981 the BTA formalized itself by adopting a constitution and, coincidentally, began to meet with tenants' representatives from the other Yorkshire Development Group flats in Hull, Leeds, and Nottingham. The residents of these other council estates had been encountering many of the same problems manifest by Broomhall Flats. This larger group dubbed itself the Yorkshire Development Tenants Action Group (YDTAG) and, through its meetings and ongoing communications, allowed activists in the different cities to compare notes on their housing conditions and political strategies. By the following year, YDTAG had generated enough attention to initiate meetings at which councillors from the four cities appeared. In Leeds on May 15, 1982, eleven councillors from the four cities discussed the problems in their respective YDG flats and pledged to work with the tenants group.[26] By this time the Leeds Council had, in fact, authorized the demolition of one of the YDG estates, Hunslet Grange, which was subsequently pulled down in January 1983. Representatives of the BTA attended the demolition ceremony in Leeds, accompanied by councillors Howard Knight and Tony Tigwell. This event was covered by the Sheffield press, a reporter noting: "After a ceremony which saw the foundation plaque torn from the wall, a chimney stack demolished and windows smashed, the crowd was treated to a cup of tea and bun."[27] At this time, tenants, councillors, and administrators in Sheffield still clung to the hope that Broomhall Flats could be repaired, but the demolition of Hunslet Grange demonstrated that there was an alternative to continued, presumably inconclusive repair work.

In addition to publicizing their situation, the BTA began to explore means of directly addressing the unusual financial burdens borne by Broomhall Flats residents. The tenants group determined that national Department of Health and Social Security (DHSS) regulations provided for an Estate Rate Heating Addition (subsidy) for occupants of council flats requiring extraordinary heating expenditures. Thirty Broomhall Flats tenants applied for this grant in 1980. BTA enlisted the support of Sheffield councillors and members of Parliament, who communicated with the DHSS and discussed the tenants' plight in Parliament. The tenants themselves visited London to present heating bills to DHSS, and later, in 1982 complained to the Parliamentary Ombudsman about the agency's slow pace in reviewing their claims. In July 1982 DHSS finally awarded the heating allowance to Broomhall tenants receiving supplementary benefits from the government—in effect, pensioners and others receiving income support. This decision was welcomed by the BTA, although it produced some dissatisfaction among their constituents. Working tenants, even of very modest income, were not eligible for the DHSS grant.[28]

Coincidental with its efforts to win heating expense subsidies for eligible tenants, the BTA also sought to reduce the tax burden on Broomhall Flats residents. Until the mid-1980s British households, irrespective of their status as owner-occupiers or tenants, paid local "rates" based on the value of the property they occupied. In August 1982, and nearly coincidentally with winning the DHSS subsidy, the BTA petitioned the council for a reduction in rates levies for Broomhall Flats tenants. This was a two-stage process, first requiring a favorable ruling by a local Evaluation Officer, then authorization by the Sheffield Council. In fact, when the BTA sought rates reductions for eight representative flats the group was confident in council's support for their initiative. In the recollection of one BTA member, the Evaluation Court hearing was little, if any, challenge:

> When it came to the day we got as many people as possible to go and we also took an excellent report from John McQuillan, Environmental Health Officer (from the staff of Shelter). We had also prepared a lot of other evidence and a display of photos so they could really see what the flats were like. Within half an hour of seeing the report we had a 20% reduction.[29]

The February 1983 Evaluation Court ruling was followed in June by the council's award of rates reductions for all Broomhall Flats tenants—with the 20 percent evaluation reduction backdated for six years. Again however, this award was not distributed equally. In this instance tenants receiving housing rent rebates from the authority were ineligible for the full 20 percent rates reduction.[30]

From 1982 the Sheffield Council was won over to the cause of BTA, although at that point all parties still anticipated that some remedy could be identified to make the estate comfortably habitable. After mid-1982 a Broomhall Project group regularly met—including tenants, councillors, and Sheffield administrative officers. The project group certainly eased tenant-council relations and, by bringing together representatives of different authority departments such as Housing and Works, seemed to improve the quality of services for the

flats. In a May 1982 report summarizing conditions at Broomhall
Flats, Sheffield's Housing Director acknowledged "structural defects,
water penetration, severe condensation and high heating costs."[31]
Nonetheless, the Housing Director's suggested course of action was to
collaborate with the Hull, Leeds, and Nottingham authorities in
preparing a petition for central government assistance in repairing
Broomhall and other YDG estates. The costs of renovation were estimated to run as high as £10,000 per flat, a figure far in excess of
Sheffield's resources, as well as far in excess of the repair expenditures
already accumulated by the flats. In fact, given the central government's lack of sympathy for Sheffield and other Labour-controlled
municipal authorities, the Housing Director was recommending an
implausible strategy.

Although it was quite unlikely that the central government would
fund repairs on the scale suggested by Sheffield's Housing Director, the
four-city discussions that had resulted from the tenant organizing at
Broomhall and the other YDG cities provoked Sheffield to reexamine
the possibility of taking legal action against Shepherd and Sons. The
other authorities were considering similar steps, and in order to establish unequivocally the extent of structural deterioration in Broomhall, in
late 1982 the Sheffield Council authorized demolition of one of the
Broomhall buildings. A private engineering firm, Eastwood and
Partners, was hired to supervise this process and prepare a report on the
flats' structural integrity. The demolition of the 22-flat Wellington block
in summer and fall of 1983 produced another round of anxiety among
the tenants. Asbestos had been used to insulate the flats, and in spite of
assurances to the contrary from the Eastwood firm, residents became
concerned that the demolition process would release dangerous quanti-
ties of asbestos fiber.[32]

Beyond the asbestos scare, Margaret Howard recalls many unpleasant moments during this period. Wilfred Eastwood, the head of the
engineering firm overseeing the Wellington block demolition, was little
interested in the concerns of the residents, who were nearly as fright-
ened by the exploratory demolition as they were demoralized by their
long fight over conditions in the flats. As for Howard, Eastwood dis-

missed her as an "interfering woman."[33] In fact, despite the unsatisfactory interpersonal relations between Eastwood and the tenants, his firm's report—released in January 1984—confirmed the substance of their claims. From the start, construction practices had been shoddy, and over the decade and a half of the flats' occupancy water seepage had produced substantial deterioration of the structural concrete. Eastwood estimated that the basic repairs needed to restore the Broomhall structures would cost in the range of £1,000,000 and would need to be completed within two years. To return the flats to first-class habitability would cost far in excess of £1,000,000.[34]

Coincidentally with the preparation of the final Eastwood report, the BTA, Sheffield Council, and other council estate tenants groups in Sheffield arranged for a visit to the city by Ian Gow, Prime Minister Thatcher's housing minister.[35] Gow's visit, on January 11, 1984, was a memorable day for Margaret Howard. The housing minister spent 45 minutes at Broomhall Flats, with Howard leading Gow through the complex. The BTA had selected particular, especially deteriorated apartments for the minister and his media entourage to inspect, but along the way Gow requested one visit to a flat that was not on the tenants' list. Surprised by the minister's impromptu petition, Howard, on the spot, had to identify a suitable flat. This she did, but with no assurance as to whether the unit's occupant would be present to welcome the contingent of officials, activists, and reporters. When the tenant answered their knock, Howard was elated; for his part, Gow was duly impressed. This "randomly selected" flat was as damp and water damaged as any of the apartments on the BTA's list.[36]

Housing Minister Gow's visit to Sheffield was well publicized, and in conjunction with the release of the Eastwood engineering survey, the seemingly inexorable chain of events that would produce the demolition of Broomhall Flats appeared very near its end. Yet among the ranks of Broomhall Flats tenants the work of Margaret Howard, Madge Rule, Lawrence Randall, and Mandy Bryce was not unequivocally appreciated. At the end of January 1984 Margaret Howard received the following unsigned letter:

Mrs. Howard-

> We said a long time ago that the Broomhall flats were
> dangerous and would colapse [sic] sooner or later,
> now the Survey as [sic] proved we were right yet you
> say they should be repaired which is stupid as it would
> be impossible to put five ton slabs right built up like a
> pack of dominoes, and the repairs would have to go
> on forever and as was stated a whole chain of floors
> could colapse [sic] at any time. [BTA president]
> Randle [sic] says he likes them and as [sic] no prob-
> lems we suggest that he goes round and sees. If any
> section(s) should colapse [sic] he could be one of the
> unlucky ones.[37]

The writer's claim is true enough. For the better part of the roughly
five-year period during which serious tenant organizing sought to
resolve the Broomhall Flats situation, the leaders of the BTA anticipated that the flats would be saved. Indeed, at the meeting of the
Broomhall Project Group in mid-January 1984, tenants and Sheffield
officials discussed a piece of equipment—a dehumidifier—recently
developed at the local technical college, Sheffield Polytechnic, which
might be used to reduce moisture in the flats. Although the dehumidifier was described as a "sophisticated bucket placed under a leak,"
Howard Knight nonetheless suggested that it might be considered "part
of a package as an alternative to demolition."[38]

With the summer of 1984 the Sheffield Council at last authorized
the inevitable. At the end of April the city's Director of Housing
reported to the Housing Committee on the steep cost of repairing and
rehabilitating Broomhall Flats.[39] Within weeks the Legal Department
advised the council that there was no chance of succeeding in new litigation against Shepherd and Sons. Still, the council could not quite pull
the trigger, and in May only ordered the evacuation of the flats. In July
the council did approve a demolition order, though even this action did
not quite close the story of the unhappy estate. Just as the construction
of Broomhall Flats was checkered by tragedy and unforeseen circum-

stance, the closing down of the estate proved tortuous. Residents were eligible for relocation grants, but by early 1985 the council—locked in combat with the Thatcher government over the setting of local rates— had no funds for these cash advances.[40] Throughout late 1984 and most of 1985 the derelict estate was subject to break-ins by vandals and squats by homeless people. A number of the remaining tenants were physically assaulted.[41] When the BTA held its last meeting, in October 1985, there were still seven people occupying the flats. The last two Broomhall Flats tenants left the complex a few weeks before Christmas 1985.

The greater portion of the Broomhall Flats residents resettled near their former homes. Throughout the late 1980s there were press accounts of proposals to redevelop the cleared Broomhall Flats site, but nearly a decade passed before the construction of a new residential estate occurred.[42] In a manner quite characteristic of the public-private partnership ethos favored by the Thatcher and Major governments, Sheffield's Housing Department co-developed a portion of the site with the United Kingdom Housing Trust. In place of the 653 brutalist units of Broomhall Flats rose 106 flats and 32 houses available for rent, some designed to accommodate the aging. In addition, on the ring road side of the site a private developer offered houses and flats for sale. The new estate's construction techniques, architecture, and site plan, were strictly traditional: two- and three-floor brick structures arranged on gently curved streets. And to further distinguish the new development from its troubled predecessor, the Broomhall Flats site was optimistically renamed Broom Springs. Although former tenants of Broomhall Flats could exercise first claim on the new rental units, after so many years there were few takers.

For the BTA's leadership, their half-decade effort to win a habitable residential environment was the culmination of their "public lives." Within a few years of the demolition of the estate, Lawrence Randell had died. Margaret Howard and Madge Rule moved to flats not very far from the estate, but in subsequent years neither woman was active in community groups. Mandy Bryce became a Sheffield Council employee, moving from community work to a policy analysis position. For Margaret Howard, the Broomhall Flats mobilization was the defin-

New housing on the Broomhall Flats site

ing moment of her long life, and yet years later she continued to express misgivings. She remained quite certain that the residential environment of the flats was intolerable, and moreover, that the authority would not have acted to remedy the situation unless prodded to action by the tenants. Yet she also realized that for many of the elderly residents of the flats, moving out was a harsh corrective measure. By trying to save their homes the BTA had indeed laid the groundwork for destroying them. In Margaret Howard's words: "Some people would say that I had won, but I felt defeated."[43]

IV

The compromise highway and traffic control measures introduced at the end of the 1970s did not bring an end to Sharrow's automobile-derived problems. Located just to the south and east of Sheffield's city centre, the neighborhood's principal streets, Bramall Lane and London Road, through the 1980s became increasingly clogged with traffic moving between central Sheffield and developing areas to the city's southeast. An additional hazard was produced by a practice described by local people as "rat running," motorists attempting to avoid main thoroughfare congestion by racing through the residential side streets of Sharrow and adjoining Nether Edge. Automobile movement, though, was not the only traffic dilemma for Sharrow. Along London Road most merchants have no space to provide off-street parking for their patrons; so beyond the temporary strategy of double-parking on the street (thus adding to the traffic build-up), visitors to Sharrow have fallen into the habit of parking on adjoining side streets. In a densely settled neighborhood lacking alley or designated off-street parking for the majority of residents, this constituted another irritant for Sharrow people. By most accounts, Sharrow's side street parking problems reach their apex on the afternoons of Sheffield United football matches, when thousands of soccer fans pour into lower Sharrow, many leaving their cars along neighborhood side streets and walking the remaining distance to the Bramall Lane football ground.

The Sharrow Traffic Campaign's origins were in the early 1980s, when Ann Wilson, a resident of the Thorp Estate, began to seek a remedy for the persistent use of her residential area as an off-London Road parking lot. The energy and tactical sophistication demonstrated by the Traffic Campaign were, in part, a tribute to Ann Wilson's emergence as a skilled activist, but the organizational network developed by the SSICCP also played a major role in sustaining this campaign. At the same time, the difficulties encountered by the Traffic Campaign in achieving the implementation of its traffic control recommendations underscore the limitations of the "campaigning" approach to public policy change.

For the first year or so that she lived in the newly opened Thorp Estate, a low-density group of houses just to the north of London Road, Ann Wilson viewed parking problems in her complex as more or less an aggravation. There were a limited number of parking spaces on the estate, and these were supposed to be for the use of residents. But soon enough following its opening—and drivers' discovery of the development's network of paved pathways—spillover parking from London Road establishments began to inundate the Thorp Estate. Alternatively, cars would be left directly in front of the estate's entrances, thus preventing Thorp residents from driving into or out from the estate. Ann Wilson's first effort to bring attention to the spillover parking problem was by contacting one of Sharrow's city councillors, Doris Askam,

which resulted in an inconclusive visit by some Sheffield Authority officials to the Thorp Estate. This was in late 1982. By 1984 Ann Wilson's
aggravation had turned to consternation when an elderly resident of the
Thorp Estate was struck by a car on London Road, a few days later
dying of her injuries. This time Ann Wilson spoke with a more forthcoming councillor, Tony Tigwell, who suggested that she discuss her
concerns at the next meeting of the Sharrow Neighbourhood Groups
Forum.[44] Sponsored by the SSICCP, this group had met irregularly
since the early 1980s but at the time was beginning to come together
more frequently—with the aim of giving more coherence to the work of
Sharrow's various residents and tenants groups.

In early 1985 Ann Wilson presented her concerns to the Sharrow
Neighbourhood Groups Forum, which included a number of other
individuals similarly perturbed by their areas' traffic woes. With the
approval of the Neighbourhood Groups Forum, Wilson set about circu-
lating petitions demanding that the Sheffield Authority attend to the
community's traffic concerns. In Wilson's words, the petition drive "didn't
get anywhere," and by the autumn of 1985 she hosted a meeting of local
groups at which she proposed a cooperative effort through which they
would systematically identify Sharrow's traffic-related problems and
draft a set of corrective measures to be forwarded to the authority.[45] Out
of this meeting grew the Sharrow Traffic Campaign.

In a process that was reminiscent of SAG's neighborhood surveys
of the previous decade, the Traffic Campaign developed a questionnaire
that was distributed in eight local areas of a few blocks each (and
including the Sheffield Authority's Lansdowne, Leverton, and Thorp
housing estates) across Sharrow. The dozen or so organizational representatives active in the campaign formulated the survey questions, with
the broad intention of seeking people's views on both traffic flow and
parking problems. The questionnaires were distributed to one in five
residences within the study areas, the Traffic Campaign complementing
this canvassing effort with a public information campaign—press
releases for the citywide newspapers and radio stations, articles in the
neighborhood newsletter, posters displayed in shop windows and other
public places, and word of mouth. Traffic campaign volunteers distrib-

uted and collected the questionnaires. This information-gathering phase of the Traffic Campaign occurred in January and February 1986, which the Traffic Campaign's report proudly noted was Sheffield's coldest winter in 39 years.[46]

Ann Wilson was the driving force and spokesperson for the Traffic Campaign, but she did not carry on this initiative without assistance. A member of the SSICCP's Management Committee, Helen Ward—along with her son Jason—handled some of the more technical aspects of the data collection and analysis. The campaigners, most having little or no experience to call upon, used the SSICCP's office computer to tabulate the questionnaire results. The SSICCP and the Sheffield Council provided small cash grants to underwrite campaign expenses. It was the job of the local area data gatherers to analyze the results of their samples. In six of the eight local areas these were residents of that particular group of streets or housing estate. Ann Wilson and Helen Ward drafted the Sharrow Traffic Campaign Report, including its overall recommendations.[47]

The spring and early summer of 1986 were devoted to the preparation of the Traffic Campaign's report. The campaign's climax was a public meeting to which representatives of local government would be invited for a briefing on the report's recommendations. Throughout the winter and spring the Traffic Campaign had publicized its activities, but a particular emphasis was now placed on the hearing scheduled for July 15 at the Duchess Road Community Centre in lower Sharrow. To illustrate the traffic and parking problems besetting Sharrow, campaigners hung maps and photographs on the walls of the community centre. Councillor Tony Tigwell chaired the July 15 meeting, which drew several representatives of the local authority including David Blunkett's successor as Labour Leader of the Sheffield Council, Clive Betts. Ann Wilson recalls approximately 200 people attending the meeting. A press account describes the good-sized community centre meeting room as "packed."[48]

The Traffic Campaign's report is an interesting amalgam of grassroots annoyance and very detailed recommendations for improvements in traffic flow and parking regulation. The campaigners' frustrations are most evident in the report's introduction:

> After years of fruitless complaints to many different authorities and organizations about parking and traffic harassment in the Sharrow area, local people decided to unite and launch a "Traffic Campaign"....The vision that local people had of the future Sharrow area was that of a multi-storey car park, spread out flat on one level—that level being their streets and roads, already pathetically congested by non-resident traffic, along with masses of industrial and commercial vehicles belonging to people working at local factories.[49]

The bulk of the 49-page report is devoted to the local area analyses, from which 48 specific recommendations were derived. For example, among the twelve St. Barnabas area recommendations are the following: to restore sidewalk and street pavements at the conclusion of ongoing housing rehabilitation work, to provide more off-street parking along Bramall Lane, to place traffic bumps ("sleeping policemen") on Kearsley and St. Barnabas Roads. The report's eight general recommendations are, conversely, rather nonspecific (e.g., that the authority consider the development of an "overall parking strategy for the area") with several constituting, in effect, procedural points (e.g., that governmental organizations agree to meet with the local groups that helped prepare this report).[50]

Veterans of the Traffic Campaign universally recall the Duchess Road public meeting as a great success. Ann Wilson was elated by the reaction of the authority representatives: "They were amazed. They knew that we were up to something, but they didn't know what. I think it was the quality of the report. We were on Cloud Nine because they rated the report as very professional."[51] Others present at the meeting note that the authority immediately accepted a large portion of the report's recommendations, although memories vary in reference to the precise number. In subsequent years Traffic Campaign documents consistently set this figure at 39; but substantively, the principal success of the public hearing appears to have been the authority representatives' general approval of the report and agreement to begin discussions with local area groups regarding specific traffic and parking measures.

Within a month the joyful mood of the traffic campaigners had begun to shift. A mid-August letter from Ann Wilson to an officer in the Highways Department begins:

> On behalf of the above named I am compelled to write to your department to say how disappointed we are for your non-communication since the public meeting on 15th July, where you personally assured campaign colleagues and myself that you and/or yours would be in touch within a week after discussions with your appropriate departments regarding future meetings with the relevant community groups in the campaign report.[52]

In the wake of this shaky start, representatives of the Sheffield Authority followed up the July public meeting with a series of local area discussions at which the detailed recommendations of the Traffic Campaign Report were examined. At the end of these meetings, in early 1987 the Sheffield Council formally "accepted" the Traffic Campaign Report and pledged to begin work on the measures recommended in the report or given priority in the follow-up authority-resident meetings.[53]

During the next several years the Sharrow Traffic Campaign evolved into a watchdog group whose activist core periodically met with authority officials to monitor progress in the implementation of traffic and parking measures, and which periodically sponsored public forums bringing together local residents and authority representatives. This was a disheartening period, especially for Ann Wilson. On the one hand, the authority did institute a variety of the small-scale measures—such as specific pedestrian crossings or localized parking restrictions—that had been recommended by the Traffic Campaign. On the other hand, it was not evident that the authority was developing a comprehensive traffic/parking strategy for the community. Moreover, the police did not distinguish themselves through aggressive enforcement of the new regulations. Most troubling of all, traffic and parking conditions in Sharrow were not improving.

In January of 1989, the Sharrow Traffic Campaign was "relaunched," but in its second life the campaign was much less forceful.[54] Ann Wilson notes, "At first there are 30 people calling officials, then its ten, then you realize that you're the only one left."[55] By this time, indeed, even Wilson's drive was sapped by multiple, overlapping responsibilities. By the end of the decade she had become actively involved in the day-to-day operations of the SSICCP, and at home she devoted increasing hours to seeing after her elderly mother. Wilson's view is that the Traffic Campaign's impact was sabotaged by unresponsive officials, who hid behind a variety of rationalizations for their inactivity, among them the lack of funds: "You can't talk money with people after we have put together a report identifying the problems. It's not our job to find the solutions. Then money comes up, and they say it will be done in 1990-blob, but we're still left with the problem."[56] Other campaign veterans offer alternative explanations for the persistence of Sharrow's traffic problems. Mick Kerrigan of the Sharrow Street Residents Group thinks that the neighborhood's complicated street system, combined with the complexity of the Traffic Campaign recommendations—48 items produced by eight different groups—made the implementation of effective measures more difficult. He also senses that turnover among the administrative officers with whom the campaign worked reduced the continuity of the authority's efforts. Further, it is Kerrigan's view that the Traffic Campaign lost its momentum following the Duchess Road Community Centre event: "We fell down in the follow-up. It wanted two or three more years. But we sort of shrugged our shoulders and said 'we did it'."[57] A third Traffic Campaign activist, Harold Gascoigne—who has long been affiliated with the Sharrow Labour Party—looks back on the campaign and observes that the Thatcher government's fiscal attack on the local authorities undermined the service delivery capability of the Sheffield municipal administration.[58]

Administrative foot-dragging and resource constraints, a technically complicated set of proposals, and the inevitable flagging of voluntary energy are the incontestable ingredients of the Traffic Campaign's "follow-up" problems. By the early 1990s few, if any Sharrow residents would contend that the previous decade had witnessed an improvement in local traffic and parking conditions. Nonetheless, but for the efforts of the Traffic Campaign, these conditions might have gotten worse. Moreover, the core of Traffic Campaign activists continue to express pride as they look back on their efforts, pointing to the good work embodied by their report and the sense of community that grows from participation in such an organizing effort.

V

The efforts of the Sharrow Street Residents Group illustrate still another variation in the ambiguous fortunes of SSICCP-supported grassroots initiatives during the 1980s. The Sharrow Street area includes several blocks of turn-of-the-century terrace houses bounded by London Road and Sharrow Lane on the north and east, and by the 1960s-era Lansdowne and Leverton estates on the south and west. Lifelong resident and leader of the residents group, Mick Kerrigan, observes that "this was always a poor area."[59] Nonetheless, among the approximately 300 households in the Sharrow Street district there are a large percentage of owner-occupiers. In part for this reason, it was one of the General Improvement Areas (GIAs) approved as a consequence of the mid-1970s Sharrow-Nether Edge planning consultation. As such, building owners could seek government assistance to underwrite up to 75 percent of their rehabilitation expenses.

The origin of the Sharrow Street Residents Group was a Wesley House meeting chaired by John Peaden in June 1980. Peaden announced that the Sheffield Authority had appropriated the funds and was now prepared to accept rehabilitation grant applications from local residents.[60] In its first year or two, the residents group attempted to fan participation in this program, but rather quickly it also became the sounding board for a typical array of neighborhood concerns: the ubiquitous traffic and parking complaints, nuisance businesses along London Road, street noise, and littering. In the group's early days, Peaden regularly attended its meetings and otherwise provided it with guidance and technical support. The residents group did not, however, have much success in advancing its principal agenda item. Although most local residents were presumably aware of the rehabilitation grants, given the deepening local economic recession and the precarious state of many families' finances, even 75 percent support for major repairs was not an attractive inducement. As a result, in 1983 the residents group resolved to petition the Sheffield Council for designation as a Housing Action Area (HAA). HAA status was reserved for neighborhoods in which there were severe physical and social problems, and whose housing required prompt upgrading. For the most economically strapped households, HAA status provided a grant covering 90 percent of rehab costs.

In early 1983 the Sharrow Street Residents Group organized a photographic project to document the decline of their neighborhood. The resulting visual documentation of the area was displayed at Wesley House in the summer of 1983. By way of the SSICCP, the residents group also made contact with two University of Sheffield faculty members, Tony Crook and Roy Darke, who agreed to supervise a student-administered survey of local homeowners and tenants. The surveying, data analysis, and report-drafting occupied much of 1984, a timeline that was considerably longer than anticipated. Nonetheless, the results of the Crook-Darke project were quite helpful to the residents group's cause. While nearly 90 percent of surveyed residents were aware of the GIA grants, over half indicated that, even with GIA support, they could not afford to do major repairs. The Crook-Darke report was forwarded to the city's Housing Department, and on February 16, 1985, the *Sheffield Morning Telegraph* published a detailed story on the report and neighborhood. John Peaden commented to the *Telegraph* reporter:

> The residents association has suspected for a long time that the area was wrongly designated. It should have been a HAA. There must be lots of areas in Sheffield that in ten years' time will be like Sharrow, unless something is done on a much bigger scale.[61]

In spite of this favorable publicity, during the next several years the residents group experienced slow going in their effort to win HAA designation. In the spring of 1985 the local Environmental Health Department conducted its own survey of the area, but no subsequent action from the authority was forthcoming. The residents group, in turn, busied itself with a variety of local issues. During 1986 and for the next two or three years, Mick Kerrigan was a leading figure in the Sharrow Traffic Campaign. At the end of 1987 the residents group's efforts were redoubled when the central government announced its intention to phase out HAAs. Over the next several months Kerrigan issued a barrage of letters and telephone calls, and along with his neighbor, Pete Fitzakerley, attended numerous meetings at Town Hall with the aim of advancing the Sharrow Street area's case as a prospective HAA.

Kerrigan's extensive personal and organizational contacts allowed him to assemble a long list of supporters for the residents group petition, including the Sharrow Labour Party, the Sharrow Neighbourhood Groups Forum, and the Sheffield Inner City Forum (an assembly of organizations representing occupants of privately owned dwellings).[62] In order for the Sheffield Council to designate Sharrow as an HAA, a necessary intermediate step was still another local survey. This step was outlined for local residents at a public meeting held at Mount Pleasant on June 14, 1988. In addition to Sheffield Authority, SSICCP, and Asian Welfare Association representatives, the residents group core of about ten people was joined by approximately 50 area residents.[63] Later in the summer the Housing Department distributed and collected its questionnaires.

By this point the Sharrow Street Residents Group was racing with time. Unless the Sheffield Authority approved its petition within the next several months, the central government's termination of the HAA program would short circuit any concerted rehabilitation program, at least in the foreseeable future. In December 1988 the Sheffield Housing Department forwarded the results of its Sharrow Street survey, accompanied by a recommendation for HAA approval, to the city council. On January 19, 1989, the Sheffield Council approved Sharrow Street's HAA status, forwarding its decision to the central government's Department of the Environment for the proposal's anticipated final ratification. However, a week later Mick Kerrigan attended a hearing at

Town Hall and discovered that, although the Sharrow Street area had won HAA designation, it was not included in the list of funded projects for the coming year. The residents group supposed that exclusion from the 1989-90 project list, given the impending termination of the HAA program, might mean that in spite of all of their efforts, there still would be no rehabilitation grants for the Sharrow Street area. Once again Mick Kerrigan turned to telephone, word processor, and in some cases, pen and paper, firing off a fusillade of protests at this oversight. At last, in March 1989 the Sharrow Street area was added to Sheffield's Housing Development Programme for 1989-90.[64]

With their area's HAA status finally assured, the residents group began to meet with Sheffield Authority officials to plan the rehabilitation program. During the 1980s the authority had introduced "enveloping schemes" as a means of providing essential repairs to older housing. Enveloping entailed roof, wall, window, and foundation repairs, with the aim of providing a basic shoring up of a house's exterior. Interior work was left up to owners. From a cost-effectiveness standpoint, enveloping rows of terrace houses permitted the authority to achieve significant scale economies. The Sharrow Street area—about half a dozen blocks of nearly uniform terrace units—was an ideal site for enveloping. Nonetheless, while there was appeal to the authority's enveloping the Sharrow Street area, notably its paying the entirety of the standard renovation package, enveloping work was a tricky proposition. The 315 Sharrow Street area houses would be renovated in a coordinated effort that would bring numerous workmen, as well as quite a large amount of building materials, into the narrow streets of this confined area. Disruption of day-to-day life was guaranteed. Moreover, in the nearby St. Barnabas area, which had undergone enveloping in 1985-86, the rehab work stretched to an unexpected two full years, and many residents complained of property damage and persistent personal inconvenience over the course of the repair effort.[65]

At a June 21, 1989, public meeting, 150 people attended a discussion of enveloping which brought together Sharrow Street Residents Group leaders, Sheffield Authority representatives, and architectural consultants. The meeting authorized the residents group to pursue the enveloping option, and in an effort to avoid the snafus that had dogged the St. Barnabas project, over the next half-year an extensive planning process ensued. In late summer the architectural firm, Ritchie and Rennie, did a feasibility study. From September 1989, a "project group" bringing together local residents, city government officials, the architects, and—after the new year—contractors, regularly met to review plans and progress. The project group meetings were well attended, sometimes by as many as 50 local residents, and in the multi-ethnic Sharrow Street area a number of focused meetings were also held. For example, before the start of rehab work, meetings for Chinese and Asian residents were held. The January 19, 1990, meeting concentrated on the particular issue of how contractors should proceed in Asian households when the male head of household was not present.[66]

In February 1990 the Sheffield Council approved a contract for enveloping the Sharrow Street area. Thirteen thousand pounds would be spent on each house. The Sharrow Street area was divided into six blocks of approximately 50 houses each. In four of these areas a private contractor, Tarmac Construction of nearby Rotherham, was to carry out the rehab work. The other two groups of 50 houses would be enveloped by the municipal government's Works Department. The timetable for completing the project was one year.[67]

If the divided contract for the Sharrow Street enveloping project was not a recipe for disaster, at the least it gave Mick Kerrigan and other leaders of the residents group plenty of opportunities to intercede among residents, local authority, and contractors. The enveloping project was beset by a predictable catalogue of complications and setbacks: resident complaints of workers' vulgarity, reports of burglaries, parents' concerns about children playing around scaffolding, delays in the completion of specific tasks. At the end of July a roof collapse resulted in no injuries, but the event was notable enough to be reported in a local newspaper.[68] Throughout this period Mick Kerrigan, often assisted by Pete Fitzakerley, performed numerous and varied tasks: organizing teams of local men to move the upstairs furniture and belongings of elderly residents, answering neighbors' complaints when the contractors' emergency numbers were not responding, locating competent and inexpensive interior decorators, generally providing liaison for the various parties involved in the project.[69]

Although the enveloping project was beset with its fair share of incidents, throughout 1990 the contractors sustained a pace of work that was close to their timetable. Only toward the end of the project, in early 1991, did the residents group's solidarity begin to break down. This was the result of a misunderstanding over individuals' option to pay for extra rehab work. The enveloping agreement permitted building owners to contract with Tarmac or Sheffield Works to do renovations beyond the specifications of the basic, £13,000 rehab package. Mick Kerrigan and Pete Fitzakerley, for example, contracted for the replacement of their old windows with new, double-glazed windows. When some of their neighbors observed the workmen making these additional improvements, they supposed that Kerrigan and Fitzakerley, having developed contacts in Town Hall and with the contractors, were receiving a "payback" for their cooperation. Kerrigan and Fitzakerley reminded their fellow residents of this arrangement, which was available to all local householders.[70] Their efforts were probably only half-successful. By May 1991, when the residents group sought to organize a street fair in celebration of the completion of the enveloping project, there was, to Mick Kerrigan's mind, surprisingly little interest in supporting this event.

In the wake of the Sharrow Street Residents Group's decade-long campaign for a systematic housing renovation scheme, their small piece of Sharrow ward has the look of a model community. The rows of terrace houses are well appointed, and an ethnically mixed population coexists quite congenially. However, the residents group has been in hibernation since the completion of the enveloping project in mid-1991. Mick Kerrigan, his wife Sue, and Pete and Carol Fitzakerley were exhausted by the demands of lobbying for, then seeing through the rehabilitation program. None of their neighbors has assumed the Kerrigans' and Fitzakerleys' role as heart and adhesive of the residents group. For the time being, at least, there seems to be no pressing need for anyone to take on these chores.

VI

The South Sheffield Inner City Community Project's high-water mark was reached in the middle 1980s. At that time SSICCP's staff numbered a dozen, including authority employees outposted to Wesley House with the mandate to work in the neighborhood. Due to the considerable number of volunteers working on one or another SSICCP project, Wesley House seemed considerably busier than this staff count might suggest. As the previous sections of this chapter demonstrate, to a greater or lesser degree SSICCP also supported the activities of various grassroots initiatives across Sharrow. A clear sign of SSICCP's repute at Town Hall and beyond was its winning a second round of Urban Programme funding for the period running from 1984 to 1988. However, by the end of the decade the South Sheffield Project had lost its momentum. The decline of SSICCP is attributable to a number of factors, both internal and external, whose interaction suggests both weaknesses in SSICCP's vision and tactics as well as broader constraints on neighborhood-grounded political action.

The simplest explanation for the decline of SSICCP is to point to its defunding and resultant destaffing in the late 1980s and early 1990s. The bulk of SSICCP's operating funds derived from its Urban Programme grant, which required a local authority match of one pound for every three central government-appropriated pounds. The Sheffield Council Family and Community Services Committee (F & CS) provided the local share of SSICCP's budget. F & CS was also one of several units that authorized the outposting of municipal staff to SSICCP. By 1987, when SSICCP applied for a third round of Urban Programme support, the project's financial support began to give way.[71] Its previous refunding by the Urban Programme, for the 1984 to 1988 interval, already had been somewhat unusual, and the South Sheffield Project's local council support was no longer unshakable. SSICCP's principal early advocate on the Sheffield Council, David Blunkett, had moved on to Parliament, while the Council was, itself, experiencing serious budgetary strain in the aftermath of the mid-1980s ratecapping dispute pitting local authorities against the Thatcher government.

SSICCP did manage to win a third round of Urban Programme support, but in this instance the funding period was only three years, with the central government's allocation decreasing ("tapering") to zero grant in the fourth year. Nor did the Sheffield Council increase its appropriation to compensate for the loss of central government aid. Moreover, in the period from 1989 to 1991, the authority removed its outposted officers from Wesley House in order to reassign them to more conventional—and in the Council's view more essential—service delivery responsibilities. In a quantitative sense, these budget constraints worked a double hardship on SSICCP, which in addition to losing the assistance of authority-assigned workers also had to cut back its own staff. Yet in John Peaden's view, the more crucial setback resulting from SSICCP's budgetary crisis was qualitative: "With people like Bob Martin and David Skinner on staff (both lost during the SSICCP staff reductions) the group could still come up with new ideas."[72] In effect, much of SSICCP's energy and creativity was jettisoned along with most of its personnel.

Even as SSICCP struggled to make fiscal ends meet, the organization also began to find that developing new programmatic operations did not necessarily complement its central substantive objective, which was to serve as an anchor for Sharrow grassroots action. For example, in response to the changing expectations of the Thatcher government, SSICCP, as a recipient of Urban Programme funding, began to give greater attention to economic development matters. In some instances, such as SSICCP's support of Commercial Improvement Area status for London Road (which gave merchants on this street access to city-financed loans for building improvements), the group achieved a considerable measure of success. But in a number of other cases—including the formation of a co-op run by unemployed people, a restaurant business training project, and the I and I Bookstore—SSICCP-sponsored economic development initiatives did not thrive. John Peaden, while asserting that in the face of Sharrow's growing economic misery of the 1980s SSICCP had to take on some of these experiments, also admits that economic development was not the original mission of the group and that SSICCP never really had a firm handle on how to promote local economic development.[73]

Programmatically, SSICCP did not simply wither away in the late 1980s. During its latter years the group began a community health project aimed at improving basic health and nutritional practices among Sharrow residents, in addition to providing them with information regarding formal health care services in Sheffield. An outgrowth of the community health project was the formation of an Asian women's organization, which besides dealing with health matters also sponsored public affairs discussions, sometimes in conjunction with presentations by outside speakers. As Sharrow's economic woes deepened, Wesley House's Citizens Advice Bureau spun off a Money Advice Centre whose principal focus was advising individuals and families facing critical financial stress. Sharrow's Money Advice Centre, in turn, was the model for a citywide financial counseling program. South Sheffield Community Transport also joined the service-providers located in Wesley House, its three minibuses available—at minimal cost—for community group-sponsored excursions. In the late 1980s SSICCP assisted the formation of the Somalian Refugee Trust, an organization raising funds to support the resettlement of Somali refugees to Sheffield. And, as we have observed, during the mid- to late-1980s the SSICCP aided two significant grassroots initiatives, the Sharrow Traffic Campaign and the Sharrow Street Residents Group.[74]

Nonetheless, SSICCP staff members and volunteers agree that by the end of the decade the organization's role in the life of Sharrow had begun to recede. Aside from the group's funding difficulties, an interestingly common contention is that Wesley House—inconveniently located on a side street off London Road, with the internal lay-out of a rabbit warren—began to be a liability. This view holds that local people, put off by Wesley House's out-of-the-way location and its unarguably confusing, gritty interior, simply lost the habit of looking to SSICCP as a community resource. John Peaden reviews these years and detects a drift away from community advocacy and toward service provision. When, for example, the Money Advice Centre was created, an extremely useful counseling service was provided to local residents, but initiatives of this sort did little to advance the neighborhood as a collectivity.[75] Staff member Chris Hodgkinson, who worked at SSICCP for a decade from the early 1980s, adds a complementary observation: "There was an element of not looking at what the community wants but what will make us (SSICCP) necessary."[76] Ultimately, as funding stress pulled apart SSICCP's various components in the early 1990s, there was not much sense—at least among Sharrow residents at large—that a coherent neighborhood institution was at risk. The strongest evidence of this is that SSICCP wound down in a remarkably subdued fashion, without protest by Sharrow residents.

In late 1992, when John Peaden's deteriorating health forced him to leave SSICCP, the group experienced a further jolt. Losing Peaden, who was the guiding force in SSICCP—and before that, the Sharrow Action Group—left the group with a debilitating leadership vacuum. But again, as with the South Sheffield Project's funding woes, this story is more complicated than it at first appears. Peaden began organizing in Sharrow in the late 1960s, and I have discussed SSICCP with no one—including Peaden himself—who claims that he operated with the same vigor 20 years later. The attenuation of Peaden's energies was not simply a matter of age or ill health. As SSICCP's financial crisis worsened, Peaden devoted more of his attention to the daunting task of seeking new, revenue-generating projects for the group. This turned out to be a largely unsuccessful quest, but nonetheless, in Peaden's last two or three years at SSICCP it occupied a substantial share of his time.

Between Peaden's declining health and the ebbing of SSICCP's staff, the group's leadership difficulties are not surprising. However, one might suppose that SSICCP's local activist core could step in to reorient their group. In fact, by the early 1990s SSICCP's neighborhood leadership was mainly composed of older Anglo veterans of the group's past campaigns and projects. Although SSICCP, most particularly John Peaden, had made quite an effort to incorporate Sharrow's immigrant and ethnic minority populations, in the long run the group had not really reached beyond its original constituency of longstanding home-owners and tenants. This failure appears to be another source of SSICCP's decline after the mid-1980s.

Strains between SSICCP and its co-owner of Wesley House, the Asian Welfare Association (AWA), illustrate this problem. AWA possessed financial support independent of SSICCP, and although in principle the two organizations cooperated in serving Sharrow, in reality they functioned as autonomous entities cohabiting the same premises. Over time a fair amount of discord entered this relationship. SSICCP-affiliated staff and volunteers came to think that AWA contributed less than its fair share to the upkeep of Wesley House. In turn, AWA personnel viewed themselves as junior partner in a relationship in which the senior partner did not engage in due consultation. Cultural factors further divided the two groups. Among SSICCP staff and volunteers was a sizable female cohort, including some Asian women. AWA was a male-dominated group, and on a day-to-day basis AWA staffers—at least in the view of some SSICCP personnel—seemed to expect that the women of Wesley House would wait on them. Ultimately, as SSICCP's fortunes waned in the early 1990s, AWA was not an especially vigorous ally.[77]

In a sense, SSICCP's loss of direction is also a matter of its having run out of things to do. Given Sharrow's declining physical environment, high levels of unemployment and poverty, and the rigors of immigrant life for its newcomers, this seems like a counterintuitive claim, but consider, for the moment, the institutional context within which SSICCP has operated. For the group's first five or six years it assisted local campaigns that took action with the aim of winning government support for measures to enhance living conditions within Sharrow. These initiatives included housing rehabilitation work, planning schemes (especially emphasizing traffic and parking management), educational programs tailored to the needs of ethnic minority students, special social services for ethnic minorities and immigrants, and neighborhood-based economic development. Although the specific objectives of these efforts varied, without exception they presumed that funding and other types of support would be forthcoming from either the local authority, the central government, or both.

In some cases, such as housing rehabilitation, quite a large part of SSICCP's agenda was achieved over the course of the 1980s. In other instances, such as economic development, the return was less evident.

But in either case, by the end of the decade neither the local authority (mainly due to its own resource constraints) nor the central government (due to alternative policy preferences) continued to provide assistance. This did not mean that the activists in local Sharrow groups—Ann Wilson or Mick Kerrigan, for example—were any less exhausted at the end of the decade. However, it did mean that after more than a decade of hard organizational work, by the early 1990s it was not obvious what SSICCP could do next.

For his part, John Peaden had explored alternative funding sources for SSICCP, but relative to the United States, foundations, "trusts," or other private sponsors have not become major players in English community development work.[78] And ironically, as I have noted, Peaden's efforts in this direction probably played some part in attenuating SSICCP's local presence. This was probably an unavoidable dilemma. In short, even though SSICCP achieved a variety of successes during the 1980s, the larger economic and institutional environments within which it operated became increasingly inhospitable. And on the ground in Sharrow, small- and medium-scale gains attributable to grassroots action seemed to be swallowed up by these larger dissonant forces. It is probably little wonder that so many of Sharrow's grassroots leaders seemed to have lost their faith and will to persist by the early 1990s. Former councillor Tony Tigwell expressed this sense of disillusion most eloquently as he contemplated his city's "terminal decline":

> The whole reason for this city was mining and steel. Without them how do you justify 500,000 people living here? When they come up with these new development schemes, I ask myself: "Why don't we just make something?"[79]

NOTES

1. Interview with John Peaden, August 5, 1993.

2. David Blunkett and Geoff Green, *Building from the Bottom: The Sheffield Experience* (London: Fabian Tract 491, 1983), p. 26.

3. "South Sheffield Inner City Community Project," pamphlet, June 1981, South Sheffield Inner City Community Project (SSICCP) Files.

4. Blunkett and Green, *Building from the Bottom,* pp. 21-24.

5. "Wesley House: South Sheffield Inner City Community Project," pamphlet, October 1987, SSICCP Files; Interview with Mick Kerrigan, SSICCP and Sharrow Street Residents Group, June 29, 1993; Interview with Mike Pye, Sheffield City Council, August 24, 1993.

6. Peaden Interview, August 5, 1993.

7. "Wesley House."

8. Peaden Interview, August 5, 1993.

9. Interview with Akhtar Kayani, Director of the Asian Welfare Association, July 13, 1993.

10. Peaden Interview, August 5, 1993; "Wesley House."

11. Department of Planning and Design, Sheffield City Council, "Sheffield Inner City Areas of Worst Deprivation," June 1979, unnumbered; "South Sheffield Inner City Community Project."

12. "SSICCP Urban Programme Application 1988-1992," September 1987, p. 4, SSICCP Files.

13. Interview with Chris Hodgkinson, July 7, 1994.

14. *High and Dry* (London: SCAT Publications, n.d.), p. 2.

15. Eastwood and Partners Consulting Engineers, "Yorkshire Development Group Type Dwellings, Broomhall: Abbreviated Version of Our Report Dated August, 1983," correspondence with City of Sheffield Director of Department of Town Planning and Design, October 24, 1993, p. 2, Margaret Howard (MH) Files.

16. *High and Dry,* p. 2.

17. "Post-War Dream Turned to Nightmare," *Sheffield Morning Telegraph,* May 2, 1984; Report of the Director of Housing to the Chairman and Members of the Housing Programme Committee," April 30, 1984, p. 2, MH Files.

18. Eastwood and Partners, "Yorkshire Development Group Type Dwellings," pp. 2-4.

19. "Report of the Director of Housing," April 30, 1984, p. 3.

20. Broomhall Community Group, "Living in Broomhall," April 1978, MH Files.

21. Interview with Margaret Howard, June 24, 1993.

22. Interview with Tony Tigwell, August 20, 1993.

23. Interview with Mandy Bryce, August 25, 1993.

24. Bryce Interview, August 25, 1993.

25. Howard Interview, June 24, 1993.

26. Minutes of Yorkshire Development Tenants Action Group, May 15, 1982, MH Files.

27. Francesca Robinson, "Timber! Victory for Flats Tenants," *Sheffield Morning Telegraph,* January 10, 1983.

28. *High and Dry,* pp. 24-25.

29. *High and Dry,* p. 21 (author's parenthesis).

30. "Cash Victory for Council Tenants," June 7, 1983.

31. "Report of the Director of Housing to the Chairman and Members of the Maintenance and Modernization Sub-Committee," May 17, 1982, MH Files.

32. Andy Waple, "Asbestos: Tenants Urge More Safety Checks," *The Star,* August 4, 1983.

33. Howard Interview, June 24, 1993.

34. David Holmes, "Flats in Urgent Need of Repair," *Sheffield Morning Telegraph,* January 21, 1984; "Report of the Director of Housing," April 30, 1984.

35. Mark Shipworth, "The Decline and Fall of a Housing Dream," *The Star,* January 17, 1984.

36. Interview with Margaret Howard, August 11, 1993.

37. Letter to Margaret Howard, January 26, 1984, MH Files.

38. Minutes of Broomhall Project Group Meeting, January 17, 1984, MH Files.

39. *The Star,* July 21, 1984; *Sheffield Morning Telegraph,* July 24, 1984.

40. Matt Youdale, "Tenants Trapped by Freeze on Cash," *Sheffield Morning Telegraph,* April 3, 1985.

41. Carole Richardson, "Isolated Tenants Are Targets for Muggers," *Sheffield Morning Telegraph,* January 22, 1985; "Extra Security at Danger Flats," *Sheffield Morning Telegraph,* August 1, 1985.

42. "Laing, Wimpey Battle over Site," *Contract Journal,* December 3, 1987; "64M Plan for Eyesore," *The Star,* July 27, 1990.

43. Interview with Margaret Howard, June 28, 1994.

44. Interview with Ann Wilson, June 23, 1993.

45. Wilson interview, June 23, 1993; Minutes of Meeting on Traffic, October 31, 1985, 14 Harwood Close, SSICCP Files.

46. "Sharrow Traffic Campaign Report," July 1986, pp. 6-8.

47. Wilson Interview, June 23, 1993; Interview with Helen Ward, June 22, 1994.

48. Wilson Interview, June 23, 1993; Pippa Andrews, "Plea to Sort Out Traffic Problems," *The Star,* July 22, 1986.

49. "Sharrow Traffic Campaign Report," p. 1.

50. "Sharrow Traffic Campaign Report," pp. 45-46.

51. Wilson Interview, June 23, 1993.

52. Letter to Rod Jones, Sheffield Highways Department, August 13, 1986, SSICCP Files.

53. Minutes of Sharrow Traffic Campaign Meetings, September 30, 1986, and January 28, 1987, Wesley House, SSICCP Files.

54. Mark Thompson, "Residents Relaunch Campaign on Parking," *The Star*, January 16, 1989.

55. Ann Wilson, Personal Communication, July 5, 1994.

56. Wilson Interview, June 23, 1993.

57. Interview with Mick Kerrigan, June 27, 1994.

58. Interview with Harold Gascoigne, July 30, 1993.

59. Kerrigan Interview, June 29, 1993.

60. Minutes of Sharrow Street Residents Group Meeting, June 3, 1980, Wesley House, Mick Kerrigan (MK) Files.

61. A.D.H. Crook and R.A. Darke, "Sharrow General Improvement Area: The Case for More Investment," University of Sheffield Dept. of Town and Regional Planning Occasional Paper #48, July 1984; Matt Youdale, "Sharrow Housing in Grim State of Decay," *Sheffield Morning Telegraph*, February 16, 1985.

62. Letter to Mick Kerrigan from Andrew Nicholson, Secretary, Sharrow Labour Party, March 15, 1988; Letter to Gary Hancock, City of Sheffield Dept. of Housing—Private Sector, from Cyril G. Tigwell, Sharrow Neighbourhood Groups Forum, March 21, 1988; Letter to Sheffield City Councillors from Harold Gascoigne, Sharrow Inner City Forum, February 9, 1989, MK Files.

63. Minutes of Sharrow Street Residents Group Public Meeting, June 14, 1988, Mount Pleasant Community Centre, MK Files.

64. Minutes of Sharrow Street Residents Group Meeting, June 21, 1989, Sharrow Lane Junior School, MK Files.

65. Helen Ward, "Who Am I? I Just Live Here!" A Report of Residents' Views on Sheffield City Council's Enveloping Scheme for the St. Barnabas Area, December 1987.

66. Kerrigan Interview, June 29, 1993.

67. Kerrigan Interview, June 29, 1993; Minutes of Sharrow Envelope Scheme Project Group, July 17, 1990, Wesley House; City of Sheffield Dept. of Works Director, "Sharrow Enveloping Scheme Phases 1 and 3," no date, MK Files.

68. Dave Devenport, "Repair Sends Ceiling Crashing into a Cot," *The Star*, July 30, 1990.

69. Minutes of Sharrow Envelope Scheme Project Group, 1990-91, MK Files.

70. Kerrigan Interview, June 29, 1993.

71. Interview with John Peaden, June 28, 1994; Interview with Roy Darke, SSICCP Executive Committee, July 4, 1994; "The Future of South Sheffield Project," memo from Roy Darke to SSICCP Executive Committee, June 6, 1994; Letter to SSICCP Management Committee from Roy Darke, Chair, November 19, 1987, SSICCP Files.

72. Peaden Interview, June 28, 1994.

73. Interview with John Peaden, September 2, 1993.

74. Interview with Brenda Glaves, SSICCP staff, August 4, 1993; Interview with Linda Duckenfield, Sharrow Community Health Project staff, August 23, 1993; Peaden Interview, June 28, 1994; "Wesley House."

75. Peaden Interview, August 5, 1993.

76. Hodgkinson Interview, July 7, 1994.

77. Kayani Interview, July 13, 1993; Darke Interview, July 4, 1994; Hodgkinson Interview, July 7, 1994; Minutes of Joint Meeting of the Management Committees of the Asian Welfare Association and the South Sheffield Inner City Community Project, June 16, 1994, Wesley House, SSICCP Files.

78. Jennifer Wolch, *The Shadow State: Government and Voluntary Sector in Transition* (New York: The Foundation Center, 1990), pp. 81-112.

79. Tigwell Interview, August 20, 1993.

CHAPTER SIX

UPTOWN AFTER RENEWAL: CONTESTED TERRITORY, HOTBED OF MOVEMENTS

Unlike Sharrow, where urban redevelopment conflict gave way to a consensus on the future of the neighborhood as well as on the means to achieve that future, in Uptown the urban renewal debate did not produce such harmony. Since the mid-1970s, the neighborhood has experienced periodic waves of upscale housing investment, and in turn, there has been a concerted grassroots effort to block or at least modify the trajectory of private for-profit development. These land use and housing conflicts have further spilled over into the political realm, making Uptown's City Council district, the 46th ward, one of the most volatile in Chicago. Political conflict is so commonplace in Uptown that it is sometimes supposed that personal animosities, organizational competition, and intergroup mistrust are inherent features of the community. In fact—and especially with Sharrow's sharply contrasting situation in mind—it is evident that what have continued to make Uptown a political battleground are, principally, its economic and locational circumstances. In a city whose economy is undergoing many of the most prominent features associated with the industrial to post-industrial shift, Uptown is a neighborhood ripe for residential upgrading. The result, within the neighborhood, has been the formation of grassroots organizations reflecting a wide array of agendas and internal dynamics. Nonetheless, by examining several of these groups we will also observe some of the same grassroots organizational traits evident in Sharrow.

II

In Uptown's post-urban renewal era the area's most controversial figure has been Slim Coleman, the founder of a dizzying constellation of local organizations, which I will characterize (with reference to Coleman's chief local ally, Alderperson Helen Shiller) as the Coleman-Shiller movement. Coleman's view of Uptown may be inferred from comments that he made in 1976:

> The idea that you're going to attract middle- and upper-income families back into the city in order to increase the tax base sounds very idealistic...as if you were going to have the Vice-President of Standard Oil living next to someone who's on disability from black lung in Kentucky. But when those folks move into a neighborhood, they don't like to live next to us. So we have to be...cleared out before they can be ready to move in.[1]

Coleman came to Chicago in the late 1960s, having divided his childhood between Texas and New Jersey before attending Harvard University. From Harvard, he moved on to New Left politics, working first with the Student Nonviolent Coordinating Committee in Cleveland. Arriving in Chicago, Coleman made contact with the Students for a Democratic Society and the Black Panther Party. In Uptown, and in some measure following in the path of JOIN and Chuck Geary, Coleman dedicated himself to harnessing the political potential of the neighborhood's white Appalachian population. To that end, in 1970 he organized a group ominously identified as the Intercommunal Survival Committee (ISC).[2]

The ISC was very much an organization of its time, and yet it also must have seemed a peculiar vehicle for mobilizing white southern emigrants in Chicago. Undoubtedly, the group also bore the mark of its enigmatic founder, who has been described as having "made a philosophical left turn about 1960 and never looked back," whose speech is a "strange mixture of Southern white and hip black."[3] The ISC functioned as a revolutionary cadre within Uptown, a core of activists sharing living space, participating in regular political education exercises, and—when holding salaried jobs—contributing their income to offset the group's expenses. The ISC published a newspaper that included commentary on local issues and national politics, at each level adopting a left-wing populist stance (sample headline, *Uptown Peoples' News,* December 1975: "Black Leaders Support Farmworkers"). Within its limited means, Coleman's group also began to provide services to Uptown's indigent population: advice, bags of groceries, assistance in dealing with landlords. From the standpoint of Uptown's future politics, the ISC, most significantly, began to organize Uptown's low-income population. In the mid-1970s Coleman—whose umbrella organization had adopted a more neighborly moniker, the Heart of Uptown Coalition (HOUC)—had assembled an Uptown Block Club Coalition—and by the end of the decade Coleman's supporters had become a significant force in 46th ward electoral politics.

During the 1960s and 1970s the 46th ward Democratic Party organization had dominated Uptown elections, although in the era of Mayor Richard J. Daley and his South Side-weighted political machine, the 46th ward Democrats were not a renowned ward organization.[4] Nevertheless, when a Coleman-supported candidate, Helen Shiller, lost by only 215 votes to the incumbent, Ralph Axelrod, in the 1979 aldermanic election, one local journalist described Shiller's performance as just short of a "political miracle."[5] What Coleman's forces had managed to accomplish in a decade's organizing was a thoroughgoing mobilization of Uptown's impoverished population, an effort sufficient to bring out 8,000 voters in the 1979 "run-off" election.[6] By contrast, when Chuck Geary had sought the 46th ward City Council seat in 1971 he collected 668 votes. In Shiller, a native of New York City who joined the ISC in the early 1970s following an undergraduate career at the University of Wisconsin-Madison, HOUC had a co-leader whose personality was more suitable to the electoral realm than the self-consciously provocative Coleman. Helen Shiller sat out the 1983 46th ward election, but in 1987 she entered the aldermanic race, and following a three-way primary election fight, narrowly defeated the incumbent (and Democratic organization supported), Jerome Orbach. Though confronted by vigorous challenges in the 1991 and 1995 elections, Shiller has retained her seat on the Chicago City Council.[7]

In addition to local electoral organizing, Coleman and Shiller have often used direct action tactics to advance their causes. For example, in the spring of 1981, Chicago Mayor Jane Byrne had sought to draw attention to the problems of public housing in Chicago by moving, for a few days, into the bleak Cabrini-Green Chicago Housing Authority complex on the city's near North Side. At the time, Coleman and Shiller were seeking city government support for the development of additional low-cost housing in Uptown, and with the media's gaze intently following Mayor Byrne's foray into public housing, Coleman led a march of Uptowners from the Mayor's Office in City Hall to the Cabrini-Green complex. Following the march to the mayor's temporary apartment, Coleman issued an invitation to Mayor Byrne suggesting that she visit Uptown.[8] Reflecting on a Coleman-organized picket of his home in 1984, Chicago Park District Superintendent Ed Kelly commented: "His (Coleman's) style of politics is constantly taking advantage of people who are not involved in politics—giving them food, putting them on a bus and getting them to go around and harass people."[9] In the fall of 1988 Helen Shiller, recently elected to the city council, was arrested for participating in a "Tent City" protest against gentrification in Uptown.[10]

By the late 1970s the Coleman-Shiller movement was sponsoring an impressive array of service-provision projects. In 1976 the Chicago Area Black Lung Association was formed to represent retired mineworkers before U.S. Department of Labor administrative law hearings. Coincidentally, Helen Shiller directed the planning of a community health clinic, the Uptown People's Health Center, which opened in 1978. A pool of attorneys staffed the Uptown People's Law Center, which represented local residents in a variety of contexts, including welfare and Social Security hearings as well as in tenant-landlord litigation. Working with several local colleges, the movement also offered alternative education programs.[11] Although maintaining a public stance that its radical politics prevented it from receiving mainstream institutional sponsorship (an unsigned article in the September 24, 1982, issue of the group's newspaper, *All Chicago City News,* claiming: "Never able to get substantial foundation funds because of their forthright stands in the community and their determination to keep control of the Coalition in the hands of the Heart of Uptown residents, the Coalition developed a unique series of self-reliant community programs."), the Coleman-Shiller movement was, in fact, quite successful in winning the approbation of legitimate outside institutions. In the mid-1980s the Law Center's newsletter, *Legal Lifeline,* was underwritten by the Borg-Warner Foundation. During the mayoral administration of Harold Washington, newspaper accounts estimate that Coleman-Shiller groups received approximately $400,000 in city contracts.[12] On February 25, 1980, the head of a prominent agency supporting grassroots groups across Chicago, the Community Renewal Society, noted in a letter to the *Chicago Sun-Times* (in reference to the Coleman-Shiller movement's efforts to combat arson fires): "The Uptown Coalition has provided a heartening example of neighborhood action."[13]

However, the Coleman-Shiller movement's provision of services has always been linked to larger political ends, which Slim Coleman has explained in this way:

> We're interested in keeping poor people together as a power base. When you scatter people into isolated pockets they remain powerless. If we can stay in Uptown long enough to empower the people, then we can do the same thing here that the Irish did in Bridgeport.[14]

Bridgeport is the South Side neighborhood that has been the home ground of several Chicago mayors, including the legendary Richard J. Daley. In practical terms, this approach has meant that Coleman-Shiller projects tend to intertwine service provision and political objectives more overtly than is typical of grassroots groups. Political controversy is frequently the result. For example, the Health Center, which opened its doors in 1978, was quickly engulfed in acrimony when the clinic's medical staff claimed that Coleman and his associates interfered with day-to-day operations, subverted their professional prerogatives, and sought to manipulate patients. Coleman countered that a community-based clinic ought to be controlled by the community. In less than two years the clinic closed.[15] A decade later an analogous conflict developed over control of one of the elected Local School Councils (LSCs)—for the Stockton Elementary School—in Uptown. In this instance, opponents of Coleman and Shiller claimed that their supporters had taken over the Stockton LSC as part of a grand strategy to dominate institutions throughout Uptown. The majority group on the LSC, in turn, argued that it wished to implement new educational techniques at Stockton and had achieved its electoral victory by way of legitimate, though aggressive campaign tactics.[16]

Frequently involved in local disputes such as the Health Clinic and Stockton School affairs, and publicly espousing a radical political agenda, the Coleman-Shiller movement has regularly been the target of mainstream politicians and the press. In the summer of 1979 a Democratic state senator, William Marovitz, and the 46th ward alderperson, Ralph Axelrod, accused the Uptown Peoples' Community Center of charging local residents for food dispensed through the federal government's Free Lunch Program.[17] A few years later, 14th ward Alderperson Ed Burke—an archrival of Mayor Harold Washington—called for state and federal authorities to investigate the tax-exempt status of the Heart of Uptown Coalition, which was outspoken in its support of Mayor Washington.[18] In August and September of 1988, the *Chicago Tribune* ran a series of articles with the provocative title, "Chicago on Hold: The New Politics of Poverty." In the series' fifth entry ("Shiller Guards Against Uptown Progress") *Tribune* reporter John McCarron, in an unmistakable echo of Slim Coleman's frequent allusions to building a poor people's power base, accused Helen Shiller of cynically employing radical political rhetoric to solidify her own electoral organization, which could only be preserved if the preponderance of her supporters remained indigent residents of Uptown.[19]

Led by an individual who includes physical intimidation among his persuasive techniques (in June 1985, Slim Coleman brought Chicago City Council proceedings to a stand-still when he rushed onto the floor of the council in response to a derogatory remark by 10th ward Alderperson Ed Vrdolyak[20]), the Coleman-Shiller movement has, in turn, played its share of political "hard-ball." Perhaps forgetful of its own origins in something as esoteric-sounding as the Intercommunal Survival Committee, in its April 1981 letter inviting Mayor Byrne to take up residence in Uptown, the Coleman-Shiller movement referred to an Uptown-based religious community, the Jesus People USA, as a "cult."[21] Later that year at its annual convention—and eerily paralleling the stance often adopted by Uptown's homeowners groups—the HOUC convention criticized the resettlement of Southeast Asian refugees in Uptown, which it characterized as an element in the larger process of driving up residential rents in the neighborhood.[22] Shortly after her election to the city council, Alderperson Shiller sought to prevent the city from channeling federal Community Development Block Grant funds to a rival local organization, the Uptown Chicago Commission.[23]

The Coleman-Shiller movement had initially crafted its vision of a future Uptown in the mid-1970s, when the Uptown People's Community Center produced a neighborhood plan emphasizing mixed residential and small business development, and proposing the immediate construction and rehabilitation of 600 units of low-cost housing.[24] This version of a future Uptown owed far more to Hank Williams Village than to the UCC's Meltzer Plan, and as such, was the immediate context for the Coleman-Shiller movement's protracted effort to use the courts to advance its program for the neighborhood. In 1975 attorneys representing the Coleman-Shiller forces filed a suit (*Leroy Avery et al. v. the City of Chicago et al.;* 501 F. Supp. 1 [N.D. Ill., 1978]) in federal district court that named the City of Chicago and private developer William P. Thompson as principal defendants. The Coleman-Shiller attorneys claimed that Leroy Avery and other low-income minority residents of the Montrose Beach Apartment Hotel were displaced through Thompson's efforts to upgrade a portion of Uptown, Thompson having been aided by city officials who had authorized a zoning change permitting the developer to build the Pensacola Place residential/commercial complex at the intersection of Montrose Avenue and Broadway.[25] Subject to a series of amendments by the plaintiffs, further modified as the result of negotiations between the plaintiffs and the different individual defendants, the *Avery* litigation was later linked by the federal district court to another longstanding legal action—the *Gautreaux* lawsuit charging that the Chicago Housing Authority had intentionally sought to segregate its largely African American resident population.

Over the decade and a half of *Avery*-derived negotiations between the Coleman-Shiller attorneys and the various defendants, the lawsuit took a bewildering series of twists and turns. By 1980, developer William P. Thompson, anxious to proceed with his Pensacola Place project, agreed to permit 50 federal Section Eight housing subsidy tenants to rent apartments in his complex, to make compensatory payments to displaced residents, and to hire local Uptowners as construction workers and retail employees (the latter to work in the commercial spaces included in the mixed use development).[26] Negotiations between the *Avery* plaintiffs' attorneys and local and federal officials were far more byzantine. The lawsuit spanned five mayoral administrations, and only during the Washington administration were city officials congenial to the *Avery* plaintiffs. However, local press accounts reported that as many as 3,000 units of subsidized housing might be built as the result of an *Avery* settlement, a figure that was more than excessive from the viewpoint of many Uptown homeowners as well as prospective upscale housing developers. As a result, in 1980 a group called Save Uptown Neighborhoods (SUN) coalesced to oppose the Coleman-Shiller movement and its *Avery* suit. SUN, whose leadership came from the Uptown Chicago Commission and several of the neighborhood's homeowners organizations, sought to demonstrate that Uptown already contained an "overconcentration of assisted housing." SUN filed its own lawsuit claiming that government officials had, through their sponsorship of local subsidized housing projects, conspired to prevent low-income residents from leaving Uptown![27]

Following Helen Shiller's election to the city council in the spring of 1987, the Coleman-Shiller attorneys and the City of Chicago neared a settlement of the *Avery* lawsuit that mandated the formation of an Uptown-based low-cost housing development corporation with $100,000 funding for two years, transferred several city-owned lots to the development body, and pledged city assistance in financing the construction and rehabilitation of several hundred units of low-income housing. Though the impact of such a development plan would seem to be modest in a neighborhood whose housing stock exceeded 30,000 units, opponents of the Coleman-Shiller movement were ill-disposed to this tentative agreement. Moreover, conventional wisdom among Coleman-Shiller foes supposed that the settlement was a payback to Slim Coleman, whose citywide voter registration efforts had played an important part in Harold Washington's 1983 election victory.

Such anxiety proved unnecessary when Harold Washington unexpectedly died in November 1987, permitting Democratic organization loyalists—who were not enamored of their new radical colleague, Helen Shiller—to reassume control of the Chicago City Council. At the first regular Chicago City Council meeting following Washington's death, on December 9, 1987, the alderperson from the 48th ward on Uptown's northern fringe called for a vote on the *Avery* settlement, which was rejected by a 29-17 count. The *Chicago Tribune* reported this action in a front-page story.[28] A year following Washington's death an amended settlement was reached by the Coleman-Shiller attorneys and local and federal officials. This agreement offered $100,000 to the *Avery* plaintiffs, but did not prescribe a mechanism for overseeing low-income housing development or release city-owned properties for this purpose. Helen Shiller described the final *Avery* agreement as "less than an iota."[29] In fact, following the final *Avery* settlement Alderperson Shiller used her aldermanic privilege to review 46th ward zoning variance requests and held up a commercial development proposal by a for-profit developer named Randall Langer and, following another complicated round of negotiations involving Shiller, Langer, and the city, delivered a number of Uptown parcels into the hands of the private developer in charge of scattered-site housing development for the Chicago Housing Authority.[30] Thus, at the end of a decade and a half legal marathon, the Coleman-Shiller forces had managed to win a small cash settlement and enough parcels of land to develop a handful of scattered site public housing units.

Within weeks of joining the city council in 1987, Helen Shiller proposed two ordinances intended to preserve the citywide stock of affordable housing. The first ordinance, primarily aimed at slowing residential displacement, required that landlords give tenants four months' notice of lease termination or rent increases greater than 15 percent. In addition, displaced tenants who could not find comparable housing would be entitled to relocation compensation of $2,000. The second ordinance proposed the establishment of a commission to oversee the development of private, low-cost housing across the city. Neither ordinance thrilled private developers. In the aftermath of Harold Washington's death, Shiller's two bills died in committee.[31]

For a time in the late 1980s Slim Coleman took up residence on Chicago's near Northwest Side, and in early 1988 he ran, unsuccessfully, for the post of 32nd ward Democratic Party committeeperson, which had been given up by veteran Congressperson Dan Rostenkowski. Following this electoral defeat Coleman returned to Uptown, but in the eyes of his opponents, without access to Mayor Washington and with the *Avery* litigation at last concluded, the Coleman-Shiller movement's "threat" to Uptown was much reduced. Nevertheless, the Coleman-Shiller movement remains a force in Uptown. The movement's office on Broadway continues to be the delivery point for a variety of social and legal services. Likewise, in mid-1992 when the City of Chicago— responding to a privately sponsored commercial development proposal to rehabilitate the mammoth old Uptown Theatre as anchor of a "Theatre District" at the Broadway/Lawrence Avenue intersection (and probably entailing considerable building clearance in order to provide nearby parking)—initiated a small-scale planning exercise to investigate this scheme, Coleman-Shiller supporters organized a vociferously hostile response.[32] Probably most emblematic of the continued vigor of the Coleman-Shiller movement has been Helen Shiller's two reelection victories, in 1991 defeating a well-financed opponent who was endorsed by Mayor Richard M. Daley, in 1995 winning a first-round victory by 1,000 votes—which is a landslide by 46th ward standards.

Since joining the city council Helen Shiller has emerged as the most visible public figure in Uptown, and in some respects she has adopted a fairly orthodox approach to her role as 46th ward alderperson. Like every other aldermanic office in the city, Shiller and her staff pride themselves in their mastery of the city bureaucracy, laboring as diligent intermediaries between local residents and the city's service delivery agencies. Shiller, who on occasion may be spotted riding atop a City of Chicago streetcleaning vehicle as it makes its rounds, takes great interest in physical infrastructure matters—street repaving, sewer upgrading, and all manner of utility hook-ups. In her summer 1994 aldermanic newsletter Shiller noted that "our ward now has the newest infrastructure of any ward of the north side of Chicago." In reference to the centerpiece of Uptown conflict, residential and commercial upgrading, Alderperson Shiller has sought to find a common ground linking Uptown's low-income and gentrifying populations:

> The goal of developing communities while keeping economic and racial diversity has been an objective of both city-wide and local government for over a decade. Virtually every Mayor, major media outlet and almost every community organization in Chicago has touted the benefits of diverse communities that continue to develop. And I am extremely happy to say that the 46th Ward is leading the city in this effort.[33]

Shiller's more charitable critics respond to such statements by noting that she "has certainly changed her tune"; less conciliatory opponents simply write off such comments as self-serving political rhetoric.

Alongside Helen Shiller's immersion in the details of sewer systems and service delivery has been a political agenda dramatically at odds with the City Council mainstream. Since Richard M. Daley's election as mayor in 1989 she has been a persistent critic of City Hall policy. Shiller has also used her stature as public official to support left-wing causes at the national and international level such as the anti-apartheid movement in South Africa. For some middle-class Uptowners, Shiller's criticism of development proposals such as the restoration of the grand old Uptown Theatre, if not self-serving, is simply inexplicable. But mistrust of Shiller is not merely a matter of her taking counterintuitive positions on local issues or retaining an aggressively radical worldview, for even in the 1990s with the emergence of a more "moderate" Helen Shiller, there is an element of ambivalence that shadows her public persona. For example—and quite unlike any other alderperson in Chicago (in which tidy commercial storefront offices are the norm)—Shiller works from a remarkably inauspicious ward office, at the rear of the building housing her printing company and sharing its parking area with a well-known lesbian bar. Shiller's aldermanic office also happens to be at the edge of the Heart of Uptown/Sheridan Park area, which has been the site of most of her organizing work and as such holds a great deal of personal meaning for her, but for many affluent Uptowners this aldermanic office is, at best, a forbidding place. Shiller's public appearances are similarly ambivalent. On the one hand, and again unlike other local officeholders, when Shiller enters a community meeting she typically greets—and engages in conversation—any number of otherwise inconspicuous local residents. On the other hand, Shiller is routinely unpunctual in arriving at meetings and, when invited to address potentially hostile audiences, such as the Uptown Chicago Commission or one of the local homeowners groups, often cancels her appearance at the last minute. Helen Shiller is something of a rarity: an essentially outgoing individual who is nonetheless uncomfortable playing the role of public official.

One often encounters a characterization of Slim Coleman that follows this general formulation: "Slim doesn't organize; he mobilizes." Even among Coleman-Shiller allies there is the sense that after 25 years' work in Uptown, once one moves beyond Coleman, Shiller, Jeri Miglietta, Marc Kaplan, and a few of their longtime protégés, this grassroots movement has not developed much breadth of leadership. In this view Coleman and Shiller can readily deliver an angry crowd to a public meeting, but over the long haul they have not nurtured a community that can act independently of its founders. Ironically, in the last few years a second generation of Coleman-Shiller activists—including Helen Shiller's son Brendan and Jeri Miglietta's son Anton—have begun to win recognition for their sponsorship of athletic and social programs serving Uptown teenagers.[34] Whether or not this Coleman-Shiller second generation indeed carries on the work of their elders remains an open question. It is also possible that the tenacity of the Coleman-Shiller movement is itself an anomaly, the consequence of

Slim Coleman's and Helen Shiller's particular approach to political leadership, as well as unique features of the constituent base they have sustained in Uptown. In any event, a quarter century after its formation the Coleman-Shiller movement remains a political force in Uptown and is, in most respects, as willfully insurgent in its middle age as it was in its youth.

III

In 1980, the Executive Director of the Uptown Chicago Commission (UCC), Herb Williams, offered the following analysis of neighborhood decline and rejuvenation:

> We ought to let the free market take care of itself, and it will do for the community what never has been done through tax dollars. We have to be realistic. It's the private dollar that has shown the improvement in Uptown. If we start drawing in middle-class property-owners, Uptown's diversity will continue. Already people of all racial and ethnic backgrounds have bought in. They won't be driven out by redevelopment. As I see it, if we can't make the community more middle-class, it is possible that we will go in the direction of a single racial area. Subsidized low income buildings in Chicago are 90% black.[35]

As one can readily surmise by comparing Williams' philosophy of neighborhood uplift with Slim Coleman's, throughout the 1970s and 1980s the UCC and the Coleman-Shiller movement were at odds. Yet one of the ironies of neighborhood-level politics is that issue- or ideologically-derived organizational conflict can mask substantial shifts in organizational make-up and tactics. A further irony in this particular instance is that the self-consciously iconoclastic Coleman-Shiller movement sustained a notably consistent organizational regime throughout this period, while the UCC underwent a substantial structural transformation.

When the UCC was organized in 1955, Uptown's business district included several banks, the offices of two national-scale insurance companies, a department store, and several other medium-scale firms. At the north end of Uptown (now Edgewater) was another notable commercial operation, the Edgewater Beach Hotel and Apartments. On the lakefront margin of Uptown a number of posh residential blocks were home to prominent Chicagoans, including city planner and mayoral advisor Ira Bach and architect John Cordwell (whose firm designed one of the city's major urban renewal developments, Sandburg Village, on the near North Side). In this context, the UCC set out to accomplish many of the same objectives pursued contemporaneously by the downtown business organizations springing up in cities across the United States, and by way of approximately the same means.

The core of the UCC's agenda was to sustain the viability of Uptown's "central business district" around the Broadway/Lawrence Avenue axis and to halt the residential blight threatening the lakefront residential areas. As for its means, the UCC pressured the city government to step up residential building code enforcement, brought together business leaders to discuss the future of the neighborhood and how they might contribute to its preservation (for example, through local initiatives such as Uptown Federal Savings & Loan's Operation Pride), sponsored programs to aid new Uptown residents (in particular, Appalachian emigrants) in coming to grips with life in the big city, and of course, lobbied the city government to authorize an urban renewal program for Uptown.

In the 1950s and 1960s the leadership of the UCC was a "who's who" of Uptown business leadership. In 1957 executives from Uptown National National Bank, Uptown Federal Savings & Loan Association, Bank of Chicago (based in Uptown), Kemper Insurance Company, and People's Gas Light & Coke Company (a citywide utility) were among the UCC's officers and board of directors.[36] The 1962 Meltzer Report sponsored by the UCC was underwritten by the following institutions: Weiss Memorial Hospital, Edgewater Beach Hotel, Kemper Insurance Companies, Combined Insurance Company of America, Benefit Association of Railway Employees, Goldblatt's Department Store, Bank of Chicago, Uptown National Bank, and Uptown Federal Savings & Loan.[37] Each of these institutions had substantial operations based in Uptown.

As I have detailed in Chapter 3, this alliance of business and institutional leadership did not, in the long run, have its way. The City of Chicago took years to approve the Uptown urban renewal project, and by the late 1960s there were voices in Uptown contending that the UCC was not representative of Uptown's rapidly diversifying population. Nevertheless, as late as June 1967 when Mayor Richard J. Daley appointed 11 members to the Uptown Conservation Community Council—the local citizens' board to review urban renewal planning— eight of the conservation council appointees were also members of the UCC.[38] Thus, on the eve of the protracted urban renewal imbroglio, the UCC was, without question, the principal community organization in the Uptown area.

With the winding down of the Uptown urban renewal conflict, the composition—and more subtly—the agenda of the UCC began to shift. As late as the early 1970s the UCC retained substantial ties to the neighborhood's business leadership. In 1972 James B. Cain, president and son of the founder of Uptown Savings & Loan, was president of UCC. UCC vice-president was William P. Thompson, the aggressive local real estate developer who would be cited in the HOUC's *Avery* suit. Among the board members was W. Clement Stone, head of Combined Insurance and that year a major contributor to the reelection campaign of U.S. President Richard Nixon.[39] However, over the course of the 1970s the UCC lost its primacy as the Uptown business community's vehicle for pursuing local rejuvenation. In the early years of the decade a consortium of banks and insurance companies established a pool of funds to finance residential mortgages in the neighborhood.[40] The UCC was given the opportunity to announce new investments in this program, but in effect, the community group was doing public relations legwork for the business concerns. By the end of the decade local financial institutions sponsored their own redevelopment initiatives, the Bank of Chicago and Uptown Federal, for example, targeting investment in the rundown area east of Broadway and north of Montrose Avenue.[41]

The Uptown business leadership's changing role in the neighborhood was registered by more than its loss of faith in the UCC. In 1971

Kemper Insurance moved its Uptown offices to Long Grove, Illinois. In 1984 one of Uptown's venerable financial institutions, Uptown Federal Savings & Loan Association, was absorbed by an out-of-town real estate developer. Although Uptown has remained a demographic "city within a city," it no longer is a satellite economy of downtown Chicago with a wide array of prominent corporate, retailing, and institutional interests. In effect, as Uptown's economic character shifted, the UCC lost its corporate patrons. To the extent that the UCC has retained any specifically business orientation, it is through its connection with local real estate interests who tend to view the UCC as Uptown's most legitimate community group.

By the early 1970s one can observe a movement in the UCC's approach to community issues, a movement that was not so much a matter of agenda as of how the group perceived the neighborhood's social and physical environments. For instance, in late 1973 the UCC's weekly newsletter, *Uptown Action,* reprinted an advertisement ("An Oasis of Sensation in the Heart of Chicago/Relax in your private room, and let an experienced servant girl envelop you in the pleasure of sensation.") for a massage parlor, the Stratford-on-Avon Club, located at 4411 North Broadway. The caption appended to the advertisement asks: "Is this the kind of "club" you want in your neighborhood?"[42] As the UCC lost its function as sponsor of redevelopment initiatives, it assumed the role of watchdog anxious to root out threats to the community. Relatedly, the UCC's vision of a desirable Uptown was losing the complexity implicit in the notion of a "city within a city" in favor of the more straightforward virtues of a solid residential neighborhood. Throughout the 1970s and 1980s the UCC was a persistent opponent of proposals to locate public housing, other forms of subsidized housing, social service agencies, and homeless shelters in Uptown.[43] Indeed, the group developed a term, "overconcentration," to describe the plight of the community, as often well-intentioned "liberals" from across the metropolitan area thoughtlessly supported the location of new facilities in a neighborhood which— in the view of UCC activists—was already awash in discharged mental patients, decaying low-cost housing, and poorly supervised social service units. For example, in a 1982 debate with a supporter of subsidized housing who happened to live in suburban Evanston, UCC member Paulette Bezazian countered "…let her have it there":

> "Save Uptown Neighborhoods" is not opposed to public housing. We're opposed to the overconcentration of it. There are many communities that don't have any assisted housing. We feel that they should receive some before we receive more.[44]

In the 1980s as Uptown's business leadership withdrew from the UCC, the organization evolved into a fairly conventional homeowners coalition. The number of institutional representatives among UCC officers and board members declined, and the organization's principal link to local residents was through a network of block clubs. The UCC retained a small professional staff and began to develop an array of programs characteristic of homeowner-oriented improvement associations: an anti-litter campaign, a building code enforcement project in which the UCC assisted property-owners in making repairs (or, if the owners were recalcitrant, seeking housing court action to correct their infractions), and various public safety campaigns, including (for a few months in 1988 and 1989) the retention of a private security service to patrol Kenmore Avenue in south-central Uptown.[45] UCC members and several of the group's affiliated block clubs were also principal sponsors of the SUN campaign, which rallied opposition to the Coleman-Shiller movement and sought to limit the scope of any settlement to the HOUC's *Avery* suit.

During the 1980s the UCC produced two reports examining housing rehabilitation issues in the neighborhood, the first a technical study of rehabilitation strategies appropriate for "common corridor" apartment buildings (typically, large buildings whose "studio" units are accessible by a single long corridor on each floor—and often subject to advanced physical deterioration), the second a broader survey of the factors affecting the local housing stock and the prospects for future renovation efforts.[46] The latter report was underwritten by federal Community Development Block Grant (CDBG) funds channeled to the UCC by the City of Chicago.

The UCC had been founded by a group of prosperous business concerns seeking to preserve their "home community" as well as their investments in that community. As such, the group originally had the fiscal backing to support unusually ambitious projects such as the Meltzer planning report of 1962. As the UCC's business sponsors stepped aside in the 1970s and 1980s, the group joined the legions of community organizations that must identify funding sources just as vigilantly as they seek to identify neighborhood improvement strategies. The UCC financed its operations via a fairly typical menu of revenue-raising techniques—membership dues, special fundraising events, and project-based government support such as the CDBG funding for the 1989 residential development survey. In recent years the UCC has also received local, state, and federal government funding to provide support services for de-institutionalized mental patients living in Uptown, to do housing rehabilitation work for older and disabled Uptown residents, and to provide a variety of services for prospective home purchasers and building rehabbers.[47]

Such work is consistent with the broad agenda of the organization, but oversight of these projects—and just as importantly, attentiveness to various associated operations, such as meeting deadlines for funding requests (and extensions of ongoing projects)—is dependent on the retention of an effective professional staff. The UCC's resident officers and board members, following the pattern that is fairly typical of such neighborhood alliances, have devoted most of their energy to representing the group in various public forums. In the early 1990s the UCC suffered a significant organizational setback when a newly hired executive director was unable to manage the UCC's internal operations. As a result, the organization lost some of its government funding, was forced to cut back staff, and ultimately reconfigured itself as a more purely volunteer-driven group.[48]

The UCC of the early 1990s is the organizational equivalent of the son or daughter of a famous parent, struggling to make a mark while laboring in the shadow of its renowned antecedent. Of course, in this instance the renowned antecedent is the UCC itself. The group does retain some links with what remains of Uptown's business leadership, but these ties are at best a mixed legacy. For example, AON Corporation (the renamed Combined Insurance Company) provides meeting space to the UCC in its corporate offices. However, AON's austere headquarters building is not a well-known Uptown site, and to attend a UCC meeting one must pass through the corporation's security check-point. To sit in on a UCC session is not to participate in the deliberations of a flourishing public body. The group itself relies on the energy of a small core of activists, many of them long-time Uptown residents. Given the seemingly interminable quality of the neighborhood's land use and political quarreling, the resilience of the UCC's leadership is regularly tested. Indeed, for UCC's longstanding homeowner activists, even the dependability of their younger, presumed allies in the area's residential upgrading is suspect. Reviewing the last 10 to 15 years of conflict in Uptown, one UCC activist noted: "I feel continuing frustration with my neighbors. The gentrifiers in condominiums are just renters. They don't take part in neighborhood life."[49] Having recently marked the 40th anniversary of its founding, the UCC persists in its efforts to build a respectable, middle-class community. Yet, 40 years of work have brought the group no closer to this goal.

IV

For nearly a decade one of the UCC's block club affiliates was the Montrose Harbor Neighbors Association (MHNA), a group whose rise and decline reveals many of the essential features of property enhancement-oriented grassroots action in Uptown. The MHNA represented a mixed, mainly residential area at the eastern end of Uptown and just south of Montrose Avenue. Its local area includes several unrenovated apartment buildings housing a largely low-income population, a few middle-income apartment buildings, several "six-flat" condominiums, and some extremely posh houses in the Buena Park historical district. The MHNA's guiding figure was Bill Clinard, who—as a renter and feeling himself priced out of his old neighborhood, Lincoln Park—had bought a house on Hazel Street in 1979. In 1986, following his retirement from Illinois Bell, Clinard obtained a real estate license and began to market residential property in Uptown.[50]

Clinard's main impetus for calling the MHNA's first meeting, in the fall of 1983, was a series of planning and land-use controversies. Montrose Avenue, just to the north of Clinard's home, is one of Uptown's several "frontier" streets. To the north a decrepit district of older apartment buildings houses a young, poor, mainly minority population. South of Montrose and east of Broadway there has been extensive residential upgrading. Montrose, itself, is a ragged commercial strip featuring taco stands, bars, mom and pop groceries, and a laundromat. When Clinard moved to Hazel Street one of the most notorious "establishments" along Montrose was the Hideaway, a basement bar just to the east of Hazel. In the mid-1970s a *Chicago Tribune* reporter had visited the Hideaway:

> ...people sat on the stools drinking beer at 9 in the morning. The floor had been mopped, the juke box was blaring, and the freezers were cooling. The beer was flowing as fast as the water had the night before when it backed in from the rear of the tavern and swirled in eddies around the crowded seats.[51]

Such an enterprise was not up to the expectations of Hazel Street's newly arriving gentrifiers, and moreover, according to Clinard he had also been contacted by several local people complaining about the sidewalk decorum of the Hideaway's habitués.

At this time the Hideaway was not the only disputed site in the Hazel Street area. Developer William P. Thompson was finally completing his large Pensacola Place residential project at the southwest corner of Montrose and Hazel, and he circulated the idea of seeking city government approval to close off Hazel Street, creating a cul-de-sac at its intersection with Montrose. Thompson's scheme generated opposition because of its impact on the already constricted streetside parking in the area. And just to the west, at Broadway and Buena Avenue, Kentucky Fried Chicken planned to open one of its take-out restaurants, which adjoining residents feared would attract undesirable customers and produce mountains of trash.

In the face of these developments the MHNA achieved some notable successes. The group closed down the Hideaway by organizing and passing a precinct-level referendum to prohibit alcohol sales. Developer Thompson gave up on his Hazel cul-de-sac plan. According to Clinard: "We circulated a few fliers, met with the alderman, and squelched it."[52] Although Kentucky Fried Chicken proceeded with its restaurant project, the chain agreed to upgrade property maintenance and trash pick-up activities.

Bill Clinard, an individual of unusual gregariousness who had cultivated numerous political contacts, was central to these accomplishments.[53] In retrospect, his colleagues in the MHNA presume that Clinard's hard work, in part, was attributable to the convergence between his business interests, as a realtor seeking to market the local area, and his personal sense of commitment to the neighborhood. Clinard's original motivation may also have derived from aggravation at the existing neighborhood organization formed by the residents of Junior Terrace and Hutchinson Street (in effect, the high-income portion of the MHNA area). This group, which limited membership to homeowners, had not permitted Clinard to join because his house included two rental units.[54]

The MHNA's ties with the UCC were direct and sympathetic. Bill Clinard organized the MHNA via model bylaws that he had acquired from the UCC. Clinard was active in UCC affairs; the UCC served as the MHNA's banker, holding the relatively small quantity of funds collected by the block club. The MHNA and the UCC also tended to join hands on local land-use disputes. In 1991 when a proposal was reviewed to open a homeless shelter in the nearby Clarendon Park Fieldhouse, both the MHNA and the UCC sent representatives to oppose the idea at the public hearing on the shelter.[55]

However, the MHNA was not merely an oppositionist homeowners group. In later years Clinard viewed the group's function as largely "social," and he made more than passing efforts to incorporate the area's renting population into his organization. The MHNA's main social event was a summertime "pig roast" staged in the alley running behind the houses on the east side of Hazel Street. For a time the group also collected members' discarded clothing for distribution at a local shelter.

Nonetheless, the main thrust of the MHNA was to protect the residential area south of Montrose Avenue. At MHNA meetings street crime and loitering, the management of a nearby children's shelter (whose residents were presumed to vandalize the neighborhood), and after 1987, anxieties generated by Alderperson Helen Shiller's public policy views were staple topics of discussion. In 1990 and early 1991, that is, in the months leading up to the 46th ward aldermanic election, several MHNA members promoted the candidacy of Shiller's main challenger, Michael Quigley.[56] Quigley had recently moved into the 46th ward—settling in the Montrose Harbor area—from the Lakeview neighborhood on Uptown's southern border, where he was a protégé of 44th ward Alderperson Bernie Hansen. Hansen's organization, with support from Mayor Richard M. Daley, sought to unseat Shiller. With Quigley's defeat in the spring of 1991 the MHNA's vigor seemed to flag. Bill Clinard had already contemplated relocating to Florida, and although he had not been an outspoken Quigley supporter, he did seem to take a cue from this election and proceed with his plans. By the spring of 1992 Clinard had sold his home and taken up residence in the sunshine state.

Rob Bagstad and Jill Donovan, a couple who rented an apartment in the Pensacola Place complex, attempted to resuscitate the MHNA following Clinard's departure.[57] Lacking the seemingly essential core commitment to property enhancement issues, Bagstad and Donovan sought to carry on some of the social functions of MHNA and to produce a newsletter updating residents on current neighborhood issues and events. Without a compelling neighborhood conflict to mobilize participation and in the face of what had always been a thoroughly fragmented residential constituency, Bagstad and Donovan could not sustain the organization. By the summer and fall of 1993, when the local area was disrupted by a series of street shootings north of Montrose Avenue, the Hutchinson Street/Junior Terrace residents had reconstituted themselves as the Hutchinson Hazel Junior Terrace & Buena Neighborhood Owner's Association, a group once again limiting membership to property owners and committed to an explicitly pro-gentrification stance. The MHNA was no longer a viable group.

V

Rather like the Uptown Chicago Commission but a generation later, there is a "paint-by-numbers" quality to the Organization of the NorthEast's (ONE) origins. However, this generational divide, along with a substantial constituency divide, has meant that the two groups' images of Uptown have been sharply at odds. But again like the UCC, ONE is a longstanding neighborhood organization whose character and fortunes have been variable. At the onset of the 1990s ONE experienced a powerful revitalization, by virtue of which it could make the strongest claim of any Uptown group to speak for most parts of this complex, politically divided neighborhood.

ONE was the brainchild of Brooks Miller and Robert Thrasher. In the early 1970s Miller headed a prominent local social services agency, Uptown Hull House, and Thrasher was an Uptown-based businessperson. Their reaction to the local political fireworks of the previous several years was to form a neighborhood coalition aiming to encompass the variety of Uptown's local areas, racial/ethnic constituencies, and political factions. Following an extended planning period that included a community survey and was financed, in part, by Uptown Hull House, ONE was launched in 1973.[58] Structurally, ONE followed the general shape of an Alinskyite "people's organization." ONE's broadest decisionmaking unit was a Delegate Assembly, comprised of representatives from the local institutions affiliating with ONE. These included block clubs, social service agencies, and religious congregations. Organizational leadership was divided between a smaller group of resident-activists serving as officers or committee chairs and the group's professional staff.[59]

ONE was also Alinskyite in its approach to the resolution of local issues, tending to view community problems as matters of institutional neglect and insufficient local resources. ONE's tactics were likewise Alinskyite. Within weeks of the group's formation, ONE demonstrators dressed as "trick or treaters" and on Halloween demonstrated outside the downtown office of Cook County State's Attorney Bernard Carey. A few months later ONE pickets circled the headquarters of

the Uptown National Bank, this time impersonating hobos and passing out cups of pea soup to dramatize the bank's Depression-style
lending practices. In 1981, a journalist's profile of the group appeared
under the title "Alinsky Lives!"[60]

ONE's aggressive use of direct action techniques and willingness to
confront local institutions such as Uptown National Bank quickly fixed
its public image as a radical group. Former ONE Executive Director
Josh Hoyt described the group's longstanding reputation as "left-wing
hippie fringe," but in fact, ONE's program and constituency were not
unambiguously radical.[61] Alongside its public demonstrations of the
1970s, the group organized a housing court monitoring program and
campaigned to "downzone" (that is, reduce permissible building
heights) the lakefront portions of Uptown and Edgewater (to the north
of Uptown). In the 1980s the UCC, itself, would begin to monitor
housing court action. Downzoning was certainly not appreciated by
development interests committed to high-rise construction along the
lakefront, but it was very attractive to homeowners and others concerned about Uptown's and Edgewater's loss of "neighborhood character" with the advance of Manhattan-style residential construction. In
the mid-1970s ONE opposed the construction of additional nursing
homes in Uptown and also sought to limit the number of residential
facilities serving deinstitutionalized persons.[62]

ONE more clearly parted with Uptown's institutional mainstream
on affordable housing issues. In the late 1970s the group produced a
report contending—contrary to the UCC's "overconcentration"
claims—that given the size of Uptown's low-income population, the
community did not suffer from an oversupply of cheap housing.
Similarly, and sharing this perspective with the Coleman-Shiller forces,
ONE was convinced that Uptown's rash of residential fires in the 1970s
and early 1980s resulted from a systematic program of arson initiated by
property interests seeking to profit from upscale redevelopment.[63]

Politically, this array of policy positions, combined with ONE's
tactical approach, meant that in spite of its founders' dream to unify
Uptown, if anything, ONE was contributing to the further fragmen-

tation of the community's organizational politics. On the one hand, UCC, whose organizational preeminence was on the wane, and whose emerging homeowner leaders were mortified by local radicalism, distrusted ONE—as it distrusted the Coleman-Shiller movement—as another group of rabble-rousing upstarts. On the other hand, given ONE's leanings toward reformist neighborhood tinkering, as embodied in downzoning, and the evidently middle-class status of many of its leaders, from the Coleman-Shiller vantage point ONE looked to be a group of radical poseurs. Furthermore, ONE had very quickly achieved a striking organizational robustness. When journalist Robert McClory visited the group in 1981 he described its offices as "sprawling." At that time the group's annual budget approached $200,000, and the staff numbered nine. As such, for other groups in Uptown it was very easy to envy ONE.[64]

In the late 1970s ONE had begun to explore the neighborhood impacts of energy issues. Initially, the group had focused its attention on the Illinois Commerce Commission (ICC), the state board that regulates utility rates, and had organized delegations to attend ICC rate-setting hearings. Out of this effort to hold down residential gas and electric charges grew projects to survey the energy efficiency of local apartment buildings and to encourage building owners to invest in energy-saving retrofitting measures. Over the course of the 1980s, ONE's energy conservation work was among its core activities.[65]

In 1985 ONE formed the North East Investment Center (NEIC), a staff unit that served as an intermediary between loan-seekers and suppliers of capital. During Harold Washington's mayoral administration, the city government, Peoples Gas, and an alliance of community organizations had developed the Chicago Energy Savers Fund, a capital pool dedicated to energy conservation-directed residential investment. NEIC also "packaged" loans and provided assistance to prospective borrowers in conjunction with several bank-financed neighborhood residential investment programs. Between 1985 and 1989 NEIC participated in loan agreements worth $8,223,567. Fees paid to NEIC for its services in assisting loan-seekers and lenders totaled $649,643. A 1990 evaluation of NEIC's operations dryly noted that it had become a "profit center" for its parent organization and, as such, "supported much of the cost of ONE's advocacy activities."[66]

In fact, rather than engaging in sustained advocacy, by the mid-1980s ONE seemed to be slipping into an introspective middle age. The group's Executive Director, Joe Bute, was not known as an especially vigorous community organizer, and beyond the NEIC unit, much of the energy of ONE proper was devoted to economic development issues. For example, two of the main documents produced by ONE during this period were a business survey of the Andersonville commercial district on the western edge of Uptown and Edgewater and an overview of the two communities' demographic and housing trends, which sought to determine the impact of gentrification forces.[67]

When ONE did seek to return to more aggressive community advocacy, the results were not gratifying. In 1986 a commercial developer pursued City of Chicago support for a retail project on Broadway, near the Uptown-Edgewater boundary. The property was an abandoned auto dealership, and the developer sought the city's authorization of a Tax Increment Finance (TIF) district, from which increased tax revenues could be used to pay off a loan underwriting construction of the planned shopping mall. ONE responded with an aggressive organizing campaign, claiming that the project would, through its effects on surrounding residential areas, lead to the displacement of low-income renters, and further, that the city government would be wasting its resources in behalf of an unnecessary strip mall. However, the November 1987 public hearing on the project was an organizer's nightmare. A large crowd turned out for the event, but project opponents were far outnumbered by supporters. A press account noted that one of the speakers who generated the most vocal approval was a woman who sided with the developer. The core of her statement: "Let my people shop." In the next few weeks the City of Chicago approved a scaled-down TIF package, and the project proceeded.[68] ONE had failed in a major organizing effort and, in so doing, had also managed to aggravate any number of local political figures and community groups.

Joe Bute's tenure as ONE director was also plagued by simple bad fortune. In September 1986, a fire struck ONE's office, destroying files, office equipment, and furniture.[69] Organizational operations were disrupted, and the group was forced to relocate. Five years later when I was given permission to look through ONE's files, what I found at the back of the group's office was still a water-stained, mildewing mess.

ONE's fortunes began to rebound in 1989, when the organization hired a new Executive Director, Josh Hoyt. Hoyt was initially quite pessimistic about the future of ONE. Rather than accepting the director's job, he at first joined the group as a paid "consultant" with the mandate to overhaul its operations. Indeed, for a time he discussed with ONE's resident leaders the possibility of renaming the group, thus divesting themselves of at least some of the ill-will ONE had generated over the years. After considerable discussion this idea was rejected. In the meantime, Hoyt coped with the group's financial burdens by reducing staff by more than half, cutting the annual budget by nearly $200,000, and moving into cheaper offices.[70] In Hoyt's mind, more troublesome was ONE's other liability, the long-term attenuation of its organizing efforts.

Hoyt, his remaining staff, and a handful of resident-activists began an extensive program of personal interviews with Uptown and Edgewater organizational leaders. This canvassing process had two objectives: (1) to identify local people's thinking about the main issues to be tackled by a renewed ONE and (2) to rekindle commitment to ONE as an encompassing neighborhood coalition. Following the initial canvass of approximately 500 people, ONE invited about 45 individuals to a luncheon devoted to discussing the future of ONE, Uptown, and Edgewater. This "proposition lunch" (the proposition: What is our next step?) was the bridge to three subsequent "community dialogues" dealing more directly with local issues. The culmination of this process was ONE's inviting the groups that had participated in this series of discussions to re-affiliate with a rejuvenated Organization of the NorthEast.

In recounting the renaissance of ONE, Josh Hoyt dismisses the idea that he applied a preconceived plan to the task at hand:

> Any organizer who uses a game plan is incompetent.
> Organizing is about context and listening. Yes, there
> are different frameworks—whether to lobby, or
> maybe to get involved in electoral politics—but a
> game plan...the answer is no.[71]

In fact, this restructuring of ONE probably would not have saved the group in the absence of new, compelling organizing initiatives, and, in the case of ONE's organizing work in the late 1980s and early 1990s, a degree of serendipity was involved in the group's successes. During Josh Hoyt's tenure as ONE Executive Director, the group devoted itself to two broad organizing campaigns. The first, which focused on local public schools, was an area ripe for organizing in the wake of 1988 state legislation mandating the election of Local School Councils (LSCs) in Chicago.

The second Hoyt/ONE organizing campaign centered on affordable housing, an issue whose ebbs and flows are an elemental feature of the politics of Uptown, and which in the late 1980s offered ONE the chance to have a dramatic effect on the day-to-day lives of thousands of Uptown residents. During Uptown's urban renewal era private developers had won U.S. Department of Housing and Urban Development (HUD) subsidies to assist their construction of ten below-market rental complexes. Under the terms of their subsidy agreements, after twenty years the owners of these buildings could "prepay" the remainder of their mortgages and convert their projects to market-rate properties. The ten HUD "prepayment" buildings in Uptown included more than 2,600 units of housing, and very few of their current residents would be able to afford prevailing market rents. All of these buildings became eligible for prepayment in the late 1980s or early 1990s, and in several cases their owners had given clear signals of their intention to exercise this option.[72]

Although tenant organizing had, for years, not been an ONE priority, Hoyt found that Susan Gahm of the ONE staff had been working with residents of one of the HUD prepayment buildings, at 833 W. Buena Avenue. Furthermore, since 1986 a coalition of local groups, including Voice of the People (VOP) and several of the Asian mutual aid associations, had been collaborating in a political campaign to publicize and curb the residential displacement resulting from upscale redevelopment in Uptown.[73] Susan Gahm made the rounds of the prepayment buildings, and sometimes in league with VOP organizers, began working with—or in some cases forming—indigenous tenants groups.

The mobilization of these tenants organizations was a daunting task. In most cases, the design and subsequent decay of these high-rise buildings had produced residential environments in which atomistic self-preservation might well structure the individual tenant's worldview. The prepayment buildings' demographic profiles further complicated the effort to build tenant self-confidence and mutual trust. Many residents were recent immigrants to the United States, and as such, often unfamiliar with citizen and tenant rights. Moreover, in several of the buildings the resident population represented a rainbow assemblage of nationalities, cultures, and primary languages. Nor could the formation of tenants organizations be directed at precisely the same objectives in each building. The buildings became eligible for owner prepayment over a five-year span of time (in two instances HUD held the properties, their original owners having defaulted on their loans). So in some instances the tenants' group sought to intervene in the prepayment process; in others the tenants engaged in more conventional efforts to pressure owners into making necessary building repairs. The physical condition of the ten buildings also varied dramatically, which itself affected the tenants' sense of priorities.[74]

As the owners of the prepayment buildings began to negotiate with HUD over the future of these buildings, the tenants groups found themselves in what amounted to a four-sided contest in which, on the one hand, they sought to win HUD's support for a transfer of the properties that would protect their interest, while on the other, they searched for investment partners willing to take over their buildings. In the case of the 230-unit apartment tower at 850 W. Eastwood, the tenants organization formed an alliance with the Chicago Community Development Corporation (CCDC), a recently organized development company formed with the explicit intent to preserve low-cost residential properties. CCDC proposed to purchase 850 W. Eastwood, make substantial renovations, hold down the rents, and give the tenants organization a substantial voice in subsequent building management. This plan, of course, was contingent upon HUD's approval and the federal agency's working out a complicated financing arrangement with CCDC. The 850 W. Eastwood tenants at first sought to win the support of the regional HUD office, but when they failed to make inroads with the Chicago-based HUD officials, turned their attention to HUD Secretary Jack Kemp. Relying on tactics reminiscent of ONE's early days—at one point sending a man dressed as a chicken to serenade the attendees of an HUD-sponsored event with a reworking of "Puff the Magic Dragon" as "Jack the Giant Windbag"—the tenants finally pressured Secretary Kemp to authorize a CCDC purchase of the building that included an ambitious tenant-management plan and a $4.7 million renovation.[75]

Predictably, there was considerable variation in the degree of success achieved by the prepayment buildings' tenants organizations. In a second building whose residents worked closely with ONE, HUD agreed to a tenant purchase plan that converted the building to cooperative ownership. Two other prepayment buildings were purchased by non-profit developers committed to programs of tenant management. In three additional cases tenants organizations managed to win substantial building renovations. In all, the prepayment building organizing campaign preserved about 1,300 units of housing for low-income residents, while also substantially increasing their residents' voice in building management. Another 500 apartments were renovated, although in these three buildings there was considerable resident turnover and the organizing efforts did not result in a markedly stronger tenant hand in building operations.[76]

Josh Hoyt gave up the directorship of ONE in 1993, but by the time of his departure the group was thoroughly reshaped and rejuvenated. ONE's contribution to the HUD prepayment building campaign was well recognized, and though its youth-family-schools organizing had not generated the same degree of public attention, the group had also had success in this area. Though the North East Investment Center had at one time been an important part of ONE's program (and a key source of revenue), because the group's leadership felt that its work did not fit so comfortably with the organizing emphasis of the new ONE, the investment center had been closed. At the conclusion of the canvassing/dialogue process to reframe the identity and agenda of ONE, more than 50 local organizations—including past ONE staples such as social service agencies, ethnic mutual aid associations, and churches, but also several banks, Weiss Memorial Hospital, and Loyola University— had aligned themselves with the group. This "recommitment," moreover, was not an idle exercise. ONE affiliates now underlined their support for the group through an annual fee schedule, running from $250 per year for small organizations to $2,500 per year for the largest groups. Though ONE's annual budget far exceeds the revenues produced by affiliate dues, these contributions did serve to solidify what just a few years before had been a very shaky financial situation. Finally, with the greater portion of its affordable housing work behind it—at least for a few years—in 1994 ONE turned to a new and vexing policy area, how to engender more economic vitality in Uptown and Edgewater. Neighborhoods and cities throughout the United States have found this to be a knotty problem. As a policy objective for a campaigning community coalition like ONE, it is virtually *terra incognita.*

VI

Voice of the People (VOP) dates from 1968. Chuck Geary was one of the group's founders, and in its first few years VOP opposed the Uptown urban renewal plan—in particular, the community college siting west of Broadway—and had a hand in producing the Hank Williams Village proposal. After Geary dropped out of Uptown politics in the early 1970s, VOP was headed by one of his allies in the urban renewal battle, Irene Hutchinson. At this point VOP began a very gradual process of organizational redirection and growth that would continue throughout the 1970s and 1980s.

With the clearance of housing around the Truman College site, VOP devoted its energies to finding relocation housing for displaced families. This operation led VOP's core of activists to turn to a related enterprise, the management of small-scale apartment buildings, typically low-rent and often near-derelict properties. VOP defined its mission, however, as not just ordering coal and collecting rent but also "improving" these buildings by making essential repairs. As a VOP report noted years later, this turned out to be a frustrating course of action:

> Unfortunately, once the buildings managed by Voice were improved, the owner would sometimes sell the building. Or, even worse, the owners would refuse to do their share of making necessary building improvements, leaving Voice of the People with the burden of managing buildings whose problems were too big and expensive for a manager to handle alone. One by one, either because a building was sold, or because Voice chose not to waste its time and money on buildings whose owners were neglecting them beyond repair, Voice's management contracts ended and Voice chose not to accept any new contracts.[77]

In 1972 a local developer handed over to VOP a run-down rooming house, which, once the group was able to acquire bank financing, VOP's members renovated—turning a 34-unit building into a six-flat of four- and five-bedroom apartments. This approach to property development—acquiring one building at a time, typically patching together a crazy quilt of financial support and carrying out thorough renovation—became VOP's modus operandi for the next decade and a half. The other distinctive feature of the VOP model of affordable housing development was the group's commitment to tenant management. The residents of VOP buildings took responsibility for basic building maintenance work, screened prospective fellow tenants, and by the 1980s, had majority representation on the group's Board of Directors.[78]

Working in the midst of Uptown's highly polarized political environment and, indeed, doing just what many middle-class Uptowners have hated to witness, the development of low-cost housing, VOP managed to win the grudging admiration of even some of the neighborhood's affordable housing opponents. In part, this may have been attributable to the group's "bootstrap" philosophy of tenant participation in building upkeep. Ironically, in order to advance its agenda of afford-able development, VOP, on occasion, did resort to political maneuver-ing. In 1984 VOP was planning the renovation of four small apartment buildings (totaling 30 units of housing) in central Uptown. One of the four buildings was owned by the City of Chicago, and in order for VOP to take over this property, Alderperson Jerome Orbach's approval would be required. Orbach informed VOP that he wished to assist their plan, but that he was being pressured by the UCC to block the property transfer. VOP, in turn, organized a campaign to support its plan by con-tacting organizations throughout Uptown and urging them to register their approval of VOP's efforts with Orbach, and for good measure, with 48th ward Alderperson Marion Volini as well.[79] VOP's lobbying effort failed, but the group did find an alternative building and was able to proceed with a modified "Hazel-Winthrop" redevelopment plan.

During this period, the tortuousness of VOP's redevelopment efforts is illustrated by the following project timeline, drawn from the group's spring 1985 newsletter (*The Voice Speaks*):

June 1982
   Voice Board identifies 4416 N. Clifton as a good building to develop.

July 1982
   Voice purchases an option to buy the building from the owner.

July 1982
   Voice submits application to the Department of Housing and Urban Development for Section 8 rent subsidies.

October 1982
   HUD accepts Voice's application for rent subsidies.

All of 1983
   Voice searches for long-term financing.

December 1983
   HUD forecloses on property, taking it away from owner.

February 1984
Voice successfully bids at HUD auction to buy the building.

June 1984
Voice gets title to the property.

August 1984
The Chicago Metropolitan Housing Development Corporation (C.M.H.D.C.) sells bonds that will finance Clifton's rehab. Voice holds Groundbreaking Ceremony.

October 1984
Voice gets mortgage money from the C.M.H.D.C. Construction begins.

May 1985
First two tiers of apartments finished. Families begin to move in.

June 21, 1985
Voice holds Dedication and Open House.

July 1985
Entire building is completed.

In short, three years were required to develop a building housing 35 families (selected from approximately 600 applicants). It is altogether likely that VOP's avoidance of political controversy was related to the small scale of its operations. By the summer of 1987, a decade and a half after the acquisition of its first building, VOP owned properties offering 91 units of low-cost housing.[80] No one could view VOP as a force with the potential to transform Uptown.

In 1984, due to his sense that the areas surrounding VOP apartments often had a substantial impact on the habitability of these properties, VOP Executive Director Tom Lenz suggested that staff member Mike Loftin begin to make contacts with the residents of buildings adjoining VOP's, and when possible, to begin forming block clubs which would include both VOP and non-VOP residents. For his part, Loftin was concerned about the increasingly evident displacement of low-income residents that was occurring as Uptown's real estate market reignited in the mid-1980s.[81] In late July 1986, an event occurred that gave greater urgency to Loftin's concerns and ultimately served to jolt VOP into another of its periodic reorientations. Real estate developer Randall Langer, who at the time was buying and rehabilitating properties in the Heart of Uptown/Sheridan Park area, evicted 33 families from an apartment building on the 4700 block of North Beacon Street. The evictees were Cambodian and Laotian refugees who had settled in Uptown in just the preceding few years. Langer, it was reported, initially had sought to drive out the tenants by allowing their building's plumbing system to decay. When the anticipated odor-driven evacuation failed to occur, Langer delivered formal eviction notices.

Loftin met with some of the Langer evictees, as well as representatives of their respective mutual aid associations, then began making the rounds of Uptown organizations with the intent of building a coalition to protest Langer's actions. Though Loftin found that support for Langer's evictees was widespread, he also discovered that there was not a consensus on how to counter the developer. One perspective suggested that the evictees seek legal support; Loftin sensed that the 33 families and their supporters ought to take more direct action. In fact, at the end of one strategy session, more or less out of frustration at their inability to reach Langer, Loftin and several representatives of the evictees walked over to the developer's offices to directly confront their nemesis. As their luck would have it, Langer was present, but at the sight of the oncoming delegation he tried to duck into an inner office. Loftin and associates caught Langer before he pulled off his escape, and a brief, inconclusive verbal exchange followed. Nonetheless, the group's realization of the developer's apprehensiveness gave them new confidence.[82] Out of Loftin's organizing resistance to the Langer evictions grew the Uptown Task Force on Displacement and Housing Development.

Initially, the Task Force focused on Langer, organizing pickets of his office and winning a measure of media attention. By 1987 it had reached a settlement with the developer, who at the behest of Alderperson Orbach (himself locked in a heated election contest with Helen Shiller and wishing for an uncontentious run-up to election day), offered a relocation allowance to each of the displaced families.[83]

However, the Task Force—whose participants were now drawn from several mutual aid associations, various social services agencies, religious groups such as the Jesus People USA and the Uptown Chicago Ministry, as well as VOP—had broadened its agenda to the larger questions of gentrification-induced residential displacement and the preservation of low-cost housing in Uptown. The Task Force pressured state and federal officials in an effort to win new Section 8 housing development in Uptown, in the summer of 1988 organizing a march to Illinois Governor James Thompson's private residence on Hutchinson Street. Working with ONE, the Task Force won the endorsements of U.S. Congresspersons Charles Hayes and Sidney Yates, as well as U.S. Senator Paul Simon, for a proposal to extend a congressionally approved moratorium on the transfer of HUD prepayment buildings. Probably the high-water mark of the Task Force's campaigning was in October 1988, when HUD allocated 52 units of Section 8 housing to Uptown, all to be developed by VOP.[84] This was, however, a shortlived victory. In 1990 VOP lost this Section 8 authorization in the wake of the federal agency's in-house fiscal scandal and program retrenchment. Having already committed $60,000 in earnest money toward the acquisition of two properties, VOP, without HUD backing, had to forfeit these funds.[85]

The Task Force, a network of activists with strong organizational backing, was an effective device for mounting the 1986-1988 campaign to publicize the pressures on Uptown's low-cost housing stock. However, the various groups and interests operating under the Task Force umbrella soon enough began to disagree over the movement's evolving agenda. For instance, an organization such as VOP, with housing to manage and a commitment to Uptown's low-income resident population, was less enthusiastic about the Task Force's other associated policy concern, homelessness. By the summer of 1988 some of the Task Force's members, notably representatives of the Coleman-Shiller movement and the Jesus People, began to advocate a Tent City demonstration in Heart of Uptown/Sheridan Park to publicize homelessness. This idea split the Task Force, which as a collective body did not endorse the Tent City, though several Task Force members and affiliated groups did join in the demonstration. [86] The Tent City was staged for a number of days in October 1988, but in the aftermath of this protest the Task Force began to unravel.

Although Mike Loftin was the principal founder of the Task Force on Displacement and Housing Development, and VOP was the affordable housing group most closely associated with the Task Force's organizing campaign, the Task Force was not simply VOP's political arm. Indeed, through its participation in the Task Force, VOP quite serendipitously discovered what would be its most important new initiatives in the early 1990s. Out of VOP's contacts with the Task Force-aligned mutual aid associations emerged the suggestion that it sponsor the development of new, cooperatively owned housing.[87] In the early 1990s this idea came to fruition via the group's International Homes Project, through which VOP worked with four Asian mutual aid associations as well as the American Indian Economic Development Association and the Ethiopian Community Association to build 28 units of cooperative housing. The ethnic and mutual aid associations joined the project planning discussions and recruited prospective purchasers. VOP took on the complicated negotiations with the City of Chicago—which provided most of the parcels for the project—and the private lenders, the Local Initiative Support Corporation (a nonprofit capital fund), the Federal Home Loan Bank, as well as architects and contractors, to arrange funding for development and purchasers' mortgages, and to oversee the construction process.[88] The owners of these townhouses were able to occupy their new dwellings in the spring of 1994.

As a result of its participation in the Task Force, VOP also began working with the tenants groups in the Uptown HUD prepayment buildings, in several instances collaborating with ONE organizer Susan Gahm. In the preceding account of ONE I have outlined the complexities of this organizing effort. VOP worked closely with the tenants group in the 920 W. Lakeside Place apartment complex, helping to build a cohesive tenants organization and to link the tenants with a nonprofit development company that pledged to retain below-market rents, renovate the building, and bring the tenants into the building management process. However, HUD (which had assumed ownership of this mortgage-defaulted building) rejected the tenant-development company purchase offer and auctioned the building to an out-of-state real estate company.[89]

Two years later in 1992, VOP formed a development affiliate (the Lakeview Towers Preservation Corporation) and, with financial assistance from HUD and the Chicago Community Development Corporation, purchased the largest of Uptown's prepayment buildings.[90] With the acquisition of the 499-unit Lakeview Towers, VOP nearly tripled the size of its property portfolio and, possibly more critically, found itself in a new position—that is, as landlord of a large and relatively decrepit rental complex. Since purchasing the building VOP has overseen an arduous rehabilitation program (with tenants temporarily shuttling from unit to unit as work progressed) and has sought to introduce to Lakeview Towers its longstanding philosophy of tenant participation in building management. VOP's relations with its new tenants have been uneasy. The group's purchase of the building resulted in a fairly byzantine restructuring of rents, which caused anxiety among many tenants (and, in fact, pushed up expenses for some). The building rehabilitation process also brought some hardship to tenants. On a number of occasions VOP has found itself at odds with the association representing Lakeview Towers residents.[91] Thus, via its very successes, VOP has catapulted itself into an entirely new organizational environment. No longer a small-scale, activist-driven group, VOP presently seeks to manage a large number of housing units in a humane fashion while sustaining a measure of its grassroots vitality. It remains to be seen how effectively VOP will traverse this difficult path.

VII

The second half of the 1980s was a critical period in Uptown. Following a lull during the early 1980s, private investment in real estate once more surged. In 1984 and 1986 local homeowners and real estate interests won approval of the Buena Park and Sheridan Park historical districts. In each instance, promoters of the historic district designation anticipated that their efforts would yield new, upscale residential development. By the end of the decade the HUD prepayment buildings were at or nearing the end of the 20-year subsidy guarantee period, after which their owners could convert their properties to market-rate rentals. In short, the neighborhood that had been scarred but not substantially upgraded by urban renewal might finally make the turn into something approximating middle-class respectability.

At the very same time, and often in response to these very developments, a series of grassroots initiatives sought to protect the interests of low-income Uptowners, and in particular, to retain as much of the neighborhood's low-cost housing stock as possible. ONE and VOP were beginning their organizing campaigns in the prepayment buildings. The Uptown Task Force on Displacement and Housing Development carried on a public campaign to shame developers such as Randall Langer and to draw public and official attention to residential displacement and homelessness in Uptown. In 1987 insurgent activist Helen Shiller won the 46th ward seat in the Chicago City Council and quickly proposed two ordinances aimed at securing low-cost housing across the city.

Nor was the "Battle of Uptown" simply a neighborhood affair. In late 1987 Chicago's two principal daily newspapers published articles entitled "Shiller & Poor vs. Yuppies in Uptown" and "Class Struggle Divides Uptown," and throughout this period, when Chicago-based media sought to explore knotty neighborhood issues, Uptown tended to attract their reporters and camera crews.[92] In a parallel fashion local activists often viewed Uptown conflicts as skirmishes in a war reaching well beyond the borders of their neighborhood. Opponents of gentrification presumed that they were seeking to block downtown banks, outside real estate speculators, and even the remnants of the old Democratic Party machine. For their part, pro-gentrification partisans viewed themselves as embattled pioneers locked in struggle to rid the neighborhood of riff-raff, often in the face of official indifference. Recalling this period—and accepting the proposition that the mayoral administration of Harold Washington was not an ally of homeowners— Bill Clinard of the Montrose Harbor Neighbors Association told me: "With Washington, whatever Helen and Slim asked for, they got."[93]

By the spring of 1991, and with Helen Shiller's reelection to the city council, a ceasefire was reached. Low-cost housing advocates were on the way to protecting several of the prepayment buildings, and VOP, along with other nonprofit developers, had begun new projects that would add to Uptown's stock of affordable housing. Although developers, homeowners, and gentrifiers had to reconcile themselves to four more years of neighborhood co-habitation with Alderperson Shiller, their cause was not altogether lost. Developers were continuing to renovate six-flats in Heart of Uptown/Sheridan Park, and at the north end of Uptown along Argyle Street and to the west on Clark Street, very substantial commercial area improvements were preceding. Indeed, some of the affordable housing advocates' victories, such as the physical upgrading of the prepayment buildings, probably made adjoining areas more desirable locations for upscale development.

This Uptown ceasefire did not represent a permanent settlement. Critics of activist groups such as the Coleman-Shiller movement and ONE persisted in their view that they—and not Slim Coleman, Helen Shiller, or even Josh Hoyt—were the real heart of Uptown. Alderperson Shiller expected local gentrification pressures to continue, and she, no more than her antagonists in the UCC, was willing to accept the proposition that well-intentioned people might still disagree on the proper course for Uptown. On the point of future investment trends, Shiller was certainly correct. As long as Uptown adjoins affluent Lakeview to the south and Lake Michigan itself on its eastern flank, retains several stops on the North-South mass transit line, and holds older buildings and vacant lots that whet the imagination of ambitious real estate developers, pressures to upgrade Uptown will persist. In the early 1990s Uptown was calm but not at peace with itself.

VIII

One of the central points of debate among community organizers is the proper balance between politically aggressive, at times opportunistic campaigning and the formation of structured, frequently service-providing organizations. Josh Hoyt has expressed this tension in the following way: "When you've got grants to administer, homes to build, tenants to manage, downtown meetings to go to, you don't reach out to the people who are unorganized."[94] One lesson that might be drawn from the experience of grassroots action during the 1980s in Sharrow and Uptown is that groups in the latter community were more successful in finding a point of balance between grassroots mobilization and structural stability. Groups such as ONE and VOP managed, when necessary, to mount effective organizing campaigns, yet coincidental with their more overtly political work, they forged durable organizational structures. In contrast, Sharrow's SSICCP remained dependent on governmental aid, and as its financial base eroded, the group's ties to the local populace withered. Relatedly, a promising organizing exercise such as the Sharrow Traffic Campaign ultimately foundered, in large part, due to its undeveloped structure.

The achievements of ONE and VOP in the 1980s and early 1990s are indeed a testament to wise decisionmaking and vigorous organizational follow-through. Nonetheless, I think that the seemingly contrasting organizing stories of Sharrow and Uptown should also be considered in relation to their respective governmental and public policy contexts. By doing so we can detect a crucial source for the divergent organizational courses taken in the two neighborhoods. To begin with Sharrow, the calculations of grassroots activists have been profoundly shaped by their expectations of the British welfare state, which even during the years of the Thatcher government, provided some mix of medical care, housing, and income support for a large portion of Sharrow's population. Moreover, even as the Conservative government of the 1980s began to reduce the scale of government social service provision, Sheffield's local Labour administration sought to retain its version of "local socialism." In these circumstances, the new initiatives and program remedies sought by Sharrow activists inevitably turned on winning governmental support. With regard to the grassroots dilemma of mobilization versus organization, mobilization tended to receive more attention. For Sharrow activists, indigenous organization-building has been secondary to inducing supportive government action.

While the foregoing calculus clearly applies to the work of the Broomhall tenants, the Sharrow traffic campaigners, and the Sharrow

Street residents' group, the SSICCP quite self-consciously set out to build a durable community organization. Nevertheless, John Peaden and his associates in the SSICCP assumed that their group could collaborate with the municipal administration and that, in particular, fundraising was not a crucial element in the forging of a long-lasting organization. By the early 1990s, as central government-generated fiscal pressure worked its way through Sheffield's municipal system, the SSICCP was undermined by this working assumption, but in 1977—or even 1985—it was not an evidently risky course of action. The decline of SSICCP turned on more than its fiscal problems, but in recent years the group's preoccupation with funding, building, and staff matters clearly reduced the energy that it could devote to community work.

Since the early 1970s, the governmental/public policy context within which Uptown groups have operated has been quite different. The U.S. welfare state never delivered the array of benefits typical of northern European industrial democracies, and, more to the point, since the Nixon administration, federal redevelopment and housing policy has given greater and greater sway to private groups. This is revealed by the new forms of downtown redevelopment that have emerged since the mid-1970s; it is also the antecedent of the wide array of affordable housing groups and other grassroots initiatives that have sprung up in low-income neighborhoods across the U.S. Context, to be sure, is not synonymous with organizational efficacy. What groups such as ONE, VOP, and to some degree the Coleman-Shiller movement, were able to do in the 1980s was to move into particular public policy "niches" and by way of aggressive organizing and the careful cultivation of private foundations, business allies, and remnant sources of governmental assistance, develop viable organizational programs and structures.

There is also a paradox revealed by these contrasting stories of neighborhood organizing. While Uptown in the 1980s has been the site of a more sustained proliferation of grassroots activism, this activism has not produced the outcome that many exponents of grassroots-ism place at the heart of their agenda, the revitalization of coherent communities. Indeed, the organizationally ebbing Sharrow of the early 1990s is a far more cohesive community than Uptown, whose thousand points of organizational light have also produced a thousand conflicting perspectives on neighborhood betterment (and decline). Unraveling this paradox is a major objective of the following chapter.

While consideration of the governmental/public policy context helps account for the different approaches to and consequences of organizing in Sharrow and Uptown, at the level of day-to-day organizational affairs there is much complementarity in the two neighborhoods' experiences. Effective leadership is crucial to grassroots success—enough vision to give direction to a group, enough sense of democracy to give the rank and file a stake in a group's success. Effective organizations require a workable financial base, but the quest for financing can divert energy and ultimately undermine broader political objectives. Agenda-setting is crucial, but, like financial security, this is a two-edged sword. A workable organizational agenda—for example, the delivery of low-cost housing units—can be at odds with certain more explicitly political imperatives, such as agitation to reduce the negative effects of upscale housing development. Balancing organizational maintenance demands and broader political goals, as always, is a difficult task for grassroots leaders. Finally, sustaining rank and file participation and morale is a ubiquitous demand, and again, formalizing organizational agendas, programs, and structures may or may not be consistent with the retention of an active membership or constituency.

For community activists, this brief recitation of universal organizing issues will not be surprising. However, there is one implication of this set of organizing concerns that I wish to emphasize. In the contemporary political climate of both the United States and Britain, there is an emerging sentiment that claims that voluntary organizations can take over many of the responsibilities once left to the state. This is a perspective with which I share some sympathy, and indeed, a central purpose of this study is to examine how grassroots action has advanced the fortunes of two urban neighborhoods. Nevertheless, the vagaries of grassroots organizational practice that I have just noted—leadership, resource availability, agenda-setting, and rank and file participation—mean that the quality of voluntary group performance typically will be mixed. In many circumstances this variability is surely an acceptable feature of community and organizational life. However, to the degree that policy-makers, intellectuals, or the public come to think that formerly governmental services—especially those that might be considered essential or fundamental in some way—can be taken over by voluntary groups, there must then be equivalent attention given to how we can insure that nongovernmental bodies deliver their "products" in an acceptably predictable, accessible, even democratic fashion.

NOTES

1. Flora Johnson, "In Order to Save It," *Chicago,* December, 1976, p. 185.

2. Ellis Cose, "These Activists Get High 'on the People'," *Chicago Sun-Times,* July 6, 1975; John Eisendrath, "Slim Coleman: The Poet, the Politician, and the Punk," *The Reader,* December 2, 1983.

3. The former characterization is by Fran Spielman and Basil Talbott, Jr., "Harvard Hillbilly Coleman True to His Dream," *Chicago Sun-Times,* June 14, 1985; the latter is from Cose, "These Activists Get High."

4. David K. Freemon, *Chicago Politics Ward by Ward* (Bloomington: Indiana University Press, 1988), pp. 303-309.

5. Hank De Zutter, "Brother Against Brother: The Bloody Fight over Uptown's Health Clinic," *The Reader,* December 21, 1979.

6. Chicago's nominally nonpartisan city council elections involve one or two steps, a "primary," which may result in selection of the alderperson if one candidate receives more than 50 percent of the votes. If not, a "run-off" election follows, pitting the two largest vote-getters in the primary.

7. Jack Hafferkamp, "Who Owns the Neighborhoods?" *Chicago,* November 1979, p. 199; John McCarron, "Shiller Guards Against Uptown Progress," *Chicago Tribune,* September 1, 1988.

8. Monroe Anderson and Philip Wattley, "Cabrini Protesters Call It a 'Police State',"*Chicago Tribune,* April 14, 1981.

9. Spielman and Talbott, "Harvard Hillbilly Coleman True to His Dream."

10. "The Uptown Gamble," special issue of *The Chicago Reporter,* November 1988, p. 1.

11. Hafferkamp, "Who Owns the Neighborhoods?"; Eisendrath, "Slim Coleman: The Poet, the Politician, and the Punk."

12. John Kass, "Class Struggle Divides Uptown," *Chicago Tribune,* December 27, 1987.

13. Donald L. Benedict, Executive Director of the Community Renewal Society, Letter to the *Chicago Sun-Times,* February 25, 1980.

14. Eisendrath, "Slim Coleman: The Poet, the Politician, the Punk."

15. Hank De Zutter, "Brother Against Brother"; Eisendrath, "Slim Coleman: The Poet, the Politician, the Punk."

16. Florence Hamlish Levinsohn, "How One School in Uptown Has Fared

Under School Reform," *The Reader,* November 8, 1991.

17. Hafferkamp, "Who Owns the Neighborhoods?" p. 195.

18. "Burke Asks Probe of Bloc Protesters," *Chicago Tribune,* June 1, 1985.

19. John McCarron, "Shiller Guards Against Uptown Progress," *Chicago Tribune,* September 1, 1988.

20. Gary Rivlin, "War Is Swell: Fast Eddie Returns, Slim Coleman Makes His Day," *The Reader,* June 21, 1985.

21. The Heart of Uptown Coalition's letter inviting Mayor Byrne to visit Uptown was reprinted in the April 28, 1981, issue of the *All Chicago City News.*

22. Korey Willoughby, "HOUC Fights Displacement, Crime," *Uptown News,* September 15, 1981.

23. Helen Shiller, "Some Basic Facts on Housing Feud," *The Sunday Star,* January 17, 1988.

24. Hafferkamp, "Who Owns the Neighborhoods?," pp. 196-197.

25. Bill Grady, "Uptown Group Charges High-Rise Plot," *Chicago Tribune,* October 9, 1975.

26. Lela Davis, "Uptown, Developer Back in Court," *Chicago Tribune,* August 5, 1982.

27. Joseph Sjostrom and Rudolph Unger, "Uptown Group Sues City, U.S." *Chicago Tribune,* April 9, 1981.

28. James Strong and Manuel Galvan, "Washington Coalition Fails in First Big Test," *Chicago Tribune,* December 10, 1987.

29. John Gorman, "Judge OKs Renters' Suit Settlement," *Chicago Tribune,* December 8, 1988.

30. Doug Cassel, "Q & A: The 46th Ward Alderman Answers Her Critics," *The Reader,* March 29, 1991; Interview with Randall Langer, Uptown real estate developer, October 22, 1992.

31. Patrick Barry and Thom Clark, "New Investment Threatens Old Housing Mix," *The Neighborhood Works,* November-December, 1987, p. 10.

32. "The Battle For Uptown," pamphlet prepared by the All-Uptown Community Rights Assembly and distributed in advance of the September 22, 1992, public hearing on the Broadway/Lawrence area.

33. Helen Shiller, "Developing Without Displacing," *Alderman Shiller's 46th Ward Report,* Summer, 1994, p. 1.

34. Paul Galloway, "The Next Upstarts," *Chicago Tribune,* September 9, 1993.

35. Jack Hafferkamp, "Uptown Revisited," *Chicago,* July, 1980, p. 126.

36. The list of UCC's officers and board members appears in correspondence between Albert N. Votaw, UCC Executive Director and General Richard Smykal, head of the City of Chicago's Community Conservation Board, dated August 30, 1957, Chicago Historical Society (CHS) Uptown Files.

37. *Uptown: A Planning Report,* prepared for the Uptown Chicago Commission by Jack Meltzer Associates, May 1962, preface.

38. "Name Uptown Council for Urban Renewal," *Chicago Tribune,* June 15, 1967.

39. Uptown Chicago Commission, *Annual Report,* 1972, CHS.

40. Don DeBat, "$5 Million Home-Loan Plan for Uptown," *Chicago Daily News,* January 15, 1970; Albert Jedlicka, "Big Mortgage Pool Set up for Uptown," *Chicago Daily News,* July 26, 1974.

41. Jack Hafferkamp, "Uptown Revisited," pp. 142-144; Manuel Galvan, "Uptown Federal Drops Parkview Plan," *Chicago Tribune,* March 1981.

42. *Uptown Action,* October 18, 1973.

43. Thomas M. Gray, "Uptown Unit Rejects More Public Housing, *Chicago Sun-Times,* May 20, 1971; Dolores McCahill and Dennis D. Fisher, "State Policy on Ex-Mental Patients Attacked," *Chicago Sun-Times,* August 8, 1978; Mary Elson, "Neighbors Fight New High-Rise," *Chicago Tribune,* October 15, 1981; Douglas Frantz, "Uptown Storefront Shelter Draws Fire," *Chicago Tribune,* January 28, 1982; Deborah Pennelle, "Activists Differ over Housing Needs," *News Star,* November 1, 1989; Phil Borchman, "It's Tough to Fight City Hall," *News Star,* May 2, 1990; Greg Hinz, "Homeless Shelter in Uptown Draws Fire," *News Star,* January 30, 1991.

44. "Public Housing Issue Heats up in Uptown," *Chicago Tribune,* August 8, 1982.

45. Paulette Bezazian, "Uptown Program to Combat Litter," *Chicago Tribune,* February 10, 1981; Dan Liberty, "Special Security: Fed-up Uptowners Hire Their Own Cops," *The Reader,* September 29, 1989; Interview with Pat Reskey, Executive Director of the Uptown Chicago Commission, November 1 and 16, 1990.

46. *The Common Corridor Building: Problems and Potential,* a redevelopment feasibility study conducted for the City of Chicago Department of Housing by the Uptown Chicago Commission, June 1983; *Uptown Residential Development Survey,* prepared by the Residential Development Organization of Uptown, A Program of the Uptown Chicago Commission, n.d.

47. Reskey Interview; Interview with Al Walavich, former Uptown Chicago Commission President, January 18, 1995.

48. Walavich Interview; Interview with Rob Bagstad, Uptown Chicago Commission Board member and Montrose Harbor Neighbors Association, and Jill Donovan, Montrose Harbor Neighbors Association, July 18, 1992.

49. Walavich Interview.

50. Interview with Bill Clinard, President, Montrose Harbor Neighbors Association, December 3, 1990.

51. Rick Soll, "All Uptown Had to Lose Was Boredom," *Chicago Tribune,* September 7, 1973.

52. Clinard Interview.

53. I first met Bill Clinard in late 1988, before I had begun this research project. My wife and I bought a condominium on Hazel Street in Uptown, and Clinard happened to be the real estate agent representing the seller. At the end of the "property closing" at a downtown financial institution (and after previously—and quite emphatically—having referred to the Hazel Street area as "Buena Park"), Clinard reached across the table to shake our hands, and still smiling, said: "Welcome to the People's Republic of Uptown." Clinard was nominally a Republican, on election days serving as a Republican Party election judge in our polling place. However, some of the MHNA charity events, which Clinard organized, were held in the office of the local Democratic ward committeeperson, Ed Rosewell.

54. Bagstad-Donovan Interview; Interview with Norm and Helene Raidl, Montrose Harbor Neighbors Association, February 4, 1995.

55. Hinz, "Homeless Shelter in Uptown Draws Fire."

56. Bagstad-Donovan Interview. Quigley's interest in Uptown was temporary. A few months after losing the aldermanic election he moved from the neighborhood.

57. Bagstad-Donovan Interview; Raidl Interview.

58. Robert McClory, "Alinsky Lives!" *The Reader,* April 3, 1981.

59. Saul D. Alinsky, *Reveille for Radicals* (New York: Vintage Books, 1969). Sanford D. Horwitt provides a concise discussion of the "people's organization" in *Let Them Call Me Rebel: Saul Alinsky His Life and Legacy* (New York: Vintage Books, 1992), pp. 172-176. Robert A. Slayton provides a lively account of the original people's organization in *Back of the Yards: The Making of a Local Democracy* (Chicago: University of Chicago Press, 1986), pp. 189-223. ONE's structure is discussed in Elizabeth Warren, *Chicago's Uptown* (Chicago: Loyola University Center for Urban Policy, 1979), p. 56.

60. McClory, "Alinsky Lives!"

61. Interview with Josh Hoyt, former Executive Director of the Organization of the NorthEast, July 1, 1995.

62. Warren, *Chicago's Uptown,* pp. 57-62; Bonita Brodt, "Group's Persistence Pays off in North Side Zoning Change, *Chciago Tribune,* October 4, 1979; "ONE 1980 Convention Report," September 1980.

63. Dan La Botz, "Group Claims Uptown Area Not 'Glutted'," *Chicago Defender,* November 11, 1980; "Uptown May Be Next S. Bronx," *Uptown News,* March 3, 1979; Rich Dieter, "Report of the Activities of the Organization of the NorthEast (ONE): July, 1980 to July, 1981," prepared for the Joyce Foundation, n.d., pp. 2-9, ONE Files.

64. McClory, "Alinsky Lives;" "ONE Not Supported by Gov't Funds," Letter from Robert Thrasher to *The Sunday Star,* August 29, 1982.

65. Stevenson Swanson, "Watts Up? Conservation Gets Boost," *Chicago Tribune,* January 22, 1981.

66. Maria Choca and Jean Pogge, "An Assessment of Options for the NorthEast Investment Center," prepared for the Organization of the

NorthEast, February 1990, p. 2.

67. The Organization of the NorthEast Community Ventures Program, "The Andersonville Commercial Area: A Business Census," March 1984; Organization of the North East, "The Future of Uptown/Edgewater; An In-Depth Look at Neighborhood Change," 1986.

68. Ben Joravsky, "A Strip Mall in Edgewater: Class Warfare, or Small-Time Tiff?" *The Reader,* January 15, 1988.

69. Arsenio Oloroso, "ONE Burned Out," *The Sunday Star,* September 21, 1986.

70. Ben Joravsky, "Community Regroup: ONE's Back in Business," *The Reader,* June 28, 1991; Hoyt Interview.

71. Hoyt Interview.

72. *Saving Our Homes: The Lessons of Community Struggles to Preserve Affordable Housing in Chicago's Housing,* prepared by researchers at Loyola University of Chicago and the Organization of the NorthEast, April 1996, pp. 1-9; Ben Joravsky, "Low-Income Housing: A Big Deal in Uptown," *The Reader,* December 8, 1989; R. Allen Hays, *The Federal Government and Urban Housing* (Albany: State University of New York Press, 1995), pp. 248-249.

73. Berry and Clark, "New Investment Threatens Old Housing Mix"; Patricia Lynn Stern, "Community Organizations and Response to Urban Crisis: Displacement in Uptown, Chicago," Radcliffe College B.A. Thesis, March 1989, pp. 56-60, 92-120.

74. *Saving Our Homes;* Interview with Denice Irwin, President of the 920 Lakeside Tenants Organization, June 24, 1991.

75. *Saving Our Homes,* pp. 18-19; Chinta Strausberg, "HUD's Kemp to Save $5.4 Million for Housing," *Chicago Defender,* October 16, 1990.

76. *Saving Our Homes.*

77. Linda Hogan, *We Can Do It: A Guide to Co-operative Building Management* (Chicago: Voice of the People, 1987), p. 7.

78. Hogan, *We Can Do It,* pp. 7-8; Hank De Zutter, "The House That the People Built: An Uptown Success Story," *The Reader,* December 12, 1980.

79. Douglas C. Dobmeyer, Letter to the Friends of the Voice, October 19, 1984; Joe Bute, Memo to Marilyn Katz, January 9, 1985; Douglas C. Dobmeyer, Letter to Joe Bute, March 5, 1985, ONE Files.

80. Hogan, *We Can Do It,* p. 8.

81. Stern, "Community Organizations and the Response to Urban Crisis," p. 56; Interview with Tom Lenz, former Executive Director of Voice of the People, November 14, 1991; Interview with Mike Loftin, former Voice of the People staff, April 13, 1992.

82. Loftin Interview.

83. Loftin Interview.

84. Jill Rehkoff Smith, "A Drop in the Bucket, but Sweet," *Uptown News,* February 21-22, 1989; Graham Witherall, "Dems Join Rally for Decent Housing," *News Star,* November 8, 1989.

85. Phil Borchmann, "Long-Awaited Rehab to Begin," *News Star,* September 18, 1991.

86. Stern, "Community Organizations and the Response to Urban Crisis," pp. 101-103; Interview with Janet Hasz, Voice of the People Resource Developer, April 15, 1991.

87. Hasz Interview.

88. "Voice Breaks Ground for New Housing—and New Era," *The Voice,* Fall 1993, pp. 1-2.

89. Ben Joravsky, "Kinder and Gentler in Uptown: Will HUD Kibosh a Promising Private-Public Housing Deal?" *The Reader,* May 12, 1989; John McCarron, "Texans, Not Tenants, Get HUD High-Rise," *Chicago Tribune,* September 1, 1989; Irwin Interview.

90. "Uptown Group Buys HUD Prepayment Building," *The Network Builder,* Fall 1992, pp. 14-15.

91. *Saving Our Homes,* pp. 22-26.

92. Tom McNamee, "Shiller & Poor vs. Yuppies in Uptown," *Chicago Sun-Times,* November 15, 1987; John Kass, "Class Struggle Divides Uptown," *Chicago Tribune,* December 27, 1987.

93. Clinard Interview.

94. R. Bruce Dold, "Look Who's on the Inside," *Chicago Enterprise,* May-June, 1993, p. 7.

CHAPTER SEVEN

NEIGHBORHOOD IDENTITY, NEIGHBORHOOD CHANGE, AND GRASSROOTS ACTION

The quarter century from the late 1960s to the early 1990s witnessed an enormous variety of developments in Uptown and Sharrow: the high-water mark and ebbing of municipally sponsored redevelopment, the rise and evolution of an array of grassroots initiatives, neighborhood change set in motion by factors working well beyond the confines of these two neighborhoods. In the two remaining chapters I turn, first, to a comparison of the Uptown and Sharrow experiences with reference to the related matters of neighborhood stability and change, devoting particular attention in the latter portion of this chapter to the complex relationship between varieties of grassroots action and neighborhood identity. In Chapter 8, I explore what Uptown and Sharrow tell us about the broader politics and urban conditions of the United States and Britain.

II

Even as we approach the end of the century, the scholarly examination and popular understanding of urban neighborhoods remains shadowed by the perspectives and terminology refined by the early twentieth-century human ecologists. For many big-city residents, the notion of neighborhood "invasion and succession" continues to be a plausible script for comprehending the processes producing widespread neighborhood decline as well as the occasional counter-example of neighborhood rejuvenation. At the metropolitan level—especially in North America and Britain—as urban regions expand, one continues to observe more affluent groups taking up residence in increasingly distant suburban communities. Surrounding downtown cores, "zones of transi-

tion" also press outward, and in or adjoining these areas a disproportionate share of metropolitan areas' poor and ethnic minority populations tend to reside.[1] Thus, overlapping the details of neighborhood
invasion and succession is the seemingly inexorable outward march of
the metropolis—led by those fittest to occupy the urban periphery,
trailed by those most recently arrived or least equipped to escape the
inner city.

The general plausibility of the ecological scenario, notwithstanding, in the last generation a variety of researchers, commentators, and
activists have contended that the ecological perspective disguises as
much as it reveals about underlying urban relationships. Among social
scientists, an army of researchers bearing the flag of the "new urban sociology" contend that the practices of economic and political institutions,
far more than organic urban processes, account for the fortunes of
neighborhoods, cities, and regions.[2] Although the question of "human
agency"—the degree to which individuals and groups can act upon and
change their physical and social circumstances—is a troubling consideration for both ecologists and exponents of the new urban sociology, for
community activists it is an article of faith that neighborhoods are not
simply the captives of immutable forces, whether such forces are understood as inherent features of dynamic metropolitan systems or globally
penetrating institutional practices. For members of groups such as
SSICCP, the Sharrow Traffic Campaign, the Coleman-Shiller movement, and VOP, acting locally does matter.

The study of gentrification can be linked in a variety of ways to
these contending views of fundamental urban processes. In the first
instance, the "upgrading" associated with gentrification—at least in the
early to mid-1970s—appeared to be a major exception to the presumed
dynamics of neighborhood invasion and succession, which specify that
more advantaged urbanites retreat in the face of less respectable groups.
At that time some urbanologists proposed that a "back to the city movement" was beginning to restore formerly downtrodden big city neighborhoods.[3] In fact, within a few years most observers of gentrification
rejected this scenario, which constituted something of an "amendment"
to the invasion/succession model. Not only were there too few suburban

émigrés to anchor a "back to the city" explanation of neighborhood reju-venation, but "agency" also reared its head to complicate the situation. If hundreds of thousands of suburban families were rediscovering the virtues of inner city living, this would certainly constitute a form of meaningful human agency. But if gentrification was typically centered on neighborhoods targeted by public policy—either as an outgrowth of emerging downtown redevelopment strategies or (in the United States) as an after-effect of the older urban renewal program—that would be another form of agency altogether. Urban renewal, in its own right, sought to forestall ecological trends via the agency of public policy, but many critics of urban renewal noted that it was a policy which—con-trary to its sponsors' claims—had secured the city for downtown busi-ness interests and more affluent residents through the expedient of removing racial and ethnic minority populations. If gentrification was itself the consequence of public policies such as land transfers or tax abatements directed to private developers, would its consequences be any more equitable? In short, observation of gentrification became a ground for testing alternative views of neighborhood change, again with the ecological and new urban sociology perspectives roughly defining the opposing camps, but with the assessment also turning on the nor-mative consideration of who gains and who loses as neighborhoods upgrade.[4] Finally, because gentrification pressures did produce an array of grassroots responses in both North American and European cities, the study of grassroots mobilization in gentrifying areas has offered the opportunity to measure the capacity of local organizations to advance neighborhood-based interests.

My original thinking in comparing Uptown and Sharrow had sprung from these considerations, specifically the opportunity offered by their contrasting cultural and public policy environments to explore alternative responses to upgrading as well as the agenda-setting and subsequent action of grassroots groups reacting to gentrification. In 1990 I had begun my research in Uptown, and in 1991, when I first vis-ited Sheffield, I sought a neighborhood sharing the general features that seemed to stamp Uptown's identity: a history of grassroots mobilization, a multi-ethnic population, some degree of ongoing gentrification.

Ultimately, having identified Sharrow as my "double" for Uptown, I concluded that although there is a trickle of gentrification occurring in the former, it has been insufficient to produce either significant neighborhood conflict or concerted grassroots organizing directed either in behalf or in opposition to such upgrading. However, by considering why gentrification has not appeared in Sharrow, I believe that certain features of Uptown's seemingly permanent state of conflict can be understood, with, of course, gentrification's special contribution to this disharmony highlighted. Thus, before turning our attention to Uptown, we ought to underline two aspects of Sharrow's situation.

Unlike Chicago, Sheffield is an industrial city whose economy has not managed the "turn" necessary to generate large numbers of jobs in corporate management, business services, communications, or travel/tourism. As the city's fabricators of steel, heavy equipment, and cutlery have declined, so have their management and service requirements. Sheffield's city centre retailers have also suffered from inter-metropolitan and suburban competition. As a result, the city's base of affluent business and professional people has not yielded a growing market for the kinds of evocative, conveniently located residential neighborhoods that have been the staple of gentrification elsewhere in Europe and North America. Furthermore, Sheffield's tight physical layout and the Sheffield Authority's decision in the 1930s to establish a greenbelt around the built-up portions of the city, have also tended to undercut gentrification pressures in neighborhoods such as Sharrow. For downtown-based businesspersons and professionals there are several older, hospitable residential areas on the city's fringes which, to this day, remain within 15 to 20 minutes' drive of Sheffield city centre. Such areas have further siphoned potential gentrifiers from Sharrow.

Uptown's, and more broadly, Chicago's contemporary circumstances are quite different. In its heyday as an industrial center Chicago's economy also sustained major banking and retailing sectors. Since the turn of the century the city has been an important center for entertainment, tourism, and conventions. In the half century following World War II as Chicago's industrial economy has decentralized, relocated beyond the metropolitan periphery, or declined due to external competition, the city

has, nonetheless, retained a substantial, downtown-centered office economy. Although speculative office development by the late 1980s had produced an oversupply of office space and plummeting commercial rents in
Chicago, as recently as the mid-1980s analysts of the downtown economy hailed the emergence of a new "Super Loop" reaching beyond the
bounds of the traditional downtown core.[5] Thus, in sharp contrast to
Sheffield, for the last quarter century Chicago's "post-industrial" economy has generated a plentiful supply of relatively young and well-paid
entrepreneurs, middle-level managers, and professionals, many of them
wishing to live in proximity to the metropolitan core.

Since the 1960s, and in tight synchronization with the emergence
of its post-industrial economy, Chicago has witnessed substantial residential gentrification, with the main line of investment following the
belt of neighborhoods running north from the Loop along Lake
Michigan. In the 1960s the Old Town section of the Lincoln Park
neighborhood was the leading edge of gentrification. Within a decade
much of the larger Lincoln Park area was "won" for the middle class.[6]
Subsequently, Lakeview—just north of Lincoln Park and with Uptown
on its northern margin—experienced widespread residential upgrading.

As I have noted in portions of Chapters 2 and 6, tempers spurred
by Uptown's urban renewal war had hardly cooled before signs of gentrification began to appear—the occasional homeowner-initiated rehab
project, the assemblage of properties by local business interests such as
Uptown Federal Savings & Loan Association and the Bank of Chicago,
articles in the daily press highlighting the architectural charms and
investment prospects offered by Uptown. For investors and developers,
Uptown's charms have indeed been numerous. Following years of urban
renewal-derived clearance and the subsequent loss of numerous buildings to fire, the neighborhood offered many vacant sites for development, and at least until the 1980s, comparatively modest real estate
prices. Though five to six miles from the Loop, Uptown straddles the
Chicago Transit Authority's main North-South elevated rail line, which
gives access to the downtown in about one-half hour. In a Lake
Michigan-conscious city, the neighborhood's access to the lake and
lakefront parks is the equal of any in the city. Finally, until Uptown's

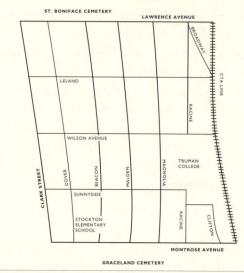

Map 7–1 • *Heart of Uptown/Sheridan Park*

grassroots mobilization was well underway in the 1980s, the neighborhood's high residential turnover and paucity of homeowners promised
to give developers a relatively free hand in acquiring property and
designing and marketing projects.

By examining the disputed Heart of Uptown/Sheridan Park area
(Map 7-1), particularly its changing fortunes in the mid- to late-
1980s, we can derive a fairly characteristic snapshot of gentrification
pressures and conflict in Uptown. Heart of Uptown/Sheridan Park
adjoins Broadway on the east, Clark Street on the west, with the
Graceland and St. Boniface cemeteries on the south and north,
respectively. In its southeast corner is Truman College, whose siting
was a central element of Uptown's urban renewal controversy.
Following the approval of the Truman College site, dozens of buildings in the surrounding area went up in flames. In 1986, developer
Randall Langer's disputed eviction of Cambodian and Laotian tenants
was from an apartment building on Beacon Street, once again in
Heart of Uptown/Sheridan Park. Yet amid this physical and social
upheaval, the area's two westernmost streets, Beacon and Dover, have
retained an impressive collection of stately houses, and scattered elsewhere among Heart of Uptown/Sheridan Park's vacant lots and aban-

doned buildings are solid single family homes, six-flats, and larger apartment complexes.

Tables 7-1 and 7-2 report investment and housing transaction trends in Uptown from the late 1970s through the late 1980s. The late 1970s and early 1980s represented a period of substantial real estate activity, which was followed by a lull from 1982 to 1985. As a rule, residential upgrading was occurring on the eastern edge of the neighborhood, and in fact, much of the investment activity at the turn of the decade was attributable to apartment/condominium conversions in lakefront Uptown. In 1984, state and federal authorities, responding to a neighborhood petition, designated the Buena Park area a historic district, this status entitling local homeowners to property tax reductions and landlords to tax credits on a portion of building rehabilitation expenditures. The historic district designation also aided marketing efforts by local realtors, and, if new developments were proposed, required that these be reviewed by the state historic preservation agency.

Table 7-1
UPTOWN, TOTAL PRIVATE
INVESTMENT ($1,000s)

1978	11,945
1979	23,968
1980	16,698
1981	24,512
1982	6,485
1983	4,076
1984	5,240
1985	6,651
1986	10,586
1987	11,955

Source: James L. Greer and Lawrence B. Joseph, *"Public & Private Investment in Chicago: A Report of the Neighborhood Information System Project,"* May 1989, Table 4-A

The Buena Park area adjoins lakefront Uptown, but within months of its receiving historic district status, the Sheridan Park Improvement Association—well to the west of previous upgrading areas—began to work on its own historic district petition. Heart of Uptown/Sheridan

Park homeowner Martin Tangora handled the research on local build-ings; politically connected attorney Philip Krone served as government liaison; and developer Randall Langer raised funds for the effort.[7] Langer was, at that time, acquiring buildings in Heart of Uptown/Sheridan Park, and it is quite likely that he, as well as other developers investing in local properties, viewed the historic district des-ignation as a means of glamorizing an area not heretofore associated with urbane sophistication. By the end of the decade Langer had pur-chased buildings holding approximately 500 units of housing, most of which he had renovated for upscale rental.[8] Beyond their preservation-ist concerns with some of Heart of Uptown/Sheridan Park's more dis-tinctive structures, proponents of the historic district also contended that resulting tax benefits would ease fiscal pressures on local property owners, which in turn, would halt the area's persistent loss of housing. Nevertheless, at the state hearing on the Sheridan Park Improvement Association's petition, representatives of the Coleman-Shiller move-ment, VOP, and three other local organizations spoke in opposition. However, even one critic of the historic district characterized the pro-posal as "very well written" and representing "outstanding" scholarship.[9] The Illinois Historic Sites Advisory Council unanimously approved the Sheridan Park Historic District on September 29, 1985. At the end of the year the district also won national landmark status.

Although its sponsors disavowed any intention to employ the his-toric district designation as a lever to push up local property values, the real estate sections of Chicago's daily newspapers assumed just such a causal connection. An article examining the Sheridan Park Historic District conflict was entitled "Uptown Uplift." A few years later, long-time *Chicago Sun-Times* real estate analyst Don DeBat titled an article on the Heart of Uptown/Sheridan Park area "Historic Rehabs Revive Sheridan Park."[10] Randall Langer quickly included references to the historic district in his promotional materials.[11] And—as Table 7-3 quite dramatically demonstrates—right on the heels of the approval of the Sheridan Park Historic District, local investment exploded. In the next few years Heart of Uptown/Sheridan Park was dotted with building renovations and apartment/condominium conversions. Brochures for

Table 7-2
UPTOWN RESIDENTIAL REAL ESTATE
TRANSACTIONS 1979-88

| | SINGLE FAMILY DWELLINGS | | 2-6 UNIT BUILDINGS | | CONDOMINIUMS | |
	No.	Median Price ($1000s)	No.	Median Price ($1000s)	No.	Median Price ($1000s)
1979	27	56.0	64	64.5	127	58.0
1980	26	64.5	28	57.5	73	60.0
1981	11	47.0	19	72.5	52	60.0
1982	5	63.5	14	69.6	54	58.5
1983	20	63.5	26	73.5	167	56.9
1984	24	69.5	25	83.0	167	56.0
1985	26	69.0	41	84.5	178	49.6
1986	45	99.9	56	95.0	246	56.1
1987	29	79.4	69	113.7	295	67.5
1988	31	88.0	54	144.0	281	63.0

Source: Neighborhood Information System Project, University of Chicago Center for Urban Research and Policy Studies

"The Dover" six-flat noted that this condominium conversion was "in historic Sheridan Park." Two blocks away, the real estate firm marketing "The Evelyn" characterized their property as "the cornerstone of the Sheridan Park historic district."

Table 7-3
VOLUME OF PRIVATE LENDING IN
HEART OF UPTOWN/SHERIDAN PARK
(CENSUS TRACT 0317)

	No. of Loans	($1000s)
1984	18	1,176
1985	13	920
1986	24	8,076
1987	25	4,158
1988	36	5,654

Source: Woodstock Institute Community Lending Factbooks, 1984-88

The historic districting effort in Heart of Uptown/Sheridan Park illustrates the essential features of a calculated campaign to pump up a local residential real estate market. As the prospects for lakefront Uptown upgrading narrowed, real estate developers—led in this instance by Randall Langer—sought new territory for focused investment. Though away from the traditionally "hot" lakefront real estate market, due to its less evidently desirable location and its peculiar post-urban renewal history, Heart of Uptown/Sheridan Park offered inexpensive properties. From an investor's perspective, a further attraction is its well-demarcated physical dimensions (a major commercial street on the west, the North-South CTA line and Truman College campus on the east, cemeteries flanking the northern and southern margins). With a nucleus of longstanding homeowners and some recent rehabbers already based in Heart of Uptown/Sheridan Park, a homeowners organization could be mobilized in short order. The campaign to win the historic district designation served to coalesce the membership of the Sheridan Park Improvement Association, while the designation, itself, forged a new neighborhood identity and offered financial incentives for investors. Once the historic district was approved, it was a matter of effectively marketing the neighborhood, with the aim—just as surely—of attracting a critical mass of new, middle-class residents whose presence would insure continued real estate activity, as of reaping immediate profits through escalating rents and property sales.

It was through a chance discussion with a Heart of Uptown/Sheridan Park rehabber that I encountered the most cogent explanation of a puzzling term I had heard a number of times in conversation and at public meetings. This was "regentrification." In the course of my conversation with this Heart of Uptown/Sheridan Park homeowner, I wondered what he thought of the division of opinion over what to call the neighborhood. Sheridan Park, not surprisingly, is the term preferred by many homeowners and most recent middle-class arrivals in the area. Heart of Uptown is an older name, often chosen by renters and individuals with recollections of the urban renewal era. My partner in conversation replied with an account of a visit to his house by descendants of its original owner. This family was driving through the neighborhood and spotted the old house. Evidently, they had

The elegant front...

...*and fortified rear of a 6-flat condominium renovation in Heart of Uptown/ Sheridan Park*

been looking for it, possibly anticipating that it would no longer be standing. When they came to his front door, the visitors engaged the current owner in discussion and produced an old postcard bearing a photograph of his (and their old family) house. What particularly struck the present owner, he informed me, was the script at the corner of the card, which indicated that the house was located in the Sheridan Park area of Chicago. The

current owner—who is engaged in extensive renovations of the old property—then explained that this card illustrated to him that he, along with
other new residents of the area, was "bringing back" Sheridan Park to its
former glory. As such, he was a "regentrifier" rather than a "gentrifier."

One of the truisms of neighborhood life is that the residential
area that can maintain a reasonably high degree of stability—institutional as well as population stability—is more likely to forge the kinds
of communal ties that in turn produce a secure and pervasive sense of
community. In such neighborhoods all can feel welcome and, being
welcome, will make contributions to the collective life of the community. Uptown and Sharrow clearly part on this matter. Sharrow,
though divided by race and ethnicity, has through its network of residents organizations, church- and ethnic-based groups, and due to the
longstanding efforts of the SSICCP, managed to carve out a generally
recognized identity and sustain a high degree of communal good will.
Uptown, quite evidently, has not. In part this is due to the latter community's polarization over an array of public policy concerns—among
them, gentrification/affordable housing conflicts, standards of public
order, the philosophical grounding of local public figures, notably
Alderperson Shiller. Further, the very heterogeneity of Uptown's
grassroots mobilizing, and the neighborhood's history of inter-organi-
zational conflict, tend to reduce the willingness of groups to cooperate with one another. In Uptown it is not at all uncommon for
organizations which, in the present, agree on a particular issue, to
nonetheless refuse to collaborate due to mistrust bred of past conflict.
However, beyond this surely significant point of contrast—Sharrow's
more successful efforts at building inclusive groups such as SAG and
SSICCP, Uptown's history of multiple, conflictual organizational
development—I will also elaborate what seems to me to be a more
fundamental, though less evident, source of their contrasting experiences of communalism and conflict.

As a site for building community organizations, Sharrow has one
clear advantage over Uptown. With its overwhelmingly working-class
population, Sharrow offers the activist/organizer a crucial unifying
"device" that may be employed to counterbalance cleavages growing out

of race/ethnicity or housing tenure (that is, renters versus owners). Social class homogeneity, as such, is not an automatic "trump" to neighborhood conflict, but certainly in the case of Sharrow, movements such as SAG, the Broomhall Tenants Association, and SSICCP have managed, by and large, to avoid the divisiveness that can grow from conflicting racial/ethnic perspectives or property interests. Indeed, the most striking contrast in the experiences of Sharrow and Uptown with municipally sponsored redevelopment was the absence of internal conflict in the Sheffield neighborhood.

Sharrow's working-class character is, further, an important component of its neighborhood identity, a matter not just of internal significance. In my search for gentrifiers and the gentrification issue, I made an effort to contact residents of the Broomhall Park area at Sharrow's southwestern edge, easily the most desirable residential portion of the ward, as well as Nether Edge up the hill from Sharrow. Nether Edge, historically, has sustained an identity quite separate from Sharrow's, but at particular points in time, such as the 1970s Sharrow-Nether Edge planning process, the two neighborhoods' fortunes have been linked. In addition to seeking accounts of gentrification-related conflict, in my interviews with these Sharrow "neighbors," I wished to ascertain whether they might articulate the kind of neighborhood-in-transition dread so common among Uptown homeowners. I was unable to induce any such comments but rather, as demonstrated by Philip Hulley of the Nether Edge Neighbourhood Group, found that residents of these more affluent areas experienced little if any stress due to their proximity to Sharrow:

> I am very conscious of a gradation in the housing, but
> I don't think that people here feel threatened. It's a
> matter of what people can afford. You do see people
> move up the hill as their finances permit it, but
> Sharrow is not in a threatening spiral.[12]

Hulley added that residents of Nether Edge recognize that they, themselves, live in the "inner city...otherwise they wouldn't stay here." A final feature that helps to explain Hulley's sense of security:

as was the case with my other Nether Edge and Broomhall Park informants, he had never received a direct contact from a real estate firm inquiring about his interest in putting his house on the market. In respect to social class identity, Sharrow is not merely an internally well-defined area. It is a neighborhood set in a larger matrix of neighborhoods whose social class character has tended to be relatively fixed. This is a local urban attribute of Britain's highly structured system of social classes, whose broader features may in many respects not be especially desirable, but which in this instance does seem to give more stability and cohesion to the day-to-day practice of neighborhood life.

Conversely, Uptown is a neighborhood in perpetual flux. At one time the residence of some very prominent Chicagoans as well as large numbers of younger office workers and thrill-seekers, the area's "aristocracy" left in the 1950s to be replaced by a variety of less prosperous groups. In the last decade a new generation of developers and property-buyers have sought, in some cases quite self-consciously, to "regentrify" Uptown. Some of Uptown's newcomers have no plans to remain in the neighborhood for more than a few years. For them, a critical consideration in observing local conditions is their property's resale value, for they are moving up the social class hierarchy, in part, through successful property exchanges and movement to increasingly more desirable residential communities.[13] Other property owners may have a long-term commitment to the neighborhood, but like preceding gentrifiers in Lincoln Park and Lakeview, they do wish to forge the community on their terms, to make it safe for the middle-class. These are not unusual aspirations, nor are they out of line with the realities of class and community mobility in the United States. However, in the context of Uptown—housing a large low-income population, having spawned many grassroots initiatives aimed at improving the community for less affluent people—Uptown's double identity—as internally, a mixed community, as externally, a ground for property speculation and individual social class advancement—creates just the environment in which one might anticipate intense community conflict.

III

There is a mythic neighborhood organizing scenario that runs as follows. A downtrodden neighborhood's residents begin to coalesce in an effort to improve their deprived material and social circumstances. Their vehicle for neighborhood uplift is a community organization, whose campaigns mobilize local residents and deliver useful goods (such as low-cost housing) and services (such as youth programming), each of these operations contributing to improvements in the quality of local life. At some point the neighborhood passes a threshold at which both resident self-confidence and material conditions have improved to the degree that the area can no longer be characterized as deprived. The community organization that has leveraged these gains, in all likelihood, continues to serve the local area, but now it operates more like a neighborhood "council," though remaining primed for more aggressive action if such is once again required.[14]

Neither Sharrow's nor Uptown's neighborhood history conforms to this scenario. In Sharrow, SAG in the early 1970s and SSICCP after the late 1970s did serve as anchors for neighborhood mobilization, conduits for negotiation with the Sheffield Authority, and at times, vehicles for service delivery. As such, these organizations and the more transitory groups and campaigns that spun off from them did manage to forge a durable sense of community in Sharrow. Unfortunately, the community-building achievements of Sharrow's local organizations were not matched by improvements in local material conditions. As the consequences of industrial decline penetrated Sheffield's neighborhood structure, Sharrow, like most of the city's working-class districts, suffered. Moreover, as the municipal government's fiscal conditions tightened in the late 1980s, it withdrew resources from SSICCP, thus destabilizing the neighborhood's principal community organization.

In Uptown, the urban renewal controversy of the late 1960s and early 1970s divided the neighborhood into warring camps and produced an array of new community organizations. Through the 1970s, as the neighborhood's demographic structure fragmented, so too did Uptown's organizational structure. A number of Uptown's grassroots groups have achieved notable success: the Coleman-Shiller movement as an electoral organization and city-wide advocate of populist causes, ONE as an assembly of various neighborhood, ethnic, and social service organizations, VOP—and more recently Lakefront SRO—as nonprofit housing developers. Nevertheless, Uptown remains a neighborhood divided by sharp cleavages, whose population includes a large proportion of individuals in dire social and material distress. On more than one occasion the neighborhood's proliferation of grassroots groups has seemed to aggravate rather than reduce its social divisions.

In the previous section of this chapter I examined how Uptown's and Sharrow's senses of identity and experiences of neighborhood change have been shaped by larger forces such as their city's evolving economic structures, the practices of real estate interests, and residents' sense of social class in relation to place of residence. The following pages approach neighborhood identity and change from, if you will, the opposite direction, by considering how community organizations have defined their neighborhood constituencies and how their approaches to organizing have, in turn, influenced broader perceptions of their respective neighborhoods.

Over the course of the twentieth century there have been two general frameworks for interpreting urban neighborhoods, the first which I term the "site" perspective, the latter, the "system" view.[15] The neighborhood "site" is an arrangement of buildings, streets, and open spaces whose physical character is the principal shaper of local social conditions. In the environmental determinism that typifies site perspectives of neighborhood well-being or ill-health, community uplift can be achieved through physical improvements. This, of course, was just what the proponents of urban renewal in the United States and the implementers of the Sheffield Authority's slum clearance program sought to accomplish. As Robert Beauregard has noted, in examining how urban experts sought to rehabilitate American cities on the eve of World War II:

> ...urban decline thus was centered on specific areas
> within cities—residential and business areas where

speculation, overcrowding, disinvestment, and physical deterioration were common—only later to become more encompassing. For many commentators, the specified causes were rooted in aberrations—a depression and a world war—and were likely to disappear as normalcy returned. Although city governments were burdened by slums and blight, and experiencing fiscal difficulties, these problems were also isolated within the city.[16]

In short, once the physical deterioration of a limited number of well-defined locations was rectified, the city's travail would be at an end. However, as urban rebuilding proceeded in the aftermath of World War II, a chorus of observers in North America, Britain, and elsewhere pointed out that site-grounded approaches to neighborhood rehabilitation were not sufficient to rebuild communities. As the British sociologists Michael Young and Peter Willmott observed in the mid-1950s: "Yet even when the town planners have set themselves to create communities anew as well as houses, they have still put their faith in buildings, sometimes speaking as though all that was necessary for neighbourliness was a neighbourhood unit, for community spirit a community centre."[17]

In a sense, the "system" view of neighborhoods may be considered a response to the site perspective's reductionism, though the core of the system perspective has a long history that reaches beyond the domain of social science analysis. Undoubtedly, the system perspective's most articulate proponents have been sociologists such as Herbert Gans, Gerald Suttles, and in collaboration, Michael Young and Peter Willmott, who in examining the attitudes and behavioral codes of inner city residents have found well-understood patterns of family life, non-familial interpersonal relations, and public decorum.[18] The system view's main features may be gleaned from Suttles' summary of social relations in the Addams area of Chicago's Near West Side:

> Neither disorganization nor value rejection are apt terms to describe the Addams area. Certainly the

social practices of the residents are not just an inver-
sion of those of the wider society, and the inhabitants
would be outraged to hear as much. Also, the neighborhood is not a cultural island with its own distinct
and imported traditions. The major lineaments of the
area's internal structure are such commonplace distinctions as age, sex, territoriality, ethnicity, and personal identity.[19]

In this passage Suttles responds to two alternative ways of interpreting Addams: the work of pre-World War II human ecologists who
might find in Addams' multi-ethnic complexity the "disorganization"
growing from immigrants' untutored immersion in the metropolis;
urban renewers who would presume, by surveying Addams' physical
conditions, that it is a neighborhood locked in terminal decline.[20]

The system view of neighborhoods is a central, if implicit feature of
the community organizing philosophy pioneered by Saul Alinsky.
Alinsky understood the sources of neighborhood decline to rest outside
individual communities, and in order for the professional organizer to
build the "people's organization" that could recharge community fortunes, it was necessary for the organizer to penetrate and develop a thorough comprehension of the neighborhood's internal order. There is the
implication in Alinsky's organizing practice that some neighborhoods
may be beyond mobilization and resurrection, but as a general rule, such
was not the case.[21] Here is Alinsky exhorting the organizer to "locate"
and comprehend the internal structures of the neighborhood:

The foundation of a People's Organization is in the
communal life of the local people. Therefore the first
stage in building a people's organization is the
understanding of the life of the community, not only
in terms of the individual's experiences, habits, values, and objectives, but also from the point of view
of the collective habits, experiences, customs, controls, and values of the whole group—the community traditions. [22]

In effect, Alinsky is instructing the organizer to put the neighborhood system to use as a vehicle for political empowerment.

Elements of the site and system views of neighborhood can be identified in the initiatives of various activists, organizers, and policy-makers who have attempted to influence the course of events in both Sharrow and Uptown. In Sharrow as early as 1972, SAG's *Views of Sharrow* report indicted the Sheffield municipal government for dis-rupting "long standing community life and ties."[23] SAG's successor organization, SSICCP, quite self-consciously pursued the agenda of reinforcing Sharrow's neighborhood system. Local residents and orga-nizations would employ SSICCP as a resource in advancing their indigenously orchestrated campaigns; authority workers affiliated with SSICCP would tailor municipal services to the particular needs of the Sharrow community.

Although in Slim Coleman's case the assertion of a threatened community is framed by a class conflict model of social relations, the system view of neighborhood has also animated much of the grassroots activity in Uptown. When Coleman observes that in gentrifying Uptown the newly arrived Standard Oil executive will object to his next-door neighbor, the disabled coal miner (page 166), he is under-scoring how the friendship and institutional networks that serve the miner are likely to be attenuated in a refurbished Uptown. ONE's Alinskyite structure quite explicitly adopts the system perspective by way of the group's building a neighborhood-wide coalition on the shoulders of existing block clubs, congregations, ethnic mutual aid asso-ciations, social service agencies, and businesses. VOP's Uptown is com-prised of a low-income renting population which, nonetheless, has a sufficient commitment to the community to wish to participate in the upkeep of residential properties.

Where this paralleling of Sharrow and Uptown approaches to neighborhood breaks down is in the anticipated response of municipal government to grassroots action. John Peaden and his fellow activists in Sharrow have operated as if they needed to remind Sheffield councillors and administrators of the character of their neighborhood. Ultimately, in seeking to secure Sharrow for its working-class population, local activists have presumed that once their case was presented, they would receive a fair hearing, and beyond that, a fair distribution of municipal resources. In contrast to Sharrow, it is correct to note that Slim Coleman, Helen Shiller, Josh Hoyt, and various VOP activists have sought to secure Uptown for a somewhat wider slice of the social class spectrum, the working class and the poor, but what has more dramatically distinguished their agenda from their peers in Sharrow is their presumption of municipal indifference, or worse, hostility. Thus, in Uptown the system perspective of comprehending the neighborhood has been linked to a more aggressively localist programmatic agenda: housing development via non-profit groups, Local School Council-initiated curricular reforms, and indigenous social service provision.

As I have already noted, the site understanding of neighborhood anchored the agenda of urban renewal in Uptown, and indeed, throughout the United States, and this perspective also governed the thinking of the Sheffield officials who implemented the city's 1960s-era housing demolition schedule. In each instance, municipally sponsored redevelopment would clear out decayed portions of the city, which—when rebuilt—would reassume a useful purpose within the larger structure of the metropolis. Uptown's contemporary gentrifiers also tend to observe a site when they view the neighborhood. The neighborhood's virtues are mainly physical in nature: the accessibility of Lake Michigan and its adjoining parks, mass transit access to the Loop, the aesthetic quality of local buildings—one of my interviewees commenting: "I think the architecture is better than in Lincoln Park."[24]

In their appreciation of Uptown's physical features, gentrifiers tend not to dwell on the possibility of social costs or conflict—a reduction in the number of inexpensive apartments, the displacement of renters, the disruption of established neighborhood networks—that might accompany the upgrading of the area. In some cases this unwillingness to link changes in the physical environment with alteration of the social neighborhood is quite hard-edged, to the effect that people who are pushed elsewhere ought not to be of anyone's concern. Sometimes more affluent Uptowners assure themselves that by having moved into a building that was previously abandoned, they have not directly displaced anyone. At a local community policing meeting, which brings together residents and representatives of the Chicago Police Department—and for this particular police "beat" has been a forum dominated by vociferously pro-gentrification voices—one of the residents caused considerable discomfort when she uttered, as if struck by this insight for the very first time: "Could it be that all we're doing is pushing these criminals into the next neighborhood?" One of the police officers broke the resulting silence by asserting that their efforts would be so successful as to move the criminals "all the way up to Evanston" (the suburban town adjoining Chicago's northern boundary). No one addressed whether or not pushing the criminals up to Evanston was but a slightly more ambitious way to disassociate physical upgrading from its social consequences.

When set beside the site perspective, the system interpretation of neighborhood, as a rule, seems to offer a more nuanced interpretation of local processes. In the latter's account of neighborhood affairs, the efficacy and stability of local organizations, the quality of public order and interpersonal relations, even Alinsky's "community traditions" are the measure of local vitality. Yet in a dynamic neighborhood context such as Uptown's, the effort to define an essential set of attitudes, networks, and behavior can lead to its own form of community reductionism. For example, the Coleman-Shiller movement's interpretation of Uptown tends to homogenize the neighborhood into its population of low-income renters— black, Latino, or white—with the core of this larger group thought to be the veterans of the urban renewal war of the late 1960s. Excluded from this sense of the neighborhood are not just recent gentrifiers, but longstanding homeowners, and even the more recently arrived Asian population. This exclusion is not really a matter of misunderstanding or hostility, rather it flows from the very political grounding of Slim Coleman's and Helen Shiller's understanding of community. Their Uptown is a constituency of impoverished and otherwise disadvantaged people whose mutual ties grow out of their mobilization as a political force. To invite others into their neighborhood—whether the determinedly family-centered and upwardly mobile Asian immigrants to Uptown, or the class-mixed and more self-help-oriented groups such as ONE and VOP—is to compromise and dilute their sense of community.

In other words, Slim Coleman and Helen Shiller would found Uptown on a kind of homogeneity, a homogeneity which strangely inverts the homogeneous neighborhood preferred by their archrivals among Uptown's gentrifiers, homeowners, and organizationally, the UCC. In the latter's site-defined neighborhood, what Uptown ought to become is a good home—well-maintained private residences, orderly streets, a decent mix of commercial outlets on the margins of the residential areas. Given the area's present demographic make-up, this sense of Uptown excludes the majority of people who actually live in the neighborhood. This Uptown is also an apolitical neighborhood, which would jettison forever the struggle that drives Coleman and Shiller in favor of the affinities that would unite a future Uptown of middle-income property owners. In such an Uptown there would be no need or room for political conflict.

IV

There is a third way of organizing one's perception of neighborhood, which I call the "stage" approach.[25] The neighborhood stage is a more contingent setting than either the neighborhood site or system. The observer presumes that the neighborhood is a dynamic set of social processes and physical features, and that the internal character of the neighborhood is to a lesser or greater degree structured by external factors such as national- or international-scale immigration trends, metropolitan economic characteristics, and municipal policy decisions. The neighborhood, itself, is a stage in the sense that an array of local actors—residents, grassroots organizations, other locally based institutions—use the neighborhood arena as a vehicle for expressing their visions of personal, family, and community life. And of course, these expressions may collide. Nonetheless, in the first instance I contend that the stage interpretation of neighborhood allows the social scientist to more adequately take into account the variety of forces shaping and reshaping urban neighborhoods. Further, it seems to me that the stage metaphor can better equip grassroots activists and organizers to apprehend their neighborhoods and build more durable and inclusive organizations. It is my sense that, in particular, as one surveys the terrain of a highly conflictual neighborhood such as Uptown, what divides at least some of its activists is more than personality, conflictual group histories, demographics, or even economics. Ultimately, a core source of conflict rests in different modes of apprehending the neighborhood.

In giving a name to a third way of interpreting neighborhoods, I have in mind the strategies that have been adopted by some of the grassroots initiatives in Sharrow and Uptown. For instance, SSICCP's ethos of inclusion combined with its loose structural framework allowed it to give voice to a wide array of Sharrow constituencies—and for a considerable span of time. I do not believe that the SSICCP ever quite carried off its ambitious effort to unite Sharrow—a portion of the neighborhood's Anglo population did not accept its ethnic inclusiveness, ultimately SSICCP co-habited a building with the Asian Welfare Association, but the two groups could not fully collaborate in their work—and as I have detailed, fiscal pressures and the group's failure to manage an intergenerational leadership transition seem to point to its eventual demise. In Uptown, ONE has persisted in its effort to structurally include a wide swath of the neighborhood demographic and institutional fabric, but as we have observed in the previous chapter, the group's programmatic twists and turns have not always allowed it to act so inclusively. Nonetheless, the late 1980s/early 1990s resuscitation of ONE has been grounded in an understanding of Uptown and Edgewater that is quite consistent with what I am calling the stage perspective. Josh Hoyt, ONE staff, and the group's resident activists did not presume that there was a community to be mobilized in the advancement of new ONE goals. Instead, the ONE activists worked to identify and forge a new set of neighborhood relationships, and out of this process an ONE agenda was derived.

Simply interpreting the neighborhood as a stage for ongoing, sometimes unanticipated local action is not a recipe for inner city salvation. Far too much depends on larger economic and political forces, and even within the context of particular neighborhoods, grassroots work—apart from grassroots theory—is a very difficult enterprise. Nevertheless, I share sociologist Janet L. Abu-Lughod's view that contemporary urbanization patterns are producing "a new type of neighborhood in which mutual tolerance and careful attention to social, physical, and temporal boundaries are required if harmony is to prevail."[26] In offering this characterization, Abu-Lughod has in mind lower Manhattan's kaleidoscopic East Village area. Uptown more than Sharrow embodies many of the salient features of this new type of urban neighborhood, though even in inner city Sheffield some of its characteristics are emerging. And though the fortunes and futures of Uptown and Sharrow remain unsettled, and despite the hardships currently experienced by residents in each, the work of groups such as SSICCP and ONE offer hope for their respective futures and provide lessons for grassroots action elsewhere.

NOTES

1. Ernest W. Burgess, "The Growth of the City: An Introduction to a Research Project," pp. 47-62 in Robert E. Park, Ernest W. Burgess, and Roderick D. McKenzie, *The City* (Chicago: University of Chicago Press, 1967).

2. Mark Gottdiener and Joe R. Feagin, "The Paradigm Shift in Urban Sociology," *Urban Affairs Quarterly* 24 (December 1988): 163-187; Mark Gottdiener, *The New Urban Sociology* (New York: McGraw-Hill, 1994).

3. Franklin J. James, "The Revitalization of Older Urban Housing and Neighborhoods," pp. 130-160 in Arthur P. Solomon, ed., *The Prospective City: Economic, Population, Energy, and Environmental Developments* (Cambridge, Mass.: MIT Press, 1980).

4. Larry H. Long, "Back to the Countryside and Back to the City in the Same Decade," pp. 61-77 in Shirley Bradway Laska and Daphne Spain, eds., *Back to the City: Issues in Neighborhood Renovation* (New York: Pergamon Press, 1980); Christopher Hamnett and Peter R. Williams, "Social Change in London: A Study of Gentrification," *Urban Affairs Quarterly* 15 (June 1980): 469-487; Sharon Zukin, *Loft Living: Culture and Capital in Urban Change* (Baltimore: Johns Hopkins University Press, 1982), pp. 23-57; Neil Smith, "Gentrification, the Frontier, and the Restructuring of Urban Space," pp. 15-34 in Neil Smith and Peter Williams, eds., *Gentrification of the City* (Boston: Allen & Unwin, 1986).

5. Mary K. Ludgin and Louis H. Masotti, *Downtown Development: Chicago, 1979-1984* (Evanston, Ill.: Center for Urban Affairs and Public Policy Research, Northwestern University, 1985).

6. Larry Bennett, *Fragments of Cities: The New American Downtowns and Neighborhoods* (Columbus: Ohio State University Press, 1990), pp. 57-69.

7. David Burnham, "Making History," *The Reader,* July 25, 1986.

8. "Developer Reflects on Uptown," *News-Star,* May 29, 1991.

9. Burnham, "Making History."

10. Delia O'Hara, "Uptown Uplift," *Chicago Sun-Times,* November 1, 1985; Don DeBat, "Historic Rehabs Revive Sheridan Park," *Chicago Sun-Times,* June 12, 1988.

11. Burnham, "Making History."

12. Interview with Philip Hulley, Nether Edge Neighbourhood Group, August 9, 1993.

13. Constance Perin, *Everything in Its Place: Social Order and Land Use in America* (Princeton, N.J.: Princeton University Press, 1979), pp. 32-80.

14. Two books that adopt this interpretive structure are Peter Medoff and Holly Sklar, *Streets of Hope: The Fall and Rise of an Urban Neighborhood* (Boston: South End Press, 1994) and Robert A. Slayton, *Back of the Yards: The Making of a Local Democracy* (Chicago: University of Chicago Press, 1986). Medoff and Sklar discuss the contemporary Dudley Street Neighborhood Initiative in Boston. Slayton's book is an oral history of Chicago's Back of the Yards neighborhood, with the latter chapters focusing on the development of the Back of the Yards Neighborhood Council.

15. Larry Bennett, "Rethinking Neighborhoods, Neighborhood Research, and Neighborhood Policy: Lessons from Uptown," *Journal of Urban Affairs* 15 (No. 3, 1993): 250-251.

16. Robert A. Beauregard, *Voices of Decline: The Postwar Fate of U.S. Cities* (Cambridge, Mass.: Blackwell Publishers, 1993), p. 90.

17. Michael Young and Peter Willmott, *Family and Kinship in East London* (Baltimore: Penguin Books, 1962), p. 198.

18. Herbert Gans, *The Urban Villagers: Group and Class in the Life of Italian-Americans* (New York: The Free Press, 1965).

19. Gerald D. Suttles, *The Social Order of the Slum: Ethnicity and Territory in the Inner City* (Chicago: University of Chicago Press, 1974), pp. 3-4.

20. Burgess, "The Growth of the City," pp. 57-58; Louis Wirth, "Urbanism as a Way of Life," in Richard Sennett, ed., *Classic Essays in the Culture of Cities* (New York: Appleton-Century-Crofts 1969), p. 62; Michael P. Smith, *The City and Social Theory* (New York: St. Martin's Press, 1979), pp. 7-12. The urban renewer's attitude may be inferred from Jane Jacobs' recollection of the Boston city planner who, based on his knowledge of the North End's aging physical environment, could not believe that there had been an indigenously generated upgrading of that neighborhood. Jane Jacobs, *The Death and Life of Great American Cities* (New York: Vintage Books, 1961), pp. 9-10.

21. Alinsky did not begin work in a neighborhood unless there was a set of indigenous organizations seeking—and willing to pay for—his services. This aspect of Alinsky's organizing technique is discussed by Charles E. Silberman, "The Potential for Community Organization," in Susan S. Fainstein and Norman I. Fainstein, eds., *The View from Below: Urban*

Politics and Social Policy (Boston: Little, Brown, 1972), pp. 274-275.

22. Saul D. Alinsky, *Reveille for Radicals* (New York: Vintage Books, 1969), p. 76. (The emphasis is in the original.)

23. *Views of Sharrow* (Sharrow Community Development Project, December 1972), p. 23.

24. Interview with Judy and Turk Glazebrook, East Graceland Organization, February 16, 1991.

25. Bennett, "Rethinking Neighborhoods, Neighborhood Research, and Neighborhood Policy": 251-252.

26. Janet Abu-Lughod, "Welcome to the Neighborhood," in Janet L. Abu-Lughod et al., *From Urban Village to East Village: The Battle for New York's Lower East Side* (Cambridge, Mass.: Blackwell Publishers, 1994), p. 28.

CHAPTER EIGHT
UPTOWN, SHARROW, AND BEYOND

Many academic studies of urban communities adopt an interpretive framework that Janet Abu-Lughod has summarized as "a 'traditional' neighborhood...attacked and destroyed by outside forces."[1] In the preceding chapters I have sought to avoid this thematization of neighborhood affairs in Uptown and Sharrow. In reference to Uptown, there never was a "traditional neighborhood" to be threatened by outside forces. Sharrow's trajectory of development, from the late nineteenth century until the 1960s, did indeed coincide with the kind of neighborhood patterning that could lend itself to a story of decline and fall. However, my interpretation of Sharrow emphasizes the creativity of its responses to redevelopment, racial and ethnic change, and deindustrialization. Moreover, even as many of the neighborhood's old ways have been modified, its residents continue to seek means to maintain its fundamental livability. Though Sharrow—like many other neighborhoods in cities of the English North—struggles to sustain itself in the shadow of a forbidding economic future, I have nonetheless sought to underline the open-endedness of neighborhood life and prospects as experienced by its resident activists.

In this book's concluding chapter I extend the notion of neighborhood open-endedness in another fashion. In various ways my research in Uptown and Sharrow has suggested insights that pertain to the larger shape of social and political life in the United States and Britain. As neighborhoods whose residents and their organizations are attempting to grapple with issues such as increasing racial and ethnic diversity, economic restructuring, physical decline, and—in Uptown's case—gentrification, Uptown and Sharrow function not merely as receptors of social trends, but also as settings for the playing out of particular versions of these social dramas. Yes, I am being artful with my metaphors because this is another implication of the neighborhood "stage," that the incidents, modes of debate, and communal arrangements that are forged in our Uptowns and Sharrows will contribute to larger structures of social life and political discourse. In the following pages I examine, in turn, patterns of racial and ethnic accommodation in relation to grassroots organization-building, the experience of female residents thrust into neighborhood activism, the "ideology of gentrification" as articulated by a number of Uptown residents, and the marginalization of left-wing populist political discourse.

II

In the preceding chapter as I sought to explain the contrasting content of neighborhood identity and conflict in Uptown and Sharrow, I gave primacy to people's sense of social class and social class relations, then noted how social class identity and residence seem to be understood differently in the two areas. Uptown and Sharrow are also multiracial, multi-ethnic neighborhoods, though in my view these local features play a smaller role in differentiating them. Nevertheless, the two neighborhoods' points of similarity and dissimilarity in reference to race relations highlight some important considerations for activists trying to build inclusive organizations in multi-racial settings.

On a day-to-day basis, Uptown's public life and intergroup relations operate on a much less civil plane than Sharrow's. The former community's many taverns, social service agencies, and socially marginalized residents give its streetlife an unruly, at times menacing quality. Moreover, the close physical proximity of opulent and appalling housing brings together the gentrifier and the day-laborer on a regular basis. Often these encounters are acrimonious, resulting in arguments over littering, parking spots, or street decorum. Moreover, like U.S. society more generally, these forms of low-level social tension are overlaid by racial and ethnic differences. The vast majority of Uptown's affluent residents are white; a sizable share of the neighborhood's impoverished population is Asian, black, or Latino. Interestingly, for all of the heated verbal exchanges and occasional physical violence that punctuate life in

Uptown, race tends not to be the cleavage that people designate as their source of conflict. Instead, affluent whites complain of the disreputable behavior of their neighbors—the hip-hoppers congregating at the corner, the Mexican American men working on their cars at the streetside, the tipsy Native Americans waiting outside a social service agency. Somewhat more commonly a young black man may lash out at an affluent couple as "white muthafuckas," but as a rule the chosen epithet for such people is "yuppie scum" or some variant.

Thus, in Uptown whites often avoid both racial- and social class-grounded interpretations of neighborhood tension in favor of what might be termed a social respectability/unrespectability axis. On occasion, such as when UCC Executive Director Herb Williams quite pointedly connected increases in the number of subsidized housing units with increases in the African American population (page 177), racial considerations come to the fore. But again, the context of Williams' remarks must be borne in mind. This was a local expert speaking on neighborhood viability in relation to real estate and demographic considerations, which he might view as matters quite separate from race relations. For Uptown's racial and ethnic minority populations, race and class are more clearly evident cleavages. "Yuppie scum" are, unquestionably, wealthier people with the wherewithal to take over Uptown's upgraded housing stock. For some younger black men, in particular, whites' race-based anxiety gives them the "edge" in street encounters, if nowhere else.

Sharrow is a more civil place. Rancorous public meetings are rare, and the day-to-day public life of the neighborhood proceeds with quiet predictability. On Friday or Saturday evenings the occasional fight breaks out at one or another of the London Road discos, but these events are more directly the outcome of mixing youth, beer, and football partisanship than the result of festering intergroup conflict. However, Sharrow is also a neighborhood in which race is a persistent topic of discussion. Older Anglo residents complain that recent arrivals, such as the neighborhood's Somali immigrants, have been advanced to the head of the waiting list for desirable council flat accommodations. Asians characterize themselves as "black" and implicate the white population in explaining the difficulties experienced by their fellow Bangladeshi, Indian, and Pakistani immigrants. Surely part of this contrast in speaking of race grows out of Sharrow's situation as a one-class community. Virtually everyone who lives in Sharrow is working class (and respectable in daily habits). Unlike Uptown's residents, especially its white population, who can suppress discomfort that may derive from living in a racially mixed area by noting contrasting degrees of social respectability/unrespectability, in Sharrow, race, ethnicity, and divergent behavioral norms associated with racial/ethnic difference are unavoidably present.

Although race overlays daily life in different ways in Uptown and Sharrow, its contribution to the structure of organizational life is more comparable. In both communities grassroots organizations are, for the most part, racially and ethnically segregated. In Uptown, the homeowner-dominated block clubs dotting the neighborhood are, with few exceptions, white organizations. The most organizationally active of Uptown's ethnic minority populations, the Southeast Asians, have devoted most of their energies to building nationality-specific "mutual aid" associations. Two of the main exceptions to Uptown's organizational segregation, ONE and the Coleman-Shiller movement, are instructive deviations from form. By design, ONE is an alliance of smaller groups: church congregations, social service agencies, ethnic mutual aid associations, and business groups. A cornerstone of Josh Hoyt's rebuilding of ONE turned on redefining Uptown's (and Edgewater's) social diversity as a source of neighborhood strength and identifying ONE as the local organization best able to accommodate the area's many interests. In recent years ONE has employed the motto "We are Many, We are ONE." The Coleman-Shiller forces also represent a racially and ethnically disparate constituency: the neighborhood's remaining Appalachian population, blacks and Latinos across the age spectrum, and younger white "radicals." The great majority of this group falls outside of Uptown's respectable middle class, and Coleman-Shiller supporters are not known as reliable participants in the neighborhood's mainstream community organizations. The upshot is that for Coleman-Shiller opponents, this interracial movement is wholly illegitimate, constituting, in effect, a band of disaffected people united only by their mutual desire to overturn the norms of middle-class Uptown.

Sharrow's organizations reveal a similar pattern of racial/ethnic segregation. The struggling residents and tenants organization in the Lansdowne Flats just above Sharrow Street, whose resident population includes Afro-Caribbeans, Asians, and Somalis, manages to attract the participation of a dozen or so older Anglo residents. Across the neighborhood, participation in the smaller residents organizations that represent a few blocks of houses tends to follow the prevailing patterns of geographic segregation. Anglos dominate most such groups; occasionally, when there is the concentration of a particular ethnic minority group such as the Asian population in the South View area, then minority participation in the local residents group follows. During the 1980s SSICCP attempted to fashion an ethnically inclusive agenda reminiscent of ONE's. However, as I have discussed in Chapter 5, SSICCP managed to achieve, at best, a formal alliance with its main partner in this effort, the Asian Welfare Association (AWA). Nor was SSICCP's commitment to racial/ethnic inclusion universally approved by the group's white constituents. From the standpoint of many in Sharrow's economically embattled white working-class population, ethnic minorities already seemed to be receiving preferential treatment from the municipal government.

Paradoxically, in spite of the contrasting character of day-to-day race relations and modes of interpreting racial matters in Uptown and Sharrow, the racial configuration of their grassroots organizations is similar. The lesson is simple but nonetheless worth emphasizing— especially at a time when racial consciousness is clearly on the upswing in both the United States and Britain. Irrespective of a neighborhood's apparent interracial harmony or disharmony, building multi-racial grassroots initiatives requires close attention to the perspectives and interests of each of the "partners" within the alliance and, more subtly, to the relationship between the group's agenda and broader community concerns. The SSICCP/AWA alliance failed because their collaboration did not evolve much beyond a set of agreements between organizational leaders. The Coleman-Shiller movement has built a long-lasting, multi-racial constituency, which still manages to contribute to neighborhood polarization. However, this latter circumstance is not simply a question of race and organization-building, or of failures in the Coleman-Shiller's approach to organizing. We return to this point in a few pages when I investigate the limits of left-wing populism in Uptown and Sharrow.

III

In both Uptown and Sharrow, women are important participants in virtually every neighborhood organization. This is a feature of grassroots politics that has drawn the attention of many observers. And within the literature of women's studies, it is axiomatic that political work directed at neighborhood-, housing-, and school-related issues represents a field where women, for generations, have had a conspicuous impact.[2] A characteristic explanation for women's prominence in neighborhood organizations suggests that this type of activism represents an extension of the "domestic sphere."[3] As such, female activists in neighborhood organizations deal with a constellation of issues that are closely aligned with central family concerns such as the amenability of the home environment and children's educational opportunities. Moreover, unlike some other varieties of political activism, neighborhood organizations are "accessible" to women who have substantial, home-based responsibilities.

In the next several pages, I examine the grassroots "careers" of three women who have been active in groups discussed in Chapters 5 and 6. Denice Irwin lives in one of Uptown's HUD "prepayment" buildings and became a leader in the campaign to prevent their conversion to market-rate rental properties. You have already met Ann Wilson and Margaret Howard, who were leading figures in the Sharrow Traffic Campaign and Broomhall Tenants Association, respectively. These three women's stories are instructive for two reasons. In the first place, the striking parallels in their experiences and understanding of political activism suggest that gender, far more than social class and race/ethnicity, structures grassroots activism in Uptown and Sharrow in directly comparable ways. Second, the experiences of these three women reveal a process of political activation that is quite a bit choppier than is sometimes implied by the "domestic sphere" scenario.[4]

Denice Irwin, a single mother of three children, moved to Uptown from Chicago's South Side in 1983. Irwin was able to rent a unit on the top floor of one of the neighborhood's HUD-subsidized apartment towers. She recalls it as "the nicest place at a reasonable price....At the time I knew nothing about HUD and subsidized housing." She also did not know that in 1979 her landlord had stopped making mortgage payments, and that in turn, essential building maintenance work had been deferred. Irwin learned of the latter situation a few weeks after moving into the building. A heavy rainstorm brought water cascading through the roof and into her apartment. When Irwin sought to have the leaking stopped, she not only discovered that the building manager would not correct the problem, but that the maintenance staff expected tenants to pay them for doing routine repair jobs. Seeking outside help, Irwin visited a Legal Aid office and was referred to VOP. Irwin, with the assistance of VOP organizer Judy Meima, began building a tenants group: "I was tired of living ankle deep in water."

Although Irwin's impetus to found the tenants group was personal, she recognized that many of her neighbors also suffered from the mismanagement of their building. Moreover, by 1987 when HUD actually began foreclosure proceedings, the tenants group realized that an HUD-sponsored auction could result in across-the-board rent increases. I have elsewhere described the difficulties presented by organizing tenants in the HUD prepayment buildings. Irwin pulled together a rainbow coalition of African and Asian immigrants, Latinos, and whites (including a number of Russian immigrants). Having pressured HUD into making stopgap building repairs in the mid-1980s, after the 1987 foreclosure the tenants organization, tried—but failed—to negotiate a purchase plan with HUD. Interestingly, in recalling this complicated series of events, Irwin identifies her most daunting challenge as attempting to work with the neighborhood group active on her building's block:

> I sat at their meeting and it was as if I wasn't there.
> You know that courtyard building down the street?
> They said that they would only rent to top-rate ten-
> ants, people from Lincoln Park or the suburbs. I asked
> them: "What's the difference between top-rate and
> second-rate tenants?" They said that only Lincoln
> Parkers and suburbanites are top-rate.[5]

Though deeply offended by such encounters—at one point one of
the block club members referring to her fellow tenants as "pigs"—Irwin
was unbowed. As she developed increasing confidence as an amateur
organizer, she decided to continue her education by enrolling at Truman
College. Irwin has since become a professional tenants organizer and
recognizes her work forming her building's tenants group as a pivotal
experience in recasting her life.

Several thousand miles to the east, Ann Wilson's circumstances and
introduction to community activism bear evident similarities to Denice
Irwin's. Wilson is also a single mother of three children, who in the
1970s moved to Sheffield from her native Nottingham. When Wilson
first decided to seek a remedy for the traffic and parking problems in the
vicinity of her flat in the Thorp Estate, she adopted the most orthodox
of means, which was to contact Councillor Doris Askam. Askam did not
think that much could be done to improve the situation, but she agreed
to visit Wilson's residential complex, accompanied by some Sheffield
municipal administrators. The visit occurred on a Sunday, and to Ann
Wilson's considerable chagrin, traffic on London Road was light and
there was no spillover parking on the estate. As Wilson recalls that day:

> Then they asked me all kinds of questions that I
> couldn't answer. After they left I went into my bath-
> room and cried my eyes out. From then I knew that
> you never go to a meeting without doing your
> homework.[6]

Indeed, prodded by her embarrassment at this event, Wilson began
to take courses in a continuing education program in nearby Barnsley.
By 1985-86, she was able to organize and lead the Sharrow Traffic

Campaign. Coincidentally, Wilson also became one of SSICCP's principal resident leaders. Wilson is proud of her transformation into a community activist but also wary of that designation. She prefers to think of herself as a "community volunteer": "Activists are frustrated women. That's probably what I am, but it's no one else's affair." By the early 1990s, although community work and caring for her elderly mother occupied much of her time, Ann Wilson hoped to build on her community experience and earn a university degree.

Margaret Howard came to grassroots activism in quite a different fashion from Denice Irwin and Ann Wilson, and yet there is no question that her work with the Broomhall Tenants Association had a comparably profound effect on her life. Before moving to Broomhall Flats with her disabled husband, Howard had worked for the Sheffield Authority, for a time serving as Town Hall Secretary of the National Association of Local Government Officers (NALGO, the labor union representing local government employees). Among Howard's most vivid memories is the indifference encountered by the tenants when they began to contact public officials. Howard at first found it extremely difficult to speak out in the presence of such important people. She recalls passing over a significant personal hurdle when she joined a delegation of Broomhall Flats residents attending a meeting in Nottingham:

> The Nottingham housing director was very condescending. Mandy (Bryce) had prepared questions to be asked by each member of the Sheffield delegation. I sat and waited for my turn, sweating and shaking. I just didn't think that I could get up there and speak. But I did.[7]

Undoubtedly, Howard's occupational experience had better prepared her for these kinds of confrontations than were Denice Irwin or Ann Wilson, and yet, she still found "talking back" to haughty administrators a fearsome undertaking. Still, Howard—like Irwin and Wilson—became the mainstay of her grassroots group. Unlike Irwin and Wilson, already in her sixties when the Broomhall Flats conflict was resolved and tending an ailing spouse, Howard did not move on to other

campaigns or occupations. Nonetheless, she fondly recalls her association with the tenants group, and noting the close relationship she developed with community worker Mandy Bryce, adds: "She's the one person
I will never forget. Mandy dragged me back to the world of the living."

Although some of the very details of their transformations into
neighborhood activists are strikingly similar, as I got to know Denice
Irwin, Ann Wilson, and Margaret Howard over time, it was their senses
of what had happened to them and what they had become that I found
most illuminating. Each was at some point overwhelmed by a feeling of
inadequacy in the face of condescending officials, bureaucrats, or fellow
neighborhood residents. From their standpoint, it was getting past this
perception of ineptitude, the idea of having trespassed onto the field of
public affairs—far more than mastering the details of public policy—
that they recognized as the principal barrier to their becoming "public"
people. Further, although Irwin, Wilson, and Howard clearly focused
their attention on matters that can be recognized as extensions of the
domestic sphere—that is, housing and local safety matters—becoming
articulate participants in even domestic sphere-related neighborhood
issues required a great deal of personal initiative.

It is also noteworthy that each of these three women, in the first
instance, had learned to cope with unorthodox domestic situations, and
in the second instance, became neighborhood activists in the context of
unsettled neighborhood situations—problematic housing in the cases of
Irwin and Howard, inconvenient and unsafe traffic conditions in
Wilson's case. In other words, each was motivated to action by the over-
turning of predictable home and neighborhood circumstances. One
might propose that in the contemporary U.S. and Britain, as well as
most other industrialized countries, it is analogous shifts in local life
that have brought so many women out of their homes and into the public realm. I believe that this proposition is further amplified by the way
in which each of these women has interpreted her movement into community activism as transformative—prompting the reconsideration of
careers or, in Howard's case, into a much more generous self-appraisal
of how she had put to use her years after leaving the salaried workforce.

IV

In Chapter 7, I examined factors contributing to neighborhood stability and change, devoting several pages to the Heart of Uptown/Sheridan Park area in order to explain gentrification as a mode of intentional neighborhood transformation. In most treatments of gentrification, this process is interpreted in such a fashion, either as a phenomenon that restructures particular areas within cities, or, as a component of city-scale redevelopment policy aimed at preserving prized historical locales, retaining middle-class residents, or reinforcing municipal revenue bases. However, I also think that gentrification may be examined in another way—as the grounding for an emergent ideology that can be linked to broader features of the prevailing political discourses of the United States and Britain.

To illustrate some of the principal features of this ideology of gentrification, I draw on the concluding two paragraphs of a letter that appeared in the *Chicago Tribune*, sent by an Uptown resident who opposes the development of additional low-income housing in the neighborhood:

> Uptown has long been the dumping ground for low-income subsidized housing. Our neighborhoods have one of the highest rates of subsidized housing in the United States. Scattered-site housing is only one of the many ways that our local government has tried to sweep its problems under the carpet.
>
> Uptown is miraculously pulling itself up by its bootstraps with the infusion of private individuals who care greatly about their homes, condos, neighborhoods, and neighbors. We don't need local politicians and newspapers trying to tell us how to improve our neighborhoods.[8]

As I have noted at various points in the preceding chapters, Uptown's homeowners and gentrifiers often characterize themselves as an embattled minority, which once again seems to be a subtext of this letter. But beyond this implied perspective, the writer makes a series of more explicit claims: that governmental action cannot be trusted, that problems such as inadequate shelter are governmental rather than societal matters (and indeed, are problems because of governmental mishandling), that private individuals—by pursuing their own interests—will produce solutions for what ails urban America. Such arguments are common currency at homeowners meetings and of anti-Helen Shiller political campaigns.

One of Uptown's more aggressively pro-gentrification homeowners groups is the East Graceland Organization (EGO), and in discussing neighborhood affairs with three of EGO's members I encountered sentiments directly paralleling those expressed in the preceding letter.[9] For example, the group's president, Joe Cain, in concluding some remarks concerning "political interference" in the neighborhood, asserted: "I have little confidence in government except to tax." Cain added: "To me gentrification is a plus. It's taking a problem environment and turning it around." As for the role of private developers in transforming Uptown: "It's like anywhere. They're out to do what they do anywhere—in Florida, Arizona. In this area it's the private sector that's brought development."[10] In a second interview with a couple who have also been active in EGO, Turk Glazebrook—responding to a question seeking a description of Uptown—commented: "It's a ghetto, which is emerging. It's a piece of real estate that has been mismanaged for years." To a query asking him to describe what is wrong with Uptown, this response followed:

> It's totally imbalanced here, with too many renters.
> The emphasis should be on people purchasing what
> they're living in. This will give people a vested inter-
> est in the area. People who rent take less of an inter-
> est than people who buy.[11]

As in the *Tribune* letter, these EGO activists assert that government is at best incompetent, at worst conniving. Conversely, private economic forces—real estate practices, the self-interested behavior of property owners—not only bring private enrichment but, in addition, collective neighborhood improvement. Finally, these local property-owners express misgivings about Uptown's misfit, renting population.

Living in a city such as Chicago—with its impressive downtown core and opulent North Side residential areas but, far more pervasively, its belts of abandoned neighborhoods and crumbling public infrastructure—it is easy enough, irrespective of one's occupation, social class, race, or housing tenure status, to think that government is failing. As one puts a fair amount of fiscal or "sweat" equity into property improvements—and also observes suspicious people on the street and other local residents who do not give such attention to their homes or apartments—there is also a temptation to demonize these others. I believe that it is in this context that one can appreciate why constructing a framework of neighborhood cleavage based on notions of respectable and unrespectable behavior—as opposed to race/ethnicity or social class—has emerged among Uptown's more affluent residents. In effect, for the exponents of this ideology of gentrification, they—as respectable, self-reliant property owners—have become the agents of urban rejuvenation.

This is a public philosophy that converges in many ways with the anti-statist, pro-market, and individualistic tenets of conservative elites in both the United States and Britain. It is ironic, but nonetheless true, that what I am outlining via the views of Uptown gentrifiers is perfectly compatible with what English scholars Nicholas Deakin and John Edwards—in describing Thatcher-era urban policy in Britain—have termed the "enterprise culture":

> Enterprise is having initiative and drive; it is taking opportunities when they arise; it is independence from the state; it is having confidence and being responsible for one's own destiny; it is being driven by the work ethic; and it promotes self-interest.[12]

Relatively little gentrification has come to Sharrow or, for that matter, any of Sheffield's neighborhoods, and in the absence of gentrification-derived conflict, I encountered only the slightest hints of this perspective among my Sheffield contacts. However, the main features of the ideology of gentrification, like those of the enterprise culture, have become prevalent, if not dominant filters for interpreting government, public policy, and national interest in both the United States and Britain. Given what I have observed in Uptown, I would propose that the sources of this worldview are more varied than just the editorial offices of *The Public Interest*, right-wing Tory insurgents, and suburban retreats in each country. In neighborhoods such as Uptown, the social stresses produced by gentrification may well resonate more profoundly than we have previously imagined.

V

Both Uptown and Sharrow have fostered persistent left-wing political activity. Since the arrival of the JOIN student activists in the mid-1960s, there has been a succession of political voices in Uptown expressing discontent with national and local public policies, and more fundamentally, with the character and consequences of capitalist economic practices. In Sharrow, not only have local Labour Party candidates won every council contest in the past quarter century, but in many instances a fraction of the electorate has chosen to vote for left-of-Labour candidates. Yet within each of these neighborhoods the most forceful strain of radical politics has been some variant of the left-wing populism that has linked activists in SAG, the Coleman-Shiller movement, SSICCP, and ONE. By casting this rainbow of people and organizations into the same ideological pot, I do not mean to characterize their political positions as interchangeable (and in a moment I will make some basic distinctions among them). Rather, by noting the continuities in their thinking—which, given the circumstances of each neighborhood appears to be a plausible mode of comprehending the political and economic world—I wish to then explore why it seems that this general perspective has, in the past decade, lost much of its persuasive power.

Left-wing populism's intellectual forebears are a diverse group including Saul Alinsky, E.F. Schumacher, and Harry C. Boyte.[13] In the 1980s, among its most articulate political advocates were Labour Party politicians such as David Blunkett and Ken Livingstone, Leader of the Greater London Council before its abolition in 1986. As a political stance, left-wing populism begins with a preference for local governance

and problem-solving, a preference deriving from distrust of the operations of large-scale bureaucracies (both governmental and corporate).
Left-wing populism's objection to many contemporary institutions,
however, turns on more than the scale of their operations. As egalitari-
ans, left-wing populists seek to fashion democratic decisonmaking
mechanisms in line with a philosophical commitment to the inherent
equality of human beings. When possible, left-wing populists seek to
achieve basic elements of economic equity (for example, the universal
provision of adequate shelter) via the medium of communal, non-
governmental structures such as consumer cooperatives. A final element
in the tactical menu of many left-wing populists is the commitment to
seek societal transformation through the agency of locally grounded,
grassroots movements.[14]

Having sketched this general picture, I do hasten to distinguish
some of the variations represented by the subjects of this book. For
example, left-wing populists in Sharrow such as John Peaden and Ann
Wilson are principally motivated by a skepticism of bureaucratic decisionmaking within government. In their neighborhood, the mid-century compact between Labour and Conservative parties—and thus
between the workforce and major capitalists—to erect a comprehensive
welfare state, remains an accepted (though currently embattled) proposition. Grassroots mobilization is required to prevent the bureaucratic
agents of welfare state policy from mishandling their responsibilities.
Left-wing populists in Uptown also distrust bureaucrats, but they tend
to perceive them as accessories to the more formidable opponents of
local initiative: Democratic Party insiders, who to this day are viewed as
an occupying force in the neighborhoods of Chicago, and business
groups—especially real estate interests—seeking to profit from neighborhood change. To further differentiate Uptown left-wing populists,
the Coleman-Shiller movement, far more than ONE or VOP, embeds
its understanding of local problems within a class conflict interpretation
of society.

In order to understand the fate of left-wing populism in Sharrow,
it is necessary to review how John Peaden and his associates won their
political victories in the 1970s and 1980s. Early grassroots action in

Sharrow had several important impacts: municipal plans were harmonized with the real interests of the Sharrow population, with the formation of SSICCP the Sheffield Council entered into a more concentrated and sensitive service delivery relationship with the local community, and within the local Sharrow Labour Party there was an infusion of new members. This new Labour blood was largely constituted of grassroots activists seeking to recast the centralized, bureaucratically engineered policies of the municipal administration. Neighborhood activist/Labour councillors such as Howard Knight and Tony Tigwell were younger than the then-dominant councillors, and they came to their political careers via paths far afield from those taken by their trade unionist elders.

Nor were such changes limited to this corner of the city. By the end of the 1970s a "New Urban Left" leadership had emerged within Sheffield's Labour Party. In the next several years under the tutelage of Councillor David Blunkett, the Sheffield Authority charted a new course that, without rejecting the long-term achievements of previous Labour administrations, sought to reconnect municipal government with the residents and neighborhoods of Sheffield. Blunkett encouraged local initiatives such as SSICCP and throughout Sheffield endeavored to make routine service delivery operations less bureaucratic. In the face of the city's suddenly declining fortunes as an industrial center, Blunkett also seized the initiative in identifying innovative, economically equitable means to recharge the city's economy: via municipal support for worker-run cooperatives, through municipal aid to promising "culture industries," by the retention of cheap mass transit. In the decade and a half since this agenda was set in motion, the local authority's achievements have been, at best, mixed. Sheffield's economic circumstances have improved only marginally, and the mid-1980s rate-capping confrontation with the central government was the prelude to a significant reduction in authority budget flexibility.

The impact on Sharrow and its grassroots organizations has been dramatic. As in neighborhoods across Sheffield, the decline of public services is palpable. More subtly though, the vigor of Sharrow's grassroots groups has been sapped by municipal retrenchment. Municipal government, of course, remains and may be pressured, but it currently has little leeway to respond to local groups. In the first instance, this undercuts Sharrow grassroots groups because they have yet to master the art of generating funds and other forms of support from non-governmental sources. But beyond matters of organizational mainte-nance, the gravest damage to grassroots action in Sharrow is the erosion of a central premise of the local populist agenda: that com-munity-building could be advanced via the responsive, decentralized delivery of welfare state-derived resources. In Sharrow, left-wing populism presumed that the local state, and in turn, the central gov-ernment, could be pressed into responsive action. There is little such hope these days. Not only are the prospects for local action grim, but at the national level not even the Labour Party is likely, in the near term, to serve as the vehicle for welfare state-style redistributionist measures. At this point in time, left-wing populists in Sharrow are confronted with the predicament of how to affirm a community-rooted vision that is feasible in a post- or at least reduced-welfare state Britain.

In Uptown, grassroots groups could never hope to win the kinds of governmental concessions achieved by their Sharrow counterparts. The municipal government of Richard J. Daley was unrelentingly hostile to their objectives; with the rollback of federal urban programming after the early 1970s, there was no other governmental promontory to seize. As a consequence, left-wing populism took a variety of forms. ONE adopted a dual strategy of building alliances with other local groups—church congregations, social service agencies, ethnic mutual aid soci-eties—and sought to organize this diverse constituency around an unfolding sequence of local issues. These included "downzoning" of near-Lakefront areas as a means of relieving redevelopment pressures, programs to aid apartment building owners in reducing energy costs, and more recently mobilizing subsidized housing tenants and promot-ing Uptown (and Edgewater) as multi-cultural communities. VOP, in contrast, concentrated on housing rehabilitation. The Coleman-Shiller movement provided services for core constituents such as disabled Appalachian immigrants and contested local elections.

The vitality of Uptown's left-wing populists has been demonstrated via Helen Shiller's elections to the Chicago City Council and by the successes of the campaign to preserve low-cost housing in the late 1980s and early 1990s. And yet the very effectiveness of this latter movement defines one of the limits of left-wing populism's broader political reach. VOP presently busies itself with managing a much-enlarged portfolio of properties, and as it refines its housing development initiatives—for example, through its International Homes cooperative project—it must also learn to work in a reasonably congenial fashion with the city government, private lenders, and foundation sponsors. Out of such relationships continued radical political action is unlikely to follow. Nonetheless, given the serious housing needs of many Uptowners, VOP's "turn" is not unreasonable.

The evolution of the Coleman-Shiller movement is similarly ambiguous. Helen Shiller has won the last three city council elections in the 46th ward, and she and Slim Coleman alike are visible supporters of labor, civil rights, and grassroots groups throughout Chicago. Nevertheless, their form of left-wing populism is not well suited to reaching beyond their Uptown-based core of support. Having operated as embattled outsiders for two decades, Coleman and Shiller conduct their operations in a subterranean fashion—depending on a few loyalists to direct their groups' activities and concentrating organizing efforts on reliable constituencies. The polarizing effect of these tactical means is amplified by the tendency of their political opponents and local media to portray them as iron-willed holdovers from the discredited 1960s. As such, Coleman and Shiller operate successfully within the confines of Uptown, but theirs is not a politics that one can anticipate transcending the specific circumstances of this corner of Chicago.

In some respects, the decline of left-wing populism as a political force—which has coincided with some very successful populist campaigns in Uptown and Sharrow—has resulted from circumstances well beyond the reach of activists in these two neighborhoods. For example, in both the United States and Britain the rightward trend in mainstream political discourse has tended to marginalize left-wing populism's localist, egalitarian, and redistributionist core values. In Britain, the withering away of the local socialism embodied by municipal authorities such as Sheffield's has, in turn, undermined the populist, but welfare state-reliant agenda of a SSICCP. Although in Uptown left-wing populists have diverged from their colleagues in Sharrow by more aggressively pursuing autonomous community development measures, as local organizations' programmatic agendas expand, their capacity to sustain political insurgency may be reduced. Or, to note Uptown's principal counter-example, which is the Coleman-Shiller movement, whose radical politics have in no way been softened by considerations such as program or organizational maintenance considerations, the very retention of a confrontational populism in a slowly upgrading neighborhood has come to be viewed not as principled political radicalism, but rather as a reflexive iconoclasm.

VI

In Uptown and Sharrow left-wing populists have successfully challenged the redevelopment initiatives advanced by their respective municipal governments, and particularly in Uptown, over a lengthy span of years have sought to balance the impacts of aggressive private real estate speculation. In each area leading left-wing populists have recognized how shifting demographic patterns recast big-city neighborhoods and have endeavored to incorporate new residents and their organizations within broader institutional frameworks. Left-wing populists in both areas have also sought to mobilize local and outside resources in order to develop neighborhood-sensitive housing, educational, and social service programs. Though typically untroubled by the intellectual complexities of the challenge, left-wing populists have even had some success in building organizational structures that accommodate the pluralistic characters of Uptown and Sharrow and which have aimed, quite explicitly, to define community in non-exclusivist terms.

Nevertheless, given the radically egalitarian tenets of left-wing populism, within the political discourse of mainstream news media, or in the local political forums of other kinds of communities, one can readily enough understand why this viewpoint receives limited credence. It is less commonly acknowledged by advocates of left-wing populism that in the last decade—and even as their colleagues in many North American and British cities have achieved some startling triumphs—ideological, economic, and governmental developments have conspired to reduce the contemporary political salience of this organizing perspective even in those places where it ought to have willing audiences, and where it has demonstrated its usefulness in reshaping local conditions.

However, I also do not wish for this summation of Uptown's and Sharrow's recent political experiences to be construed as the story of two "nontraditional" communities under siege by unfriendly outside forces. At the present time the remnants of the SSICCP's leadership are struggling to recast their organization as a "community trust," which may enable it to renew its contributions to Sharrow life. Tony Tigwell, after retiring from the Sheffield Council and reducing his participation in Labour Party politics, has turned his attention to organizing a Sharrow-based credit union. In Uptown, ONE is moving on to new campaigns, while a housing group that was formed in the mid-1980s, Lakefront SRO, is making great strides in the provision of shelter for very low-income people. In short, though their contributions to broader political debate may have entered a period of diminished returns, grassroots activists in each neighborhood persist in their efforts to define practical, humane solutions to local problems.

The thematic element that links the various discussions in this chapter is the notion that the kinds of political dialogue and conflict, the varieties of grassroots activism, and the solutions to local problems forged in neighborhoods such as Uptown and Sharrow do merit outside attention. As a researcher whose main concerns center on processes of neighborhood change and the impacts on neighborhoods produced by public policy and grassroots action, I have also been struck by several broader implications growing from this parallel examination of two neighborhoods: that contrasting patterns of day-to-day race relations can yield similar race-grounded organizational networks, that in two culturally contrasting neighborhoods the experience of women activists can be remarkably comparable, that local issues and organizational dilemmas can reveal such close parallels to larger trends in ideology and political discourse. One might think of these two neighborhoods as laboratories for the United States and Britain of the next century. As the racial and ethnic diversity of these two societies increases, and as the social and economic consequences of winding down the welfare state begin to manifest themselves more clearly, conditions within neighborhoods such as these will offer crucial insights regarding the futures of their larger societies. Though at present many Americans and Britons may not recognize these interconnections, the fates of our Uptowns and Sharrows are likely to be most instructive in helping us anticipate the fates of many other communities in each country.

NOTES

1. Janet Abu-Lughod, "Conclusions and Implications," in Janet Abu-Lughod et al., *From Urban Village to East Village: The Battle for New York's Lower East Side* (Cambridge, Mass.: Blackwell Publishers, 1994), p. 350.

2. Kathleen McCourt, *Working Class Women and Grassroots Politics* (Bloomington: Indiana University Press, 1977); Ronald Lawson and Stephen E. Barton, "Sex Roles in Social Movements: A Case Study of the Tenant Movement in New York City," Signs 6 (No. 2, 1980): 230-247; Sheila Rowbotham, *The Past Is Before Us: Feminism in Action Since the 1960s* (Boston: Beacon Press, 1989).

3. Sandra Morgen and Anita Bookman, "Rethinking Women and Politics: An Introductory Essay," in Anita Bookman and Sandra Morgen, eds., *Women and the Politics of Empowerment* (Philadelphia: Temple University Press, 1988), pp. 13-15; Judith N. DeSena, "Women: The Gatekeepers of Urban Neighborhoods," *Journal of Urban Affairs* 16 (No. 3, 1994): 271-293.

4. The following profiles are based on interviews, numerous follow-up conversations, published accounts, and organizational records.

5. Interview with Denice Irwin, June 24, 1991.

6. Interview with Ann Wilson and Margaret Howard, August 11, 1993.

7. Wilson and Howard Interview, August 11, 1993.

8. Mike Pailon [sic], Letter to the *Chicago Tribune*, August 9, 1994. Even Uptown's pro-gentrification advocates seem to suffer from a lack of respect at the hands of Chicago's daily newspapers. The correct spelling of this surname is Pavilon.

9. In 1990 members of the East Graceland Organization were parties to a heated debate that included Alderperson Shiller, Shiller's chief opponent in the upcoming city council election, and the Chicago Cubs baseball club. Their conflict centered on alternative proposals for upgrading some derelict property alongside Chicago Transit Authority right-of-way. In the summers of 1988 and 1989, EGO had retained a private

security force to patrol Kenmore Avenue as well as some adjoining areas. Ben Joravsky, "Park 'n' Lot: *Tribune* Proposal Makes Hysterical Bedfellows," *The Reader,* November 23, 1990; Dan Liberty, "Special Security: Fed-Up Uptowners Hire Their Own Cops," *The Reader,* September 29, 1989.

10. Interview with Joe Cain, President of the East Graceland Organization, December 19, 1990.

11. Interview with Judy and Turk Glazebrook, East Graceland Organization, February 16, 1991.

12. Nicholas Deakin and John Edwards, *The Enterprise Culture and the Inner City* (New York: Routledge, 1993), p. 2.

13. Saul D. Alinsky, *Reveille for Radicals* (New York: Vintage Books, 1969); E.F. Schumacher, *Small Is Beautiful: Economics as if People Mattered* (New York: Harper & Row, 1973); Harry C. Boyte, *The Backyard Revolution: Understanding the New Citizen Movement* (Philadelphia: Temple University Press, 1980).

14. For a discussion of the main tenets of left-wing populism, see Robert Fisher, *Let the People Decide: Neighborhood Organizing in America* (New York: Twayne Publishers, 1994), pp. 210-233. Also note the discussion of "an alternative social policy" in David Blunkett and Geoff Green, *Building from the Bottom: The Sheffield Experience* (London: Fabian Tract 491, 1983), pp. 20-27. In the mid-1980s one of the Greater London Council's principal innovations was its extensive support for voluntary sector groups. See Jennifer R. Wolch, *The Shadow State: Government and Voluntary Sector in Transition* (New York: The Foundation Center, 1990), pp. 151-185.

APPENDIX

Much of the information that I collected on Sharrow and Uptown was derived from personal interviews. This is my roster of interviewees, whose contributions to this book I wish to acknowledge. In several instances these individuals spoke to me at various times in addition to the formal interviews identified below.

Sharrow

Doris Askam, Sharrow Ward Councillor; 8-14-93

Mandy Bryce, formerly Broomhall Tenants Association (BTA) community worker; 8-25-93

Roy Darke, South Sheffield Inner City Community Project (SSICCP); 10-28-91, 7-4-94

Fatima Deria, Somali Community Centre; 8-19-93

Linda Duckenfield, Sharrow Community Health Project staff; 8-23-93

William Emery, Broomhall Park Association; 9-1-93

Arthur Fellows, Lansdowne Residents Association (LRA); 8-7-93

Joan Flett, Nether Edge Neighbourhood Group (NENG); 8-17-93

Harold Gascoigne, SSICCP; 7-30-93

Brenda Glaves, SSICCP staff; 8-4-93

Geoff Green, formerly of Walkley Action Group; 7-1-94

Chris Hodgkinson, formerly of SSICCP staff; 7-7-94

Margaret Howard, formerly of BTA; 6-24-93, 8-11-93, 6-28-94

Philip Hulley, NENG; 8-9-93

June Johnston and Joan Lane, formerly of Shoreham Street Action Group (SSAG); 7-1-93

Akhtar Kayani, Asian Welfare Association; 7-13-93

Mick Kerrigan, SSICCP and Sharrow Street Residents Group; 6-29-93, 6-27-94

Howard Knight, former Sharrow Ward Councillor; 7-14-93

John Peaden, SSICCP staff; 11-18-91, 8-5-93, 9-2-93, 6-28-94

Mike Pye, Sharrow Ward Councillor; 11-14-91; 8-24-93

Madge Rule, formerly of BTA; 6-30-93

Joe Stevenson, Broomhall Community Group; 9-3-93

Cyril Tigwell, formerly of SSAG; 8-13-93

Tony Tigwell, former Sharrow Ward Councillor; 8-20-93

Andy White, LRA; 8-10-93

Helen Ward, formerly of Sharrow Traffic Campaign (STC);
6-22-94

George and Gillian Webster, formerly of BTA; 6-24-94

Ann Wilson, SSICCP and formerly of STC; 11-25-91, 6-23-93,
8-11-93, 6-20-94

Immacolata Zydorchiewicz, Italian Community Centre; 8-11-93

Uptown

Rob Bagstad and Jill Donovan, Montrose Harbor Neighbors
Association (MHNA); 7-18-92

Brian Bakke, Uptown Baptist Church staff; 2-11-91

Paulette Bezazian, Uptown Chicago Commission; 6-13-91

Keith Brown, Board of Directors—Organization of the
NorthEast (ONE); 7-24-92

Dan Burke (by telephone), Chicago Community Development
Corporation; 2-25-91

Ben Burton, MHNA; 7-28-92

Jean Butzen, Lakefront SRO staff; 9-12-91

Dennis Cadieux, Jesus People U.S.A.; 7-15-92

Joe Cain, East Graceland Organization (EGO); 12-19-90

Bill Clinard, MHNA;12-3-90

Warren Friedman, formerly of ONE staff; 1-24-95

Tom Fuechtmann, formerly of ONE Board of Directors; 7-8-92

Judy and Turk Glazebrook, EGO; 2-16-91

J.R. Graves, CMS Property Management; 2-2-93

Janet Hasz, Voice of the People (VOP) staff; 4-15-91

Peter Holsten, Oakwood Development Corporation; 1-4-91

Josh Hoyt, formerly of ONE staff; 7-1-95

Denice Irwin, 920 W. Lakeside Tenants Organization; 6-24-91

Mike James, formerly of Jobs Or Income Now (JOIN); 7-20-95

Marilyn Katz, formerly of JOIN; 1-27-95

Randall Langer, Combined Property Management Corporation; 10-22-92

Tom Lenz, formerly of VOP staff; 1-14-91

Mike Loftin, formerly of VOP staff; 4-13-92

Kathy Logan, ONE staff; 10-31-90

Luz Martinez, VOP staff; 12-19-90

Manuel Melendez, Comite Latino staff; 4-8-91

Yvonne Murry, American Indian Economic Development Association staff; 5-6-91

Ha Nguyen, Vietnamese Association of Illinois; 6-17-91

Helene and Norm Raidl, MHNA; 2-4-95

Pat Reskey, UCC staff; 11-1-90 and 11-16-90

Dennis Sakurai, Southeast Asia Center staff; 11-23-90 and 12-11-90

Kompha Seth, Cambodian Association of Illinois (CAI); 1-24-91

Helen Shiller, 46th Ward Alderperson; 10-19-92

Al Walavich, Board of Directors—UCC; 1-17-91, 1-18-95

Becky Yane, CAI staff, 7-8-92

Erku Yimer, Ethiopian Community Association; 7-27-92

INDEX

Abercrombie, Patrick, 48

Abu-Lughod, Janet, xiii, 238, 240-241, 261

Alinsky, Saul, 15-16, 23, 96, 188, 211, 232-233, 235, 239, 254, 262

Andersonville, 36, 38, 44, 190, 212

Argyle Street, 35-37, 39, 41-43, 81, 204

Asian Welfare Association (AWA), 126, 128-129, 151, 159, 161, 164, 237, 245

Askam, Doris, 143, 248, 263

Leroy Avery et al. v. the City of Chicago et al. (the *Avery* litigation), 171-174

Back of the Yards Neighborhood Council (BYNC), 15-16, 18, 239

The Backyard Revolution, 12-13, 23, 262

Bagstad, Rob, xii, 186, 210, 264

Baudelaire, Charles, 8, 10

Beauregard, Robert, 230, 239

Bessemer, Henry, 46

Betts, Clive, 124, 133-135, 145

Blunkett, David, 51, 73, 124-126, 129, 145, 155, 161, 254, 256, 262

Boyte, Harry C., 12, 15, 23, 35, 254, 262

Bramall Lane, 58, 64, 100-101, 107, 110-111, 113-114, 121, 142-143, 146

Broomhall Flats, 55, 114, 127, 130-142, 249

Broomhall Tenants Association (BTA), xii, 130-142, 205, 227, 246, 249

Bryce, Mandy, 132-134, 139, 141, 161, 249-250, 263

Burgess, Ernest, 8, 22, 238-239

Burnham, Daniel, 30, 69

Bute, Joe, 190-191, 212

Byrne, Jane, 24, 168, 171, 209

Cain, Joe, 252, 262, 264

Castells, Manuel, 13-14, 20, 23, 73

Cermak, Anton, 32

Chicago, 3-4, 6-8, 14-16, 18, 22-24 25-44, 54, 65, 67, 68-71, 75-84, 86-90, 92, 94-96, 117-119, 165-213, 216, 218-226, 228, 230, 235, 238-239, 247, 251, 253, 255, 258, 261

   industrial development, 27-29

   planning and housing initiatives, 29-31, 33-35, 67, 77-78, 90, 117

   politics, 31-35, 119, 203-204, 254-259

   post-industrial development, 218-219

The City and the Grassroots, 14, 23

City Trenches, 16, 24

Clinard, Bill, 183-186, 203, 210-211, 213, 264

Coleman, Slim, 91, 165-170, 173-174, 176-177, 204, 208-209, 233-236, 244, 258

Communitarianism, 14

community, 6-18, 226-228, 231-236

Community Development Block Grant (CDBG) (US), 181-182

community organizing, 15-16, 204-208, 232-233, 254-259

   and women, 246-250

The Conservation Society, 108, 118

The Corridor (Uptown), 36-37, 42, 56, 77-78, 83, 92-94

Cronon, William, 27, 68

Daley, Richard J., 3, 31-33, 70, 76, 82, 86, 167, 169, 179, 257

Daley, Richard M., 34-35, 119, 174-175, 186

Damofle, Urania, 83, 86, 93

Deakin, Nicholas, 253, 262

The Death and Life of Great American Cities, 11-12, 23, 239

Defoe, Daniel, 44, 71

Department of Health and Social Security (DHSS) (UK), 136-137

Department of Housing and Urban Development (HUD) (US), 192-194, 197-198, 200-202, 212-213, 246-247

Donovan, Jill, xii, 186, 210, 264

Downs, James C., Jr., 76, 80-81

Drabble, Margaret, 50-51, 73

Edgewater (Chicago), 35, 43, 178, 188, 190-191, 195, 211, 237, 244, 257

Edwards, John, 253, 262

enclave consciousness, 16-17

Etzioni, Amitai, 14, 23

Evans, Ethel, 23, 102, 116, 119

Fellows, Arthur, 58, 73, 263

Fisher, Robert, 15, 23, 210, 262

Flett, Joan, 118, 121-122, 263

Gahm, Susan, 192-193, 201

Gans, Herbert, 11, 23, 231, 239

Gascoigne, Harold, 148, 163, 263

Geary, Chuck, 85-86, 88, 95, 166-167, 195

General Improvement Area (GIA) (UK), 104, 126, 150, 163

gentrification, 20-21, 63, 87, 119, 168, 190, 203-204, 216-219, 226-227, 238, 241-242

   ideology of, 251-254

   in Heart of Uptown/Sheridan Park, 220-226

Glazebrook, Turk, 240, 252, 262, 265

Green, Geoff, 22, 73, 102, 120-122, 161, 262-263

Hank Williams Village, 86-87, 115, 171, 195

Heart of Uptown Coalition (HOUC), 167, 171, 179, 181, 209

Heart of Uptown/Sheridan Park, 36, 42-43, 75, 77-79, 83-84, 86-88, 92-94, 176, 199-200, 204, 220-226, 251

Heeley (Sheffield), 4, 74, 101-102, 110-113, 117, 121-122, 124-126

Heeley Bypass, 101, 110, 112-113, 117

Heeley Residents Association (HRA), 110, 112-113, 117, 122

Hodgkinson, Chris, 129, 157, 161, 263

Housing Action Area (HAA) (UK), 104, 109, 126, 150-152

Howard, Ebenezer, 9, 22,

Howard, Margaret, xii, 133-134, 138-142, 161-162, 246, 249-250, 261, 263

Hoyt, Josh, 188, 191-192, 194, 204, 211-212, 234, 237, 244, 265

Hulley, Philip, 227, 239, 263

human ecology, 215-217

Hunslet Grange (Leeds), 136

Hyde Park (Chicago), 31, 77, 90

Inner Ring Road, 65, 100-101, 107, 109, 111, 114

Intercommunal Survival Committee (ISC), 166-167, 171

Irwin, Denice, xii, 212-213, 246-250, 261, 265

Jacobs, Jane, 11-12, 23, 239

Jobs or Income Now (JOIN), 82-83, 85, 91, 166, 254

Katznelson, Ira, 7, 16, 22, 24, 69

Kelly, Ed, 168

Kelly, Edward J. (Chicago Mayor), 32-33, 70-71

Kemp, Jack, 194, 212

Kemper Insurance Company, 76, 79-81, 91, 178, 180

Kennelly, Martin, 32

Kerrigan, Mick, xii, 148-149, 151-154, 160-161, 163, 264,

Knight, Howard, 134-136, 140, 256, 264

Lakefront SRO, 230, 260

Lakeview (Chicago), 186, 202, 204, 219, 228

Lambert, Harold, 98-99, 120

Langer, Randall, 173, 199, 203, 209, 220, 222-224, 265

Le Corbusier, 10, 22-23

left-wing populism, 246, 254-259, 262

Lenz, Tom, 198, 212, 265

Let the People Decide, 15, 23, 262

Levi, Julian, 77

Lincoln Park (Chicago), 3, 31, 183, 219, 228, 234, 248

Loftin, Mike, 198-199, 201, 212, 265

London Road, 54, 56-59, 64, 74, 101, 103, 107, 110-115, 142-144, 149, 156-157, 243, 248

The Making of the English Working Class, 46, 72

Mann, Peter H., 59-60, 74, 101

Martin, Bob, 127, 134, 156

Meltzer, Jack, 78, 94

Michie, Bill, 124

Montrose Harbor Neighbors Association (MHNA), 183-186

The Moor (Sheffield), 54-55, 57, 74, 101

Mount Pleasant (Sheffield), 55, 103-104, 120, 129, 151, 163

Nature's Metropolis, 27, 68

neighborhood, 6-18, 215-217, 226-228
  site, 230-231, 233-235
  stage, 236-238, 241-242
  system, 230-236

New Urban Left, 124, 256

new urban sociology, 216-217, 238

New York City, 16, 22-23, 27, 167, 261

NIMBYism, 16

North East Investment Center (NEIC), 189-190, 194

Ogden, William B., 27

Orbach, Jerome, 167, 197, 199

Organization of the NorthEast (ONE), 89, 187-195, 200, 201, 203-206, 211-212, 230, 233, 237, 244-245, 255, 260

overconcentration (of subsidized housing), 172, 180-181, 188

Peaden, John, 5, 101-105, 116, 120-125, 127, 129, 149-150, 156-158, 160-161, 163-164, 206, 233, 255, 264

Pugh, Jerome, 78

Quigley, Michael, 186, 211

race relations
  in Chicago, 29, 33-34, 67
  in Sharrow and Uptown, 42, 64, 242-246

Randell, Lawrence, 134, 140-141

rate-capping, 53, 256

regentrification, 224-226

Reich, Robert, 17, 24

Rule, Madge, 134, 139, 141, 264

Sander, Joe, 3-4

Save Uptown Neighborhoods (SUN), 172, 181

Sawyer, Eugene, 34

Seyd, Patrick, xii, 53, 73, 74

Shabat, Oscar, 87

Sharrow, 4-6, 18-22, 26, 54-68, 73-74, 97, 99-131, 133-135, 137, 139, 141-165, 205-207, 215-218, 226-230, 233-234, 237-239, 241-249, 251, 253-261

demographic character, 60-61, 63-64
early development, 55-56
effects of deindustrialization, 56-57, 62, 115
Sharrow Action Group (SAG), 62, 102, 115, 122-123, 127, 158
Sharrow and Heeley Neighbourhood Association (SHNA), 4-5, 102, 121
Sharrow Street Residents Group, xii, 149-154
Sharrow Traffic Campaign, 143-149, 205, 248-249
Sheffield, 4-6, 8-10, 12, 14, 16, 18, 20-22, 24-26, 28, 30, 32, 34, 36, 38, 40, 42, 44-68, 70-74, 76, 78, 80, 82, 84, 86, 88, 90, 92, 94, 96-128, 130-158, 160-164, 166, 168, 170, 172, 174, 176, 178, 180, 182, 184, 186, 188, 190, 192, 194, 196, 198, 200, 202, 204-206, 208, 210, 212, 216-220, 222, 224, 226-230, 232-234, 236, 238, 240, 242, 244, 246, 248-250, 252-254, 256, 258-260, 262-264,
cutlers, 45-46, 55-56
highway proposals, 100-101
industrial development, 46-47, 49-54, 218
planning and housing initiatives, 48-49, 67, 97-99
politics, 46-48, 51-53, 115-120, 254-259
Sheffield United Football Club, 58
Shiller, Helen, 44, 91, 166-177, 186, 199, 203-204, 208-209, 213, 226, 234-236, 252, 258, 261, 265
Simmel, Georg, 9, 22
South Sheffield Inner City Community Project (SSICCP), 121-122, 125-129, 134, 143-145, 148, 150-151, 155-164, 205-206, 216, 226-227, 229, 233, 237-238, 245, 249, 254, 256, 259-260
The Spirit of Community, 14, 23
Stockton Elementary School, 170
Suttles, Gerald D., 71, 231-232, 239

Thatcher, Margaret, 51-54, 66, 114, 123, 135, 139, 141, 148, 155-156, 205
Thompson, E.P., 46, 72
Thompson, William Hale (Chicago Mayor), 32
Thompson, William P., 171-172, 179, 184
Tigwell, Tony, 134, 136, 144-145, 160-161, 164, 256, 260, 264
Tilly, Charles, 21
Truman College, 36, 87-88, 195, 220, 224, 248

Uptown, 3-6, 18-22, 26, 35-44, 64, 66-68, 70-71, 75-85, 87-97, 99, 105, 115, 117-120, 165-193, 195-213, 215, 217-224, 226-230, 233-239, 241-247, 249, 251-255, 257-261
demographic character, 38-42
early development, 35-36
neighborhood conflict, 43-44, 88-94, 202-204, 233-236, 242-246
Uptown: A Planning Report (The Meltzer Report), 78-80, 94, 117, 119, 171, 178, 182, 209

Uptown Area People's Planning Coalition, 84-85, 87, 115
Uptown Chicago Commission (UCC), 43, 76-84, 88-94, 96, 117, 171-172, 177-183, 185, 187-189, 197, 204, 209-210, 236, 243
Uptown Conservation Community Council (CCC), 3-4, 82-88, 93, 115, 117
Uptown Federal Savings & Loan Association, 80, 84, 180, 219
Uptown Task Force on Displacement and Housing Development, 199-201, 203
The Urban Programme (UK), 125, 155-156
urban renewal (US)
in Chicago, 31, 67
in Uptown, 3-4, 75-94, 115, 117, 119-120, 195, 229
urban social movements, 13-14, 20

Views of Sharrow, 74, 104-105, 115, 121, 233, 240
Voice of the People (VOP), 42, 84, 89, 193, 195-206, 212, 216, 222, 230, 233-234, 236, 247, 255, 257-258
International Homes project, 201, 258

Walkley (Sheffield), 4, 102
Walton, John, 21, 24
Washington, Harold, 34-35, 70, 169-170, 172-174, 189, 203, 209
Wesley House, 55, 126-129, 149-150, 155-157, 159, 161, 163-164
Williams, Herb, 177, 243
Willmott, Peter, 11, 23, 231, 239
Wilson, Ann, xii, 143-148, 160, 162-163, 246, 248-250, 255, 261, 264
Wilson Avenue, 33-34, 42, 75, 83-84
Woodlawn Organization, The (TWO), 15
World's Columbian Exposition, 28, 30

Yorkshire Development Group (YDG), 130-132, 135-136, 138, 161
Young, Michael, 11, 23, 231, 239